f**P**

CREATING WEALTH

RETIRE IN TEN YEARS USING ALLEN'S SEVEN PRINCIPLES OF WEALTH

Robert G. Allen

FREE PRESS

New York London Toronto Sydney

FREE PRESS
A Division of Simon & Schuster, Inc.
1230 Avenue of the Americas
New York, NY 10020

First Free Press Edition, 2006

FREE PRESS and colophon are trademarks of Simon & Schuster, Inc.

For information about special discounts for bulk purchases,
please contact Simon & Schuster Special Sales:
1-800-456-6798 or business@simonandschuster.com.

Manufactured in the United States of America

10 9 8 7 6 5 4 3 2 1

Library of Congress Cataloging-in-Publication Data
Allen, Robert G.
Creating wealth: retire in ten years using Allen's seven principles of wealth /
Robert G. Allen.
p.   cm.
Includes index.
1. Finance, Personal.
I. Title.
HG179 .A444   2006
332.024'01—dc22   2006045239

ISBN-13: 978-1-4516-3158-6

This publication is designed to provide accurate and authoritative information, not legal advice. Events and laws may change after publication. The author and publisher specifically disclaim any liability, loss, or risk, personal or otherwise, which is incurred as a consequence, directly or indirectly, of the use and application of any of the contents of the work. Before acting on any suggestion presented in this book, legal or other professional assistance may be advisable.

The verse on page 243 comes from "The Road Not Taken" from *The Poetry of Robert Frost*, edited by Edward Connery Lathem. Copyright 1916. © 1969 by Henry Holt and Company Inc.; copyright 1944 by Robert Frost. Reprinted by permission of Henry Holt and Company Inc., publishers.

The chart of key factors in gold and silver prices on pages 176–77 is used by courtesy of Investment Rarities, Inc.

To my wife, Daryl,
and my three children, Aimee, Aaron, and Hunter,
who are the true wealth of my life

Contents

Part Four \ Perpetuating Wealth: Spreading the Risk

Part Five \ Real Wealth

PART ONE

The Foundation

CHAPTER 1

We Were Programmed to Fail from the Moment We Were Born

Practical men, who believe themselves to be quite exempt from any intellectual influences, are usually the slaves of some defunct economist.
—JOHN MAYNARD KEYNES

Why is it that money seems to flow to some people like a magnet—and seems to be repelled from others? This question has always intrigued me. And I was determined to discover the answer.

I began to examine my own experiences in creating personal wealth. I talked with dozens of people: poor, well-off, and wealthy. Each person taught me something. I began to notice common threads and patterns. What I discovered was astonishing!

Let me share with you a whole new way of thinking about money and a proven method of acquiring wealth. In the process, I will put to rest (hopefully forever!) an incredible number of myths and misconceptions about what it takes to make—and keep—great wealth.

As I will show you, most of what we know about money is based upon false assumptions. As the nineteenth-century humorist Josh Billings so aptly put it: "The trouble with people is not that they don't know, but that they know so much that just ain't so."

How do people get to know so much misinformation about wealth? They are programmed. Of course, there is really nothing sinister about it. There is no conspiracy afoot to brainwash unsuspecting people into thinking "poorly." Actually, much of it is nothing more than the common sense of past generations taken to extremes. These widely held sacred-cow notions about saving, spending, borrowing, and investing are taught by well-intentioned teachers in our finest universities, in our newspapers, on television, from our pulpits, and in our homes. We take them for granted just as people used to assume the world was flat or that the sun revolved around the earth.

As a consequence, only a small percentage of the millions who try ever join the ranks of the wealthy. How can they? They are building on a shaky foundation.

I'll never forget a radio interview I did in Pittsburgh. The host and I spent some time talking about the road to wealth. The host's assistant, a young woman, listened intently. After the interview she questioned me. "Mr. Allen, all of what you say sounds interesting, even feasible. But it goes against everything my parents have always taught me!"

I asked, "How are your parents doing financially?" She replied, "Terribly. They are really strapped for money." Then she laughed at what she had just said. She understood.

Granted, it isn't easy to let go of our programming. There are lessons we feel we have learned from the Great Depression of the 1930s, the Great Recession of the 1970s, the Great Stagnation of the 1980s, or the great stock-market booms and busts of the last twenty years. But we don't have to be like the monkeys in a story I heard recently. It seems that in Africa, the natives use an ingenious method for catching monkeys. They hollow out a coconut shell by cutting a small hole at one end. The hole is small enough to barely allow a monkey's hand. Inside the hollowed shell they place a few peanuts. They connect the coconut shell to a thin, strong cord and wait in hiding for the monkeys. When a monkey discovers the nuts inside the shell, he reaches in and grasps them in his fist. But the hole is too small to allow the tightly clenched fist to escape. At this precise moment, the native pulls on the cord, and the monkey, who won't let go of those peanuts to save his life, is caught.

Too often, we hold tightly to our own peanut ideas for fear that we may lose them—when all the while it is these very ideas that hold us captive and prevent us from achieving financial freedom.

Well, what are these false assumptions? And how can we learn to let go of them? Let's examine the nine most prevalent faulty assumptions about wealth. As you study them, notice how each one contains a grain of truth.

False Assumption 1: Having a Job Is Good and Leads Ultimately to Wealth

I asked a young telephone receptionist in Columbus, Ohio, to tell me her idea of the most important factor in wealth acquisition. She replied, "A good job, a great job, a fantastic job." I was surprised by how often this same answer was given by those whose income is average or below. Millionaires rarely respond this way.

It is commonly held in our society that finding a good job, working hard, and moving up the ladder to more responsibility will eventually take us to golden retirement years of wealth and happiness. The fact of the matter is that a job merely supports the habits we have (like eating), but it rarely leads to wealth. As one shrewd observer put it, "Wealth is when small efforts produce large results. Poverty is when large efforts produce small results."

No matter how much you love your job, expecting it to make you wealthy is like looking for gold in a salt mine. If your large efforts are only producing small results, you had better check the road map. You may be on the road to poverty.

The answer is not to work harder, but to work smarter. A job should be looked upon as a temporary inconvenience. It is a method for generating cash flow for living expenses while you are setting up an automatic pilot (more on this in chapter 5). Thus, having a job is necessary for a while, but don't forget the other part of the equation. Your ultimate goal is to acquire ownership of a generous source of income that flows to you regardless of your job. Accomplishing that goal is what this book is about.

False Assumption 2: Saving Your Money Is a Good Investment

How many millionaires do you know who have become wealthy by investing in savings accounts? I rest my case.

But don't get me wrong. Saving money is good. In fact, it is important to the wealth-building process. It's not the money saved that is important. It is the discipline required to save it. But you can't expect your savings to carry you to wealth. And this is the fact that is so widely misunderstood. Assuming only minimal inflation and taxes, it doesn't take a PhD in finance to realize that any dollar that earns less than about 10 percent per year is a losing venture. At best, it is the slow liquidation of wealth.

"But," you say, "savings accounts and certificates of deposit are safe, and the money comes easy." And I reply, "Does it make you feel safe and secure to know that every day you are getting poorer and poorer?"

One of my grandfather's favorite sayings was, "Early to bed, early to rise; work like hell, and economize!"

There is nothing wrong with economizing. There is a place for it in the scheme of wealth. However, if your goal is to become wealthy, you must learn how to save *smart.* The money you save is only parked temporarily in liquid, interest-bearing accounts, waiting to be invested in a better place. This smart money is then shifted into long-range, less-liquid investments (more on this later), which generate wealth-producing rates of return—rates well in excess of 20 percent per year. Anything less is tantamount to treading water in the swimming pool on the deck of the *Titanic.*

False Assumption 3: Debt Is Bad—Avoid It Like the Plague

Have you ever heard this before? There is truth to the statement, but it depends on the kind of debt we are talking about. If we are talking about consumer debt, yes. Avoid it like the plague. Avoid borrowing money to buy the "appearances of wealth," which lose value and are often worthless before the debt is repaid.

But investment debt is another story. In fact, self-made wealth never comes without going into debt. I repeat: *You can never become wealthy without going into some form of investment debt.* And probably a lot of it.

It is true that debt is terrifying to most of us. It signifies bondage. And ironically, the only way we can develop a sizable nest egg and stay out of long-term financial bondage is to go into short-term debt. You can actually borrow your way to wealth. Chapter 9 on leverage shows that the key to wealth is the wise use of investment debt. It will help you understand the importance of debt. Even to love debt.

There is no other way short of theft or inheritance. And that brings us to our next false assumption, which is the reason most of us fear debt in the first place.

False Assumption 4: Security Is Good

Our entire society is obsessed with security. We demand social security, job security, seniority, and federal deposit insurance. But security is only an illusion. Let me illustrate: A few months ago a fireman friend of mine was called out to fight a large brush fire. He and his cohorts rushed to the closest fire hydrant, connected their water hoses, and ran to the flames. But when they turned on the water at the hydrant, nothing happened! The water lines had not been properly connected by the developer. All they could do was stand there and watch the blaze, helpless.

Those who place too much faith in security often end up trying to put out fires with empty water hoses. Would you feel financially secure if you had to rely on an almost insolvent social security system?

How dangerous it is to assume that security is good! The more you love security, the more likely you will avoid risk. And if you avoid risk, you also avoid opportunity, because risk is the price you pay for opportunity. You can't hate risk and hope for freedom.

Risk is an essential part of progress. Learn to view it positively, as an essential step in the road to wealth.

I was driving down a California freeway recently and heard a radio advertisement for a local bank. Its slogan was, "Come in out of the risk."

If I could rewrite this commercial, I would say, "Come out *into* the risk. For that is where you find the opportunity. There is no such thing as security. There are only varying degrees of risk."

False Assumption 5: Failure Is Bad

I used to be ashamed of my many failures and mistakes. And I have made plenty of them! I used to have a recurring nightmare: A crew from *60 Minutes* is waiting to interview me at my office about my remarkable success in business. But Mike Wallace has uncovered some of my whopping failures along the way, and he is getting ready to expose them to the world. What horror!

But as I became more mature, I realized that failure is part of success. A very important part. If you develop a positive mental attitude about failure, you can learn a great deal from it. You will develop ingenuity, flexibility, and an ability to create new ways of achieving goals. When you fail for a time to obtain something you really want, you join the ranks of some pretty important people—like Abraham Lincoln and Thomas A. Edison. Do you know of any successful person who has risen to the top of his or her field without some failure?

Herb True, the renowned professor of management at the University of Notre Dame, once said, "What people don't realize is that successful people often have more failures than failures do. But they keep going." You don't drown by falling in water. You drown by staying there.

Failure is not bad. In fact, one good failure can teach you more about success than four years at the best university. Failure can be the best thing that ever happened to you.

False Assumption 6: Wealth Is Measured in Material Possessions

Wealth is not money. Money is just the appearance of wealth. The form but not the substance. Wealth is thoughts, not things. You can be wealthy without having lots of money. And you can be rich and not be wealthy.

Now, that may be a bit confusing, but it's true. Wealth is a state of mind—an attitude. Author Hollis Norton says it well: "Broke is a temporary condition. Poor is a state of mind."

Let's test this hypothesis. Henry Ford was once asked what he would do if he lost all of his possessions. He replied, "I'd have them all back again in five years." In other words, he might be temporarily broke, but he would never be poor. He had a wealth of experience and knowledge to draw upon. And above all, he had a positive attitude about his ability to create wealth and knew that if he had done it once, it would probably be easier the second time.

I have been quoted as saying, "Send me to any city in the United States. Take away my wallet. Give me $100 for living expenses. And in seventy-two hours I'll buy an excellent piece of real estate using none of my own money." How can I do this without any of the trappings of wealth? It is easy when you learn the principles of wealth and are not afraid to use them.

In the next chapter we will talk about developing the wealthy mindset that makes all of this possible.

False Assumption 7: The Government, My Employer, or Someone Else Is Responsible for My Financial Well-Being

When our forefathers arrived on these shores, there was no welfare system. Each person was responsible for his or her own financial welfare. When the pioneers crossed the plains, there were no unemployment benefits. They had to scratch out their own existence. When thousands of immigrants landed here in the early 1900s, they came seeking only the opportunity to work and to be free. Somewhere between then and now, there has been an almost imperceptible—and, I think, destructive—shift in public thinking. People have ceased to assume personal responsibility for their financial well-being and assume that the government is responsible. Today we expect government to bail out everything from defunct major corporations to insolvent municipalities.

But government is not the answer. The answer lies in us. We alone are responsible for our ultimate financial welfare. The sooner we realize this, the quicker we can start on the road to wealth.

False Assumption 8: Acquiring Wealth Is a Win-Lose Game

Since the beginning of time, the acquiring of wealth has been viewed as a win-lose game—a dirty business in which the acquirer takes advantage of the acquiree, usually in an illegal or immoral way. Many people think that one has to be a greedy SOB to "make it."

But I believe you don't have to be filthy to be filthy rich. I don't have to steal from your pile in order to create a large pile for myself. There is such a thing as creating win-win wealth.

In reality, there is an infinite source of wealth. We just have to learn how to tap into it. When I tap into the infinite source of wealth, I don't reduce the possibility of your becoming wealthy. I probably enhance it. We'll discuss this in great detail in later chapters.

False Assumption 9: It Takes Money to Make Money

My book *Nothing Down* destroyed this dangerous myth. It does take money to make money—but it doesn't have to be your own money. In this book I will explore, in more depth, the principles of borrowing and leverage to create personal wealth.

And you can become wealthy starting right from where you are now, in ten years or less.

So there you have them: the nine most dangerous obstacles to the wealth-building process. Now that you know what they are, I'll show you how to rid your life of them.

CHAPTER 2

Developing a Wealthy Mind-Set

"She was born under a lucky star."
"It's not what you know but who you know."
"He was born with a silver spoon in his mouth."

Many people, because of their programming, assume that wealth is a result of luck, connections, or inheritance. The last thing that people want to hear is the plain, simple fact that the rich think differently than the poor. They are programmed differently. They have different expectations with respect to money. They have what I call a wealthy mind-set.

How do you develop a wealthy mind-set?

The first step is to understand that from your programming you make assumptions, and these assumptions become your reality. It is as if there were a filter between you and your world—the filter of the mind. Information that is transmitted to you from the world must pass through this filter. And as it passes through, it is colored, filtered, and changed to match the assumptions or the expectations you have about how the world works—or ought to work.

Let me digress here to tell you about a classic research experiment that will perhaps clarify how this business of assumptions works. Researchers placed a large pike fish in an aquarium with several dozen minnows. For a time, the pike ate the minnows to his heart's delight. Then the researchers separated the pike from the schools of smaller fish by placing a glass partition in the aquarium. Now the pike could see his lunch through the glass but, try as he would, he could not reach it. Finally, after dozens of unsuccessful attempts, he gave up. Then the researchers removed the glass, allowing the smaller fish to swim freely around the pike. But this time he didn't even notice them—and starved to death in the midst of a feast.

The pike had allowed himself to be programmed into thinking that the minnows were out of his reach forever. This programming became an assumption that colored the filter through which he viewed the world. It became his reality. When conditions changed and the assumptions were no longer valid, he could not adapt. It was a fatal mistake.

In the same way, rigidly held assumptions can be dangerous to your wealth.

One way to loosen your hold on outdated or incorrect assumptions is to learn where they come from. Observe. Listen to the conversations of friends, relatives, and neighbors when it comes to investing money. Pay attention to the advertising on television and radio and in print. Whenever you recognize some faulty programming, make a mental note.

For instance, I heard a politician make the following statement during a recent election campaign: "You've got to learn to think smaller. You've got to learn to be satisfied with less!" Can you see the folly in this kind of thinking? A person concerned with financial independence needs to do exactly the opposite: think bigger, not smaller. And never be satisfied with less.

While you are observing the source of incorrect programming, you should also be observing the results of incorrect programming. What happens to the wealth of individuals who avoid risk and cling to security?

Don't forget to also notice those who are successful in amassing material wealth. Which rules direct their thinking? What are their attitudes toward risk, debt, working for someone else, and security? What are their assumptions? How do their assumptions color their world? Green!

All I'm asking you to do is to look at the way the world of money really works. Notice who is winning and who is losing. And why. Avoiding the lemming mentality is the first step in guiding your own financial destiny.

Next you need to replace false assumptions with correct ones. I call this process "developing a wealthy mind-set." There are five distinct steps in this process.

Step 1: Set Realistic Goals and Write Them Down

A study at Yale University pointed out the value of goals. In 1954, Yale graduating seniors were asked if they had set any specific written financial goals. Only 3 percent had done so. About 10 percent had specific goals but hadn't committed them to paper. The rest had no specific goals. Twenty years later, they were resurveyed. Guess which group was most successful? You guessed it: the 3 percent outperformed the other 97 percent combined!

Now, I'm not suggesting that you can't become wealthy without goals or that you will automatically "make it" if you do have goals. But, as the survey suggests, they certainly help.

Why write your goals down? A goal that is not written down is a wish. A daydream. When you are serious enough to commit your goals to paper and read them regularly, you energize your commitment and creativity.

Step 2: Visualize Your Goal

One of the most revolutionary advances in sports training is the use of imagery. The coach of the Stanford University tennis team attributes an NCAA tennis championship to the use of imagery. The president of the company that worked with the Stanford team describes the process: "A tennis player, for example, is filmed performing his shots. The film is then edited so that only the perfectly executed strokes remain. After receiving instructions in mental imprinting for memory retention, the athlete sits before a larger-than-life video screen and watches the successful strokes repeated over and over. The athlete's computerlike memory stores those images in muscle memory, as if the athlete had physically practiced those skills in a state of perfection for hundreds of hours. Eventually, the perfect memory trace becomes so ingrained that the athlete is able to duplicate it automatically under the pressure of competition."

When our perfect computerlike subconscious mind is repeatedly shown mental pictures of our most desired goals on the videotape of our mind, the memory becomes so dominant that we are able to re-create it in reality.

When should you do this visualization? According to psychotherapist Émile Coué, a French expert on the subject over fifty years ago, the best time is just before drifting off to sleep and just after waking up in the morning. At these times, the conscious, rational mind is calm, and the subconscious mind can be influenced more easily.

Dr. Coué is best known for his positive-thinking phrase "Every day in every way I am getting better and better." He felt that by programming the all-powerful subconscious mind with even this general positive affirmation, amazing things could result. And he seemed to be able to prove it by his research.

Step 3: Affirm Yourself

After visualization comes affirmation. If goals start the motor of our mind-set, then affirmations are the fuel to keep the motor running. I am referring, of course, to a constant flow of positive information about wealth and how to obtain it. This may come by reading such masterpieces as *Think and Grow Rich* by Napoleon Hill and *The Magic of Thinking Big* by Dr. David Schwartz. Or it may come as you read quotes from great men, like those in chapter 20. All of this builds confidence and self-esteem, qualities that many of us lack. It takes a lot of self-esteem to go against the grain. And if you expect to be successful, you have to dare to be different.

I will share with you an affirmation program that I wrote and read regularly to myself during my MBA studies. Although I had graduated high in my class with a BA degree, I was sure the master's program was way over my head. From early childhood, I had believed that I was poor at math. I had even flunked algebra in high school. So when it came to a highly intensive business program including calculus, economics, and statistics, I barely kept my nose above water. It helped, during these demoralizing times, to read the following statement:

A SIXTY-SECOND COMMERCIAL TO ME

Bob Allen, you're great! You are a unique, new kind of person that the world has never before seen and will never see the likes of again. You were born to do good. You were born to succeed. You were born to bless others' lives. You were born to be great because you've got what it takes to be great:

You're enthusiastic.
You're optimistic.

You're organized.
You're a hard worker.
You're happy.
You're master of yourself.
You're a child of God.
You're a leader.
You're a big thinker.

And blessed as you are with all of these talents, there isn't a thing in the world that you can't do. With God as your partner, you will never fail.

Now, reading this didn't produce miracles. (Although, for me, just being able to graduate was a miracle!) But I did become one of the best average students in my graduating class. In a real way, I wrote my own program and fed it into the computer of my mind. And I've been a fan of affirmation techniques ever since.

Step 4: Replace Luck Thinking with Probability Thinking

Some people just seem lucky, don't they? And others not so lucky.

I don't doubt there is such a thing as luck. But most of us give luck far too much credit. I don't think much about luck anymore. I pretend that it doesn't exist. I would rather look upon luck as a low or high probability of success. And you can always work on increasing your probability of success. If you don't have the right skills, you can learn them. If you aren't trying hard enough, you can try harder. In this way, you increase the probability that luck will smile on you.

I think that this is reflected in the success of my first book, *Nothing Down*. The odds against a first-time author's book becoming a best seller are astronomical. Out of fifty thousand books published each year, only a handful make it to the bestseller lists and stay there for any length of time. Despite those odds, *Nothing Down* remained on the prestigious *New York Times* bestseller list for over one hundred weeks and has now sold over one million hardcover copies.

What did I do differently? I tried, at every turn, to increase the probabilities of success. Years before, I had a written goal to write a book someday. I had no idea what I would write about. In the meantime, I became an expert in the little-known field of investing in real estate with little or no money down. Then I decided to write about it. Luckily (?) I picked a subject that a lot of people were interested in. I wrote a rough manuscript and had a professional editor polish it for me. I had a professional designer prepare a beautiful book jacket. Before a soul in the publishing business had set eyes on my manuscript, I had already spent $2,000 to make it look like a book worth publishing.

Next, I chose not to send my precious manuscript through the normal channels. The probability of having a manuscript accepted through normal channels is almost nil. I needed a better idea. Instead I flew to Atlanta to the annual publishers' and booksellers' convention and presented my idea directly to several publishers. I got a very good reception. This built up my confidence.

But I didn't want just any publishing house. I wanted the best. For real-estate books, there is none better than Simon & Schuster. I waited for the right moment to approach the president of Simon & Schuster, my heart in my throat. He recognized the value of my book. In the ensuing weeks, we signed a contract. I was going to be a published author!

But that wasn't all. When the book finally appeared, I made myself available for an extensive publicity tour. I appeared on every radio or TV show that would have me, no matter what time of day or night. The idea caught on. The rest is history.

Now, I don't want to mislead you. It might seem, in retrospect, that I had everything under control. But this is not the case. I had no idea what was going to happen. All I knew was that I had a written goal to write a book and have it published. Every step along the way, I tried to increase the probability of success.

I know for certain that the better your attitude and the harder you work, the luckier you get.

Step 5: Take Action

Many would-be successful people have everything they need to become wealthy, but they just haven't mastered the final step: action. They can't seem to make the leap from theory into practice.

Why do so many fail to make this all-important leap? Perhaps they feel they aren't ready. Perhaps they feel disorganized, unsure, afraid. No matter what the reason, if they fail to act, they fail to succeed. I wonder which is worse, to try and fail or to fail to try.

I had a wonderful role model. Paul Jewkes was a millionaire entrepreneur whom I was privileged to work with for a few months after I got out of college. He said something to me one day that I will never forget:

"I would rather see a crooked furrow than a field unplowed!"

When it came time to buy my first piece of real estate, and I sat there with the seller in his home, petrified, my hand shaking, knowing nothing about the dangers and pitfalls of buying real estate, and realizing that I would be risking everything I had, I remembered what Paul had said—and I signed my name. I jumped off the cliff, so to speak. And that one decision, that one simple action, started me on the road to wealth. I hate to think where I'd be if I had failed to act.

So there you have all the ingredients for a wealthy mind-set. It consists of a mind devoid of unwealthy assumptions. It is the creation of a person who is disciplined enough to set goals, to visualize them, to affirm them regularly, and to increase the probability of success through positive action.

In the next chapter, we'll add to our basic wealth attitudes some fundamental principles about wealth building. After that we'll get to the specific ways of making money.

As architects of wealth, we need to lay a solid foundation.

CHAPTER 3

A Fool and His Money Are Soon Parted: Master the Seven Principles of Wealth

The men who can manage men manage the men who can manage only things, and the men who can manage money, manage all.

—WILL AND ARIEL DURANT, *The Lessons of History*

Is there any truth to the old proverb "A fool and his money are soon parted"?

I confess that if my own experience is any clue, the answer has to be yes. You don't have to dig too deep into my financial history to count the many times that this "fool" and his money have been parted too soon. And it has only been after serious study and painful experience that I have begun to be less "penny-wise and pound-foolish" (with occasional relapses, I might add).

Yes, a fool and his money are soon parted. But why is that?

Because a fool doesn't know how to manage money!

Contrary to popular opinion, the rich don't always get richer. George Gilder, one of the architects of supply-side economics, gives us some reasons why in his brilliant book *Wealth and Poverty:*

"With few notable exceptions, which are always in the news, fast movement up or down [the wealth ladder] in two generations has been the fate of the American rich.

" . . . Why can they not pass the grail on down without spilling most of its contents? Well, as they say, there are many a slip, and death and taxes take their toll of potential heirs and their money . . . Fortune hunters abound near the funerals of the rich.

"When the money is actually passed on, the part that escapes charity and philanthropy often ends among large numbers of prodigal sons and daughters to whom the average return on capital is a concept easier to understand than to achieve, even in those cases where the children have some interest in keeping their wealth. The receipt of a legacy, it turns out, often erodes the qualities of entrepreneurship that are needed to perpetuate it. Spending turns out to be far easier than choosing and maintaining those select forms of capital with yields greater than their costs."

In other words, it's not all that easy to make money grow. Even when you inherit a lot of it. To prove this point to you, I decided to undertake a little research project to determine what the average person would do with sudden wealth. With the help of professionals, a questionnaire was designed and sent out to several hundred randomly selected individuals across the country, in every major city. Here is the question we asked them to respond to:

If you were to receive from an inheritance $100,000 tax free, what dollar amounts would you spend in the next year in the following categories:

_____ Gold, silver	_____ Medical/dental
_____ Recreation	_____ Precious gems
_____ Reduce debts	_____ Automobile
_____ Bank savings	_____ Buy own home
_____ Commodities	_____ Treasury bills
_____ Bonds	_____ Recreational vehicle
_____ Collectibles	_____ Charity or church
(antiques, stamps,	_____ Go into business
art, etc.)	_____ Give to family
_____ Stock market	_____ Mutual funds
_____ Money market funds	Down payment
_____ Vacation	on real-estate
_____ Mortgages	investment
	What kind _____
	Price _____

Take a few minutes to complete the questionnaire yourself. It will make the explanation more meaningful. If you like, you may substitute your present net worth for the imaginary $100,000 gift.

Each sample investor can choose from among twenty-two different investments. You might wonder why a recreational vehicle is listed here as an investment. In the pure economic sense, anything that you "spend" money on is an investment. So you "invest" in the vehicle, and it goes either up or down in value. And if you spend your money on a vacation, you automatically lose your opportunity to spend that sum in the stock market.

Experts in each of these twenty-two areas gave me their best educated guesses as to the ten-year-growth outlook for their specialty investment. I also asked them to predict a realistic yearly growth rate. With this information, it was easy to determine what each sample investor's "shopping basket" full of investments would be worth in ten years.

Below you will find a listing of the twenty-two investments divided into six major categories, with annual projected growth rates.

Classification of investment	Investment	Projected annual growth rate
Hard assets	Gold, silver	15%
	Precious gems	17.5%
	Collectibles	15%
Liquid money	Bank savings	3–8%
	Treasury bills	3–6%
	Money market funds	3–9%
Passive capital	Stock market	10%
Growth investments	Bonds	10%
	Commodities	25%
	Mutual funds	10–13%
	Discounted mortgages	15–25%
Active capital	Buy own home	10%
	Real-estate investment	10%
	Businesses	15%
Consumer	Vacation	0%
	Medical/dental	0%
	Reduce debts	0%
	Recreation	0%
	Recreational vehicle	0%
	Automobile	0%
Nonmonetary	Give to family	0%
	Charity or church	0%

You will notice that I have assigned a value of 0 percent to all consumer and nonmonetary investments. Obviously there is more to wealth than just money. Giving away or sharing our wealth brings enormous emotional dividends often more satisfying than numbers on a financial statement. However, in the purest economic sense, it is difficult to prove that these items yield monetary results.

Before we examine the results of the survey, let me ask you to guess what percentage of the people in our survey were able to double their initial $100,000 investment within a ten-year period. Ten percent? Twenty? Thirty?

Would you be surprised to learn that only *one*—yes, only one out of one hundred—would end up in ten years with at least $200,000? (This person would have $202,000, to be exact.) There were no millionaires! Not one! *And forty people out of one hundred weren't even able to hang on to their original $100,000.* Is it any wonder, then, why so few Americans (the vast majority of whom don't have the same $100,000 head start) ever "make it" financially?

Remember what the wise sixth-century BC Chinese philosopher Lao Tzu said: "Give a man a fish, and you feed him for a day. Teach a man to fish, and you feed him for a lifetime." In other words, if you could redistribute the wealth of this nation to every citizen, the odds are that the bulk of it would be squandered or lost within a generation. Any approach that doesn't teach the principles of wealth is doomed to failure.

The Seven Wealth Principles

With this in mind, let's have a look at a couple of the survey investors and follow them through a ten-year-growth cycle to see how their investments grow. From this analysis we should be able to discern some basic wealth principles. These wealth principles, coupled with the attitudes of a wealthy mind-set, will form the foundation of your wealth pyramid and ultimately make it possible to retire in as little as ten years.

Our first investor is a middle-aged comptroller. His portfolio of investments looks like this:

Investment	Category	Value in ten years
$78,000	Bank savings	$168,396
$2,000	Debt reduction	$0
$11,000	Charity	$0
$3,000	Automobile	$0
$5,000	Business	$20,228
$1,000	Vacation	$0
$100,000		$188,624

Not bad! Our investor will be pleased to learn that he has almost doubled his beginning nest egg. But wait a minute. Haven't we forgotten something here? What about taxes? For simplicity, let's assume that our investor is in a 20 percent tax bracket and that the interest that has accrued in his bank savings should be reduced by 20 percent to account for taxes. That leaves him with $154,716 in the bank instead of $168,396. We'll assume that the business net worth, because of favorable tax breaks, is still intact. Therefore, the adjusted net worth is only $174,944. Does this sound correct?

Not quite. We forgot inflation. His dollars will be worth less in ten years. At 5 percent inflation, his dollars would be worth $107,400. Even with a very low inflation rate, this investor would end up with about as much as he started out with. Not quite as attractive as it first appeared. That isn't creating any great wealth, is it?

That brings us to the first of seven wealth principles that we can determine from this survey.

Wealth Principle 1: Don't Count Your Dollars Until
They Have Passed through the Strainers of Taxes and Inflation

Always think in terms of "real" dollars, not funny money. Those are the only dollars that you can really spend. Your dollars have to compound at a rate that is at least equal to the rate of inflation plus taxes—and that's just to break even! No matter how small the rate of inflation may appear, it is an invisible destroyer that must be reckoned with.

Our second example comes from a schoolteacher. His investment portfolio looked like this:

Investment	Category	Value in ten years
$50,000	Stock market	$129,687
$5,000	Vacation	$0
$20,000	Money market funds	$47,347
$5,000	Charity	$0
$10,000	Mutual funds	$33,946
$10,000	Automobile	$0
$100,000		$210,980

You should be catching on by now. The $200,000 has not yet passed through the strainers of taxes and inflation. After taxes, the teacher will have $188,784, and 5 percent inflation reduces this figure to about $110,000. This investor did marginally better than the first.

Can you see areas where each of these investors might have done better? Do they have all of their money working for them? No. Some of their money was invested in nonproductive areas. Our teacher put 20 percent of his money into investments earning zero rate of return. On the average, our survey investors spent 27 percent of their $100,000 inheritance on items that would be worthless in ten years. And that difference is significant over a ten-year period.

That brings us to the next investment principle.

Wealth Principle 2: Make Maximum Use of Your Assets and Sacrifice to Invest in Things That Go Up in Value

Every dollar you spend is invested in something that goes either up or down in value. Unfortunately, most people spend most of their surplus assets on the "appearances of wealth": fancy cars, fine clothes, stereos, TV sets. These items make them look rich, but in reality they become poorer each and every day.

People who are already wealthy can afford to spend a certain amount of their income frivolously, but the beginning wealth seeker cannot afford this luxury quite yet. What is the answer? Avoid, as much as possible, spending any money for consumer goods that go down in value.

Never borrow money to pay for a car, a boat, or a stereo. If you do have to buy such items, always pay cash. Thus you discipline yourself. From this point on, you will borrow money only to make money.

In our parents' day, it was not unusual to defer the purchase of luxuries for many years. In our day, what were luxuries to our parents are necessities to us. When choosing between sacrifice and instant gratification, the wealth seeker chooses sacrifice, and the poverty seeker chooses instant gratification. The poverty seeker wants what he wants, and he wants it *now!* The wealth seeker knows that if he can just wait and invest for the future, he will eventually be able to buy whatever he wants. In the meantime, he tries to make every dollar count.

Before buying anything, the wealth seeker learns to ask tough questions such as: What will this item be worth ten years from now? Will this item enhance my goal of retiring on schedule, or will it detract? Is this item something that I need, or is it merely something that I want?

Whether you are starting with $100,000 or $100, the principles are the same.

Let's look at another survey investor:

Investment	Category	Value in ten years
$10,000	Gold	$40,456
$10,000	Precious gems	$50,000
$35,000	Bank savings	$75,562
$1,000	Rare coins	$4,046
$10,000	Money market funds	$23,674
$34,000	Consumer items	$0
$100,000		$193,738

This investor's mistakes are obvious. He is not using his $100,000 to the maximum; only $66,000 of his money is working for him. The rest, $34,000, earns zero interest and is virtually worthless in ten years. Even assuming no taxes on his gold, gems, and coin investments, this investor has a ten-year real-dollar value of about $105,000.

But this example is interesting for another reason. Notice how he spread his investments. Most of our survey investors spread their money among three or more investments. They were "diversifiers." That brings us to our next investment principle.

Wealth Principle 3: *Don't* Diversify! Concentrate All of Your Eggs in the *Right* Basket

Diversification is a widely misunderstood concept. Any financial adviser will tell you not to put all of your eggs in one basket. You may agree, saying, "If I put all of my money in a bad investment, I will lose everything." That makes sense, doesn't it?

Not when you study what the wealthiest of multimillionaires, Andrew Carnegie, said on the subject: "Put all of your eggs in one basket, and then watch that basket."

Carnegie understood this basic rule of wealth. There is a time to diversify and a time to concentrate. If you are just beginning to create wealth, you concentrate. You pick a strong investment and throw your whole energy into it. Don't dissipate your energies in a dozen different directions. Become an expert, and when you fail, learn from your failures; add this precious knowledge to your storehouse and proceed to correct the mistake in the future.

As proof of the power of concentration, we find that the top three performers in the survey had concentrated 100 percent of their assets into only a few strong investments.

So what about diversification?

It is just another word for insurance. But as a wealth seeker, you should diversify *only a small percentage* of your assets into low-risk investments such as savings accounts. If your strong suit should happen to go sour, you will have a small amount to fall back on. Just enough to prime the pump and set you back in the game.

To repeat, then: invest heavily in your strong investment. Make it the workhorse of your program. Keep only a small amount on reserve.

In the next wealth principle, we learn why people are so prone to diversify and not to concentrate.

Wealth Principle 4: Wealth Seekers Are Always on the Offensive, Not on the Defensive

My survey confirmed the fact that most Americans are inordinately concerned with security, and that faced with risk, failure, or debt, they will opt for low-yielding "safe" investments. We all know that these kinds of investments don't produce wealth. Most investment advisers place too much emphasis on preserving your assets, surviving with your assets, or protecting your assets. The average investor is given to believe that the worst thing that could happen is to lose his capital. And in this way the uneducated investor is placed on the defensive. He is more concerned with saving his money than with making it grow. In my opinion, any investment adviser who is overly concerned about preserving your assets does you a great disservice.

Remember the parable of the talents? The Lord gives five talents to one servant, two talents to another, and one talent to another. Upon returning, the master finds that two of his servants have done very well with their "investments." The first has increased his portfolio from five talents to ten. The second has also doubled his talents, from two to four. But the last was afraid. He did not want to take a risk and he therefore buried his talent. Christ's words are explicit. To him who was afraid he said:

"Thou wicked and slothful servant . . . Take therefore the talent from him and give it unto him which hath ten talents . . . And cast ye the unprofitable servant into outer darkness."

Isn't that an interesting choice of words: "unprofitable servant"? The profitable servant is on the offensive. He is willing to risk to make his talents grow. The unprofitable servant is on the defensive. He wishes only to preserve, to protect, and therefore neither he nor his assets grow. And the wealth slips through his fingers and is given to those who understand this principle.

Our survey showed that 40 percent of our sample investors were unprofitable servants. They either broke even or lost all or a part of the "talents" they were given. Another 39 percent increased their assets, but not significantly. If you use the Bible as a guideline, only one person in our survey was "profitable."

But is there a place for defense? Of course. Any football coach can tell you that a good team must be balanced with both offensive and defensive units. But the saying goes: The best defense is a good offense.

Wealth Principle 5: Money Must Multiply at Wealth-Producing Rates of Return

The following table tells an important story:

RATES OF ANNUAL GROWTH NEEDED TO COMPOUND VARIOUS AMOUNTS INTO $1 MILLION

Annual Rate of Growth

Starting cash ($)	5 yrs	10 yrs	15 yrs	20 yrs	25 yrs	30 yrs
$100,000	59%	26%	17%	12%	10%	8%
$75,000	68%	30%	19%	14%	11%	9%
$50,000	82%	35%	22%	16%	13%	11%
$40,000	90%	38%	24%	18%	14%	11%
$30,000	102%	42%	26%	19%	15%	12%
$20,000	119%	48%	30%	22%	17%	14%
$10,000	151%	59%	36%	26%	20%	17%
$5,000	189%	70%	42%	30%	24%	19%
$4,000	202%	74%	45%	32%	25%	20%
$3,000	220%	79%	47%	34%	26%	21%
$2,000	247%	86%	51%	36%	28%	23%
$1,000	298%	100%	59%	41%	32%	26%

When you are traveling at wealth-producing rates, you have to take more risks.

What are wealth-producing rates? It depends on how much money you have to start with, and when you want to achieve your goal. Study the chart to see how fast you will need to travel. For example, if you have $5,000 in beginning capital today and want to turn that into $1 million within twenty-five years, then your money must grow at an average yearly rate of 24 percent *after taxes and inflation.* If your goal is to be wealthy in ten years or less, you need to find investments that grow at 40 percent, 50 percent, 60 percent, even 70 percent *per year* on the average. And that is very difficult.

You'll recall that our survey investors were investing in assets which had rates of return nowhere near wealth-producing rates of return. In essence, they were just treading water.

I think the following graph clearly illustrates this problem:

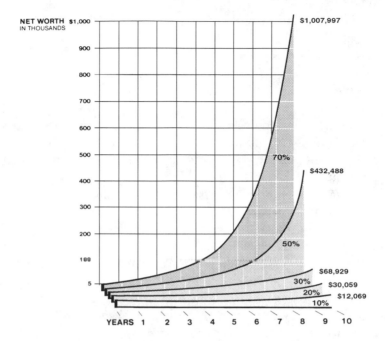

NET WORTH $1,000 IN THOUSANDS ... $1,007,997

70% $432,488

50%

$68,929
30% $30,059
20% $12,069
10%

YEARS 1 2 3 4 5 6 7 8 9 10

$5,000 COMPOUNDED AT VARIOUS RATES FOR TEN YEARS

How do we find investments that grow at such high rates of return? None of the twenty-two choices in the sample seemed to qualify. I'm sure that you already know the answer.

Use leverage. Leverage is debt. There are no safe investments that earn up to 100 percent per year over a long period of time without the use of leverage. You'll remember I said in the first chapter that it is impossible to become wealthy without going into debt. The wise—very wise—use of leverage will accelerate most investments to wealth-producing speeds. We will cover the basics of leverage here and go into more depth in chapters 9 and 10.

Since leverage is such an important tool, let me give you an example of how it accelerates a stock purchase from 10 percent to 100 percent return on investment (ROI). Suppose I want to buy some stock in ABC Corporation at $10 per share. I have $1,000, which will buy one hundred shares. If the stock increases to $11 per share, I have made a profit of $100 on my one hundred shares—a 10 percent return on my money. Suppose, instead, I borrow from my banker $1,000 secured with a personal note. I add this borrowed money (debt) to my own $1,000 and buy two hundred shares at $10 per share. If the stock goes up $1 per share, my profit is $200. But I have invested only $1,000 of my own money. Therefore the return on my investment is 20 percent (disregarding interest on the bank loan). If the stock goes up in value by $5, my profit is $1,000, or 100 percent on my invested dollars. Conversely, if the stock drops $5 per share, the leverage principle cuts in the opposite direction, and I *lose* 100 percent of my money! Leverage is therefore more risky. The faster you go up, the faster you can also go down. But no matter how frightening using leverage may seem to you, using it is absolutely essential if you ever hope to be wealthy.

Interestingly, almost 40 percent of our survey respondents indicated that they felt that debt was bad! And they showed it by their investment decisions. They had not acquired wealthy mind-sets because of their fear of debt.

In fairness, no one ever completely loses fear of debt. But wealthy thinkers learn how to control it, just as a surfer learns how to control the churning power of a wave.

I will explain this more fully later, in my chapter on leverage, but bear in mind that leverage is only temporary.

Five to ten years of wise debt buys you a lifetime of debt-free existence. And the price is well worth it.

Let's look at another survey investor. Her portfolio looked like this:

Investment	Category	Value in ten years
$10,000	Bank savings	$21,589
$15,000	Stock market	$38,906
$15,000	Money market funds	$35,511
$35,000	Consumer items	$0
$25,000	Down payment on $100,000 property ($25,000 down and $75,000 mortgage)	$140,893
$100,000		$236,899

Assuming no taxes on the real-estate investment, due to favorable tax laws, no principal reduction on any loans, and appreciation equal to inflation, this investor ends up with only $104,541 in real dollars.

Now that you understand the first five principles of wealth, do you think that you could improve on the above investment portfolio? Let's give it a try.

First of all, let's reduce the amount of money spent on consumer items. Instead of $35,000, we'll sacrifice a bit and spend only $10,000. That will free up $25,000 to be put to work.

Next, remembering the purpose of diversification, let's put only $10,000 into liquid "insurance" funds instead of $25,000 (bank savings plus money market funds). That will free up another $15,000.

Let's take the $40,000 that has been freed up from these two sources and add it to the amount of money we can use to buy real estate, for example. We'll keep our stock market portfolio at $15,000.

Our new portfolio will look like this.

Investment	Category	Value in ten years
$10,000	Money market funds	$23,674
$15,000	Stock market	$38,906
$10,000	Consumer items	$0
$65,000	Down payment on $250,000 property ($65,000 down and $185,000 mortgage)	$354,731
$100,000		$417,311

After taxes, this amount is reduced to $409,795. And after inflation, it is $189,814. Much better! Once you begin to apply the principles, things start to happen.

Is there a way to increase this even further? Let's look to the last principle again. Leverage is debt. Let's increase the debt on the real estate we purchase. Instead of buying only $250,000 with $65,000 down and $185,000 debt, let's buy more real estate and have more debt. What would happen if we bought $500,000 worth of real estate using our $65,000 cash as a down payment? The property would be rented out for enough to cover the mortgage payments on the new debt. Because of favorable tax incentives, the equity in the property would not be taxed until sold.

This one change improves the ten-year real-dollar net worth to over $300,000 in real dollars ($324,016, to be exact). Now we're starting to get somewhere. All it took was a little fine-tuning, a little sacrifice, and a lot of leverage.

But if it's all that simple, why isn't everybody rich? Well, it's *not* all that simple. Leverage, the powerhouse of any investment plan, must be used carefully and only in conjunction with the right investments. And that brings us to our next wealth principle:

Wealth Principle 6: Choose Investments That Are Both Powerful and Stable

If you could design the perfect investment, which of the following attributes would you like it to have? Put a checkmark beside your choices.

Very Liquid
No Management Headaches
Stable Growth Rates
Easily Leveraged
Hedge against Inflation
Hedge against Deflation
Good Tax Shelter
Easily Portable (in other words, fits in a briefcase)
Generates Steady Cash Flow

One thing is certain: there is no such thing as the perfect investment. And if anyone tells you that he has found such a beast, caveat emptor. He's probably selling something.

However, it is possible to find a perfect combination, or portfolio, of investments that together could display the attributes necessary in the creation of wealth. Let's look again at the major investment categories to see if we can recognize any wealth-producing attributes (see page 20).

What are the most important attributes in the creation of wealth?

In my opinion there are two: *power* and *stability.*

By power, I mean the ability of an investment to grow at high wealth-producing rates. What makes an investment powerful? The reasonable use of leverage, or debt. Examine the table below to find which investments are generally regarded as leverage vehicles.

By stability, I mean the ability of an investment to grow steadily, surely, relentlessly upward in value without broad fluctuations up or down in price. Here again, the chart points out several investments that are generally regarded as being stable in price.

But the key to finding a wealth vehicle is to find one that is *both* powerful and stable. Our choices are narrowed considerably. We see that only certain collectibles (such as high-quality rare coins), discounted mortgages, and real estate qualify.

	Liquid	Stable	Leverage	Inflation hedge	Deflation hedge	Tax shelter	Portable	Cash flow	Management
Hard assets									
1. Gold	X		X	X	X		X		
2. Silver	X		X	X	X		X		
3. Coins	X	X	X	X	X		X		
4. Art			X	X			X		
5. Antiques			X	X			X		
6. Stamps			X	X			X		
Liquid money									
1. Savings	X	X				X		X	X
2. Treasury bills (T-bills)	X	X				X		X	X
3. Money market funds	X	X				X		X	X
Passive and growth capital									
1. Stocks	X		X					X	X
2. Mutual funds	X	X	X					X	X
3. Commodities	X		X	X					
4. Bonds	X		X			X		X	X
5. Discounted mortgages	X	X	X			X		X	X
Active capital									
1. Business			X			X		X	X
2. Real estate		X	X	X		X		X	X

Why is it necessary to have both stability and power? Well, let's look at some of the investments that don't have both of these attributes.

Money market funds are relatively stable and safe but are not powerful enough to generate wealth-producing rates of return because of the lack of leverage. (Starting with $5,000 and assuming a 20 percent yearly interest rate, it would take you almost thirty years to make your first million.)

Commodities are very powerful and can produce spectacular gains, but because commodity markets are notoriously volatile (unstable) they can also produce spectacular losses. In other words, you can easily double or triple your money in two out of ten commodity trades, but you lose money in the other eight. Overall, maintaining high rates of *average* growth over a long period of time is very difficult if not impossible.

Many investments are powerful. Many are stable. But only a few are both powerful and stable. Real estate is both powerful and stable. But that doesn't mean it's perfect. For instance, it is not liquid. It may take months to sell.

Isn't this disadvantage enough to cause us to look elsewhere? Actually, the illiquidity of real estate is its most redeeming virtue. The only way for an investment to achieve liquidity is to give up something of value.

What price do other investments pay to achieve liquidity?

Take stocks. The stock market is a potentially powerful investment vehicle because of the use of leverage ("buying stock on margin"), but in order to achieve liquidity, the stock market relinquished its stability, as evidenced by the rather frequent fluctuations up and down in value. Yes, you can get your money out quickly, but you run the risk of taking a loss.

What about bank savings? Once again, they are marvelously liquid. And wonderfully stable. But they are pitifully weak. They can't produce wealth—only perpetuate it.

Stability is more important than liquidity. When I hear an investment adviser tout the liquidity of his particular investment, I can be sure of one thing: that the touted investment is either not powerful enough or not stable enough to be considered a wealth-producing investment.

Most investment advisers deal in "when-to" investments. The key to becoming wealthy in a "when-to" investment is to learn when to buy and when to sell. Timing is of the essence. If you buy low and sell high, you make a killing. If you get the formula backward, you get wiped out. These advisers would like to have you believe that they have, through their years of training and experience, developed a sixth sense for when things should be bought and sold. "Stick with me, kid, and I'll let you peer into my crystal ball [expensive newsletter] for the secrets of when to buy this and when to sell that." And wealth will be yours, of course.

I would rather point you in the direction of "how-to" investments (such as real estate) that increase steadily in value without broad fluctuations in price and are powerful enough through the prudent use of leverage to generate wealth-producing rates of return. What is important with how-to investments is not *when* to buy them but *how* to buy them—and hold onto them long enough. The secret to becoming wealthy in how-to investments has less to do with buying and selling—just buying and more to do with buying and buying.

How-to investments are rarely liquid, are always management-intensive, require a higher degree of expertise—but they produce wealth.

What makes real estate so stable? It is the law of supply and demand. Real estate, especially residential property, is a commodity in critical shortage and one for which there is an enormous demand. It is a necessity, not a luxury. People can't print up a hundred thousand homes as they might print up a stock offering.

That's why I continue to say:

Don't wait to buy real estate. Buy real estate and wait.

I have often conducted spontaneous surveys to reaffirm that statement. Recently, while speaking at an investment conference in San Francisco, I asked the following question: "How many of you know a millionaire personally?"

Out of one hundred people, perhaps fifty raised their hands.

Then I asked, "How many of those millionaires became wealthy by investing in gold?" Maybe two hands went up.

"How about commodities?" Maybe one hand.

"How about savings accounts?" The whole room broke out in laughter.

"How about the stock market?" Maybe two hands.

The response was the same for diamonds, antiques, gold coins, mutual funds, and bonds.

"How about businesses?" Perhaps twenty-five people raised their hands. Then I asked, "How many of you know someone who lost his shirt investing in a business?" Perhaps fifty hands went up.

"How many of you know someone who became a millionaire by investing in real estate?" Maybe thirty or forty hands went up. "All right, then, how many of you know someone who lost his shirt investing in real estate?" Only a few hands went up.

THE SEVEN PRINCIPLES OF WEALTH

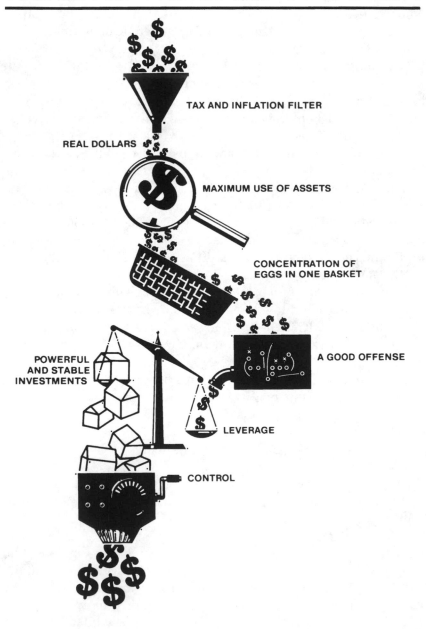

TAX AND INFLATION FILTER

REAL DOLLARS

MAXIMUM USE OF ASSETS

CONCENTRATION OF
EGGS IN ONE BASKET

POWERFUL
AND STABLE
INVESTMENTS

A GOOD OFFENSE

LEVERAGE

CONTROL

The response is the same every time I have done this informal survey.

Most when-to investment markets produce millions of small losers and a handful of large winners. Real estate produces millions of small and large winners and only a handful of losers.

Now, from this discussion it may seem that I am totally opposed to all when-to investments. Not so. There is a time and a place.

We are definitely in uncharted waters when it comes to investing during this decade. In the next chapter, I'll show you how a wise wealth seeker in an age of turmoil invests carefully to hedge against the realities of an uncertain future.

But first, let's talk about the final principle of wealth.

Wealth Principle 7: Control Is Essential

How many times have you heard of people who have lost a bundle? Think of them. You will probably find a common thread running through all the stories. Usually somehow, somewhere along the line, they transferred ultimate control of their money to someone else. And this someone took the money and through ineptitude, dishonesty, bad luck, or a combination of all three, lost it.

I have learned this lesson well. My education in this principle cost me over $200,000 largely because of two disastrous mistakes made in the same year. In both instances, I relinquished control to individuals who overestimated the potential profits and underestimated the costs and time necessary to make the investment work. And I paid the bill.

From that experience, I want to teach you a lesson that will save you thousands of dollars in the next twenty years. Over the decades, you will be approached by hundreds of well-meaning individuals with investment propositions. There will be tempting offers. But you must remember the principles of wealth. You concentrate heavily on your strong suit. *And nothing else.* And you never relinquish control over your investments. You have to watch over your little basket of fragile eggs very carefully. No one can do it for you until you can afford to hire your own staff. And even then, you have to supervise carefully.

A fool and his money are soon parted. Why? Because he doesn't understand investments. He doesn't understand leverage, or compound interest, or control. And as long as he doesn't understand these things, his wealth is in jeopardy.

But once he begins to understand these things and puts them into practice, he significantly increases the probability of success.

Now let's discuss strategy.

PART TWO

The Creating-Wealth Strategy

CHAPTER 4

Launching Yourself into Financial Self-Reliance

"The rich are different from you and me."
 —F. SCOTT FITZGERALD

"Yes, they have more money."
 —ERNEST HEMINGWAY, "The Snows of Kilimanjaro"

Sunday, April 12, 1981.

T minus one minute.

Tens of millions of people around the world were tuned to their televisions and radios.

T minus thirty seconds.

In the stillness of the early Florida morning, two million people near the launch site focused their eyes on the distant space vehicle.

T minus ten seconds. Nine. Eight. Seven. Would it fly?

Six. Five. Four. Three. Two. One. *Lift off!*

And so the first manned Space Shuttle lifted off for a successful voyage around the earth. Two days later, the reusable spacecraft landed safely on a dry lake bed at California's Edwards Air Force Base. The headline in the *New York Times* read, "Columbia Returns: Shuttle Era Opens!"

The common folk were temporarily awed. It was neat, but not as neat as landing a man on the moon. (After that, what can you do for an encore?) And with each successful launch and landing of the Space Shuttle, public interest dwindled; it became taken for granted, along with every other spectacular success. People return to their daily routines after this temporary titillation, this welcome break in the monotony. Back to the grindstone, the rat race. And in the locker rooms and lunch halls, they will talk about success, and hitting the jackpot, and luck. "One day my ship will come in." "One day I'll strike it rich." Not a second thought about the years of preparation that go into most successes. The sacrifices. The planning. The coordination. The sleepless nights. The prices paid.

For every person whose ship has come in, you will find five hundred who dream the same dreams but don't even bother going down to the dock.

The journey from financial bondage to financial freedom is much like launching a spacecraft into orbit. It takes careful planning and coordination. Anyone wishing to launch a financial spaceship into permanent orbit high above the monetary troubles of normal life and beyond the gravitational pull of inflation and taxes should be well prepared for it.

In a nation of almost 300 million people, there are fewer than 8 million millionaires. Fewer than 3 people in 100 have reached the magic million mark, the orbit of financial success. Why so few? Because so few understand the principles of wealth and how to organize these principles into a coherent, coordinated investment plan.

There are four specific stages in the wealth-building trajectory.

Stage 1: The Prelaunch Stage

The prelaunch stage is the preparation stage. So few wealth seekers ever get past this stage of the game.

I read a message scrawled on a locker-room wall: "The will to prepare to win is more important than the will to win." Preparing usually means doing those kinds of things that failures don't like to do. It means studying and learning. It means reading books, going to seminars. It means not being afraid to corner experts and ask foolish questions. I can always tell which of my seminar students have the will to prepare to win. They are the ones who stay to the end, listening and asking questions, always soaking up the last drop of knowledge, making the extra effort.

It is also vital in the prelaunch stage to get your house in order. Do you have adequate health and life insurance? Are you overburdened with short-term debt and exorbitant monthly payments? Now is the time to clean up your financial statement. Sell that boat you no longer use but are still making payments on.

Check into your credit rating. Go online or go down to your local credit bureau and ask to see your credit file, even if it costs a few dollars to do so. Ask the bureau's advice about how to clean up those "slow pays" on your record. Is there a way to challenge the report? Often a poor credit entry can be successfully challenged and eliminated. Don't be embarrassed. If you don't face it now, it will surface later on at a more critical time.

Getting your house in order also means getting your family to agree to the sacrifices that may be necessary for a few years. This may be the hardest part. For some reason, partners in a marriage often tend to be of the opposite financial philosophy (programming). One is generally risk oriented, the other risk averse. Left untended, these philosophies can build tensions that can ruin a marriage in short order. You may decide, after careful consideration, that the marriage is more important than the money. It always is. As religious leader David O. McKay wisely said, "No success can compensate for failure in the home."

My brother, Richard, tried to involve his family in each real-estate purchase. "Stephanie," he said to one daughter, "this duplex will help pay your way through college." "Matthew," he said to one son, "this home may be yours someday, so you had better help me take care of it." In this way, he taught them principles of wealth through personal experience. It is much better to have your family with you than against you.

Stage 1 is also a time to reevaluate. Perhaps you realize that you've devoted a decade or two to the wrong kinds of investments. Maybe you have been motivated by the need to be secure, which led you down the disastrous road of low-yielding investments in an inflationary environment. Maybe, like a drunken gambler, you sank your last nickel into $50 silver or $850 gold. Maybe you bought high into the stock market and don't want to sell low. Maybe you lent your life savings to your brother-in-law on a "sure thing" business opportunity that turned out to be a sure thing to lose your life savings and a brother-in-law. You are not alone. Just chalk it up to education. As I said earlier, I have deposited over $200,000 into my "education" bank account. And that hurts! But life goes on. This is the time to lick your wounds, swallow your pride, and change directions. Drastically, in some cases.

Will you have the courage to change? Will you be able to find the time to reeducate yourself and then put another program into action? These are the tough questions that need to be asked in the prelaunch stage.

This is also a time to set goals and write them down, as we discussed in chapter 2. It is a time to prepare yourself mentally for the liftoff. Now is the time to prepare budgets. Now is the time to visit your banker to lay the groundwork for a long and healthy borrowing career.

As one wise man put it, "One small good deed is better than a grand intention." This prelaunch stage is a time of many small, practical, mundane, seemingly insignificant actions that slowly compound our grand intentions into the realities of grand deeds.

All of this takes sacrifice. So few of us are willing to pay the price, and paying the price is what the next stage is all about.

Stage 2: The Liftoff, or the Struggling Stage

How many trillions of dollars have been lost by those traveling down (gambling on) the wrong road to wealth? The wreckage is incalculable! Why is so much time lost and so much money wasted? We learned the answer in the last chapter: because people choose the wrong investment vehicle. You don't launch spaceships with firecrackers. You launch them with Titan booster rockets that are proven and tested. Real estate is such a booster rocket. It is powerful and stable enough to propel your net worth into orbit.

There are many different real-estate investment programs that could be devised to create a large net worth within ten years. For our purposes here, I would like to set a *minimum* goal for you: you should be prepared to buy at least one single-family house per year for the next ten years. Assuming that you buy each property right and plan on minimal appreciation, this should conservatively produce a $500,000 net worth. Two houses per year could produce a $1 million net worth or more in ten years.

With this figure in mind, let me design a sample investment program for you. We'll assume that you can invest $10,000 per year in real estate and that you have the time to find, buy, and manage two single-family houses per year for the next ten years. (If you have less time or money than this, you will be interested in the chapters on leverage.) Try to invest in modest homes or condos whose value is below the median price for your city. The median price is where half the homes are more expensive and half the homes are less expensive. In other words, stay on the less expensive side of the line. At the end of the period you will own twenty houses, each rented out to a tenant.

Don't get sidetracked by the numbers or by the size of the plan. Most people can't imagine buying two houses per year for ten years. I make it sound as if buying a house were as simple as buying a loaf of bread. Obviously, it's not. But for now, just learn the concept. I'll get into the details of buying and selecting property later.

Let's assume that in many areas of the country well-selected properties appreciate 10 percent per year on the average—although there will be years when 10 percent per year seems extremely high and other years when 10 percent seems very low. We are hoping for a ten-year annual average of 10 percent. If you are worried about future real-estate appreciation, relax. In chapter 6, I'll show you several ways of making money in real estate assuming zero appreciation—even assuming falling real-estate markets. You can always improve your chances of building a profitable long-term real-estate portfolio by becoming an expert at finding bargain properties or negotiating bargain prices or fixing-up properties. I highly recommend this approach.

Suppose you bought one house per year for ten years. Your first house cost $150,000, and every house thereafter cost 10 percent more each year. This investment program would have the growth trajectory outlined in the chart on page 46.

The first few minutes of a NASA space launch are the most critical. During these few minutes the mighty booster rockets groan and strain to lift the space vehicle beyond the earth's enormous gravitational pull. Then the boosters are no longer needed and are jettisoned. The ship falls into a natural orbit, and the breath of a baby is all that is needed to propel it.

So it is with the struggling years of stage 2. We groan and strain under the enormous influence or gravity of our antiwealth programming. It is hard to break away. Instead of the usual instant gratification, these first years are years of sacrifice in which the results don't seem to justify the effort. According to the chart, after three years of sacrifices, your net worth is about $100,000. And it is just over $400,000 in five years. To say this another way, after having used up half the time allotted to reach your goal, you are less than halfway there. That can be discouraging. The gravitational pull of the world is very strong here. The get-rich-quick myth starts to wither and die about the third year, when you realize that becoming financially independent is not fun anymore. This is where we lose most of the crowd. Mission aborted. The price demanded has exceeded the ability to pay. Many drop out, content to tell stories about the "big one that got away."

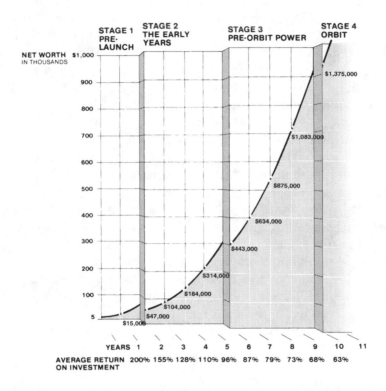

THE FOUR STAGES OF WEALTH

These first few years are also fraught with the temptation to find a quicker, easier route. The impatient are quick to abandon ship for the first fool's-gold investment opportunity that comes along. I keep a beautiful pyrite (fool's gold) paperweight prominently on my desk. Whenever someone approaches me with a "surefire" money-maker, I just look at my fool's gold and politely decline. For every solid booster-rocket investment, there are ten thousand imitations being bandied about. Now is not the time to change horses in midstream. It is the time for persistence. As the chart shows, it is only in the fifth year and beyond that your wealth starts to gather momentum. The reason why is that you made the commitment to concentrate almost all of your investment energies into one and only one investment vehicle. You put almost all of your eggs into the right basket. Now don't forget to watch over it.

You may have noticed that I said you put *almost* all of your eggs into real estate. I suggest that only 90 percent of your available assets be placed there. What do you do with the other 10 percent? Buy insurance. Not the kind of insurance you might think. You need to buy "staying power" insurance. Remember Murphy's Law: anything that can go wrong will go wrong. If you are maintaining a buying program of two single-family houses every year for the entire ten-year period, you are bound to encounter problems along the road. You may invest in a property in the wrong location and be forced to sell at a loss. You may miscalculate the negative cash flow from one of your properties. You may have trouble with one of your tenants for a period of time. You need to be prepared to solve these problems with cash. You wouldn't want to die of thirst just inches from a fountain!

Therefore, you should maintain a liquid emergency insurance fund. I call this my staying-power fund. I suggest that you work toward a savings account equal to three monthly mortgage payments for every property you own. This money should be as liquid as possible and should earn the highest interest rate allowable. This savings account doesn't produce wealth but helps preserve wealth in times of crisis. In the first year, if your two houses have monthly mortgage payments of $1,000 each, you would work toward an emergency fund of $6,000 ($1,000 x 2 properties x 3 months = $6,000). In the second year this would double. By the fifth year, with ten homes in your portfolio, you could have as much as $30,000 in your staying-power fund.

If you are well into your buying program already and don't have such an emergency fund, don't panic. I must confess that I personally have never maintained such accounts until recently. You should plan to create a fund as soon as it is feasible. Any windfall cash should go first to your emergency fund and second to your real-estate investment program. I think this is only wise.

This is done to insure you against the small chance that a string of bad luck (if you believe in such a thing) might wipe you out. You need staying power, and that comes only in the form of liquid cash.

To recap, then, stage 2 of wealth consists of the following:

1. Concentrate as much as 90 percent of your assets in real estate.
2. Buy a minimum of one property per year for ten years.
3. Maintain a staying-power fund equal to at least three monthly payments for every property you own.

Stage 3: The Powerful Pre-Orbit Stage

It is during the last five years of our sample investment trajectory that things really start happening—and fast! Every year after the fifth year, your net worth increases by at least $100,000. There aren't many folks who make $100,000 per year. In the last two years, your net worth increases by more than $200,000 per year! Your spaceship is gathering momentum.

Although we are still very much involved in buying at least two properties per year, we have some other things to worry about. What about the economy? Will there be a temporary decline in real-estate prices? What about a depression?

You might ask, "Bob, why haven't you concerned yourself with these questions before now? After all, we're pretty heavily invested into real estate." The answer is simple. Up until the fifth year, you don't have enough to lose to bother with such questions. You are trying to create wealth, not preserve it. You only worry about preserving it once you have something to preserve. Otherwise, you find yourself caught up in being on the defensive instead of on the offensive. Once you cross over the $250,000 line, you slowly begin to change from a liberal stance to a more conservative one. You begin to ask questions like, "How much time and effort would I waste if I lost everything?" Although the probability of a calamity like a deflationary depression is small—certainly, at this writing, less than 10 percent—we need to hedge against the worst case.

Don't get me wrong here! I am not a doomsayer. I am a realist. I play the probabilities. I view my investment portfolio as a vehicle that I am trying to steer safely along the road to wealth. I feel fairly comfortable about my ability to guide my vehicle, but in case of an accident I maintain an adequate insurance policy. No prudent driver would be caught without one. My staying-power fund has been my only insurance protection up till now. Now, in the third stage of wealth, I am going to buy some more insurance. This time I am going to buy some "prime the pump" insurance.

If our economy does go off track for a while in a 1930s type of deflationary depression, and real-estate values plummet, I want to be able to salvage at least some of my net worth in order to get me back in the game. Thus, I will want to be invested into deflation hedges such as bonds, cash, or precious metals.

Start small with your prime-the-pump fund. Perhaps you should get in the habit of buying an ounce of gold (one Krugerrand) for every additional real-estate property you add to your portfolio. Or you may decide to own the equivalent value of silver: between forty and fifty ounces. Rather than gold coins or bullion, you may venture into numismatics, or rare coins with proven silver and gold content. I favor this alternative, discussed in detail in chapter 13.

In the last years of the third stage, you may wish to increase your precious-metals holdings to the equivalent of three ounces of gold for every one of your properties. It would be ideal to have as much as 10 percent of your portfolio invested in such "bad news" hedges.

In this third stage of wealth, you may also choose to look differently at how you invest the cash in your staying-power fund. Up until the fifth year, this fund amounted to a minimum of three monthly payments for every property owned. In the sixth year and beyond, you should look seriously to having at least 10 percent of your assets in liquid-money form. Rather than maintaining these funds in savings and loan (S&L) associations or in money market funds—many of which are risky, since they invest in corporate notes—you should carefully select liquid funds that invest solely in government notes and obligations such as treasury bills (see chapter 14). In this way, you insulate your liquid assets even further from the small chance of an economic collapse.

I emphasize that, in my opinion, there is a only a minute probability of such a calamity, so I maintain only a minor portion of my portfolio to hedge against it.

And, even in a depression like the last one, the formula for buying real estate will not change. Only the prices will change. Cash will be king, bargains will abound. Even if you lost 80 percent of your real-estate net worth, the remaining 20 percent of your deflation-proofed portfolio would give you a great head start on everyone else.

Once you are covered with a staying-power fund and a prime-the-pump fund, you can forget about them. *These are not investments any more than you could call term life insurance an investment.*

Once you are insured, you can forget about the small probabilities of great disasters (defensive posture) and get on with the far greater probability of making some money (offensive posture). If defensive assets like cash and precious metals increase in value, so much the better. If not, we chalk it up to the cost of buying insurance.

Where does all of this insurance money come from? If you have been careful, it may come from the positive cash flows from some of your older properties. You may even decide to mortgage one of your older properties and put the borrowed money into one of your insurance funds. Your mortgage costs could be mostly offset by the return on your money market certificates. It may also come from prudent savings. Any extra cash should be distributed according to the guidelines of stage 3:

1. 80 percent real estate
2. 10 percent liquid paper assets such as treasury bills
3. 10 percent precious metals

In the ninth and tenth year, or as you approach your retirement goal, you will begin to prepare for the next stage.

Stage 4 is so important that we will devote the entire next chapter to it.

CHAPTER 5

The Automatic-Pilot Principle

A man's wealth is not in the purse he carries. A fat purse empties if there be no golden stream to refill it. Arkad has an income that constantly keeps his purse full, no matter how liberally he spends.

—GEORGE S. CLASON, *The Richest Man in Babylon*

I hate the word *retirement*. It sounds so final. To many it connotes a declining standard of living and social insecurity. I would rather use a more positive term.

Since I am a private pilot, I have adopted the term *automatic pilot*. If you're familiar with flying at all, you know that an automatic pilot is an instrument the pilot uses to make flying a lot easier. It is not used during takeoff, when the pilot must concentrate on every detail. However, once at cruising altitude, the pilot can set his course, speed, and altitude, turn on the automatic pilot, and presto—the plane takes over! The pilot is now free to do other things. This does not mean he can forget his job. He must occasionally check his gauges and instruments. But the pressure of flying has been significantly reduced.

Your goal, as a creative investor, is to launch your ship into financial orbit and then put it on automatic pilot. You then have the cash flow and the time to devote to the pursuits you think are most important. This is the domain of stage 4 of wealth.

In our sample investing program, you have been buying two single-family houses each year for a ten-year period. In the tenth year you should be the proud owner of twenty single-family houses with equities of approximately $1,375,000.

In addition, you should have at least $100,000 in liquid cash, plus an equal amount in other liquid investments.

Now, what are you going to do with all of this wealth? My bet is that you probably aren't going to feel all that wealthy. Real estate is a wonderful wealth generator but a terrible cash-flow generator. As they say, "It's all on paper." And paper won't put groceries on the table. You need cash flow. It will be necessary to make some changes.

In order to make these changes, you're going to change the way you have been doing things. The guiding principles during the first three stages of wealth are completely different from those in the fourth stage. The first three stages are wealth-*building* stages. The fourth stage of wealth is the wealth-*perpetuating* stage. Let's review these principles:

Wealth-Building Principles during the First Three Stages of Wealth

1. Always think in terms of profit after taxes and inflation.
2. Sacrifice to invest in things that go up in value. Avoid consumer items.
3. Don't diversify; concentrate your eggs in the right basket.
4. Be on the offensive, not the defensive.
5. Have your assets growing steadily at wealth-producing rates. That means debt and leverage.
6. Choose investments that are both powerful and stable.
7. Maintain maximum control over your investments.

During the fourth stage, the above principles will be reversed for a time. Here are the new principles:

Wealth-Perpetuating Principles during the Fourth Stage of Wealth

1. Jettison the debt! You read me right. Get rid of your booster rockets. They have served their purpose well. More on this in a minute.
2. Lower your compound rates of return from wealth-producing rates (above 25 percent) to wealth-perpetuating rates (below 25 percent).
3. With lower growth rates, you will need to do more careful tax and inflation planning.

4. For a time, you will think defensively, not offensively.
5. You will be more prone to diversify your assets than to concentrate them.
6. Pay less attention to the need for sacrifice. If you want something nice, buy it. You've earned it. You can afford it. Who cares if it goes down in value?
7. You will maintain less control over your investments. You will either choose investments that require less personal involvement or hire your own inhouse management team, as I have done. You will never relinquish complete control, just day-to-day supervision.
8. During the first three wealth-building stages, you will probably want to keep your present job and do your investing on the side. Once you put your investments on automatic pilot, this may change. If you don't enjoy your job, quit. Your investments can now carry you.

The emphasis during the first three stages is on equity growth and wealth building. In the last stage, it will shift to cash flow and wealth perpetuation. Let's have another look at the annual rates of return of our investment choices:

Hard assets		Liquid money	
Gold, silver	10%	Bank savings	3–5%
Precious gems	17.5%	Treasury bills	5–10%
Collectibles (antiques,			
stamps, art, etc.)	15%	Money market funds	2–5%

Passive capital growth		Active investments	
Stock market	10%	Buy own home	10%
Bonds	5–12%	Real estate	
Commodities	25%	investments	10%
Mutual funds	10–13%	Businesses	25%
Discounted mortgages	25%		
Tax-lien certificates	10–20%		
Stock options	25%+		

It would still be wise to maintain your insurance funds: 10 percent in liquid-money investments yielding the highest short-term interest rate, as well as perhaps another 10 percent in precious metals. The remaining 80 percent of your assets should be shifted into investments that, in the words of financial adviser Howard Ruff, "beat inflation and taxes plus a little bit more." Although this figure will change, you should probably aim for a target yearly growth rate between 10 percent and 25 percent for the major portion of your assets. The higher the better.

Using 10 percent as a minimum guideline, you can diversify your wealth into many areas. There are several excellent when-to investments, such as the stock market, mutual funds, and the bond market—if you know what you are doing. I personally would stay away from commodities. They are terribly risky, and the novice can lose his shirt.

Some collectibles, such as fine art, numismatics, and rare stamps, have excellent supply-and-demand features, which ensure steady price increases to the prudent expert. And many people consider them satisfying hobbies as well.

In the active-investment area, discounted mortgages have marvelous potential, as I will explore in chapter 12. If you want real estate without any of the hassle of managing it, you might look into many of the excellent real-estate limited partnerships available; see chapter 15. Or you might do as I have done and stick with real estate and its related businesses—but without relying as heavily on debt or leverage as before.

The main thrust of your investing will be to preserve your wealth while generating a cash flow sufficient for you to retire on. To provide a better picture of the automatic pilot aspects of the fourth wealth stage, let me share two alternative investment plans among the hundreds of possibilities.

Plan 1: Own Your Real Estate Free and Clear

During the first ten years, we have become used to being highly leveraged—deeply in debt for our real estate. Let's see what happens when we completely reverse this philosophy. Let's sell off the first ten houses we purchased, with their combined gross equities of around $765,000. Your goal is to sell for cash. This may take two or three years to accomplish. The maximum tax bill would be 20 percent of the profit. By spreading the sales over several years, this bill could feasibly be reduced to $115,000, leaving you with $650,000 in cash. Use this cash to pay off the remaining $641,000 in mortgages on your other ten houses. You are now the proud owner of ten free-and-clear single-family houses worth $900,000.

What about retirement? Each house will rent for between $750 and $1,000 per month after expenses. That equals as much as $10,000 cash flow per month, or $120,000 per year. Depending on inflation, this would be worth, in real dollars, at least $5,000 per month, or $60,000 per year. Not a king's ransom, but I'm sure you can manage.

What about inflation? The homes will continue to keep pace with inflation, so your net worth will rise steadily. Your rents should also rise over the years, although perhaps not quite as fast as inflation.

Now, what about income taxes? Your homes will generate some tax shelter, although the higher your income, the less your income can be sheltered from taxes.

In order for you to pay lower taxes, you would have to buy more real estate. "But wait a minute!" you say. "I just sold ten houses. Why do I want to buy some more?" You sold the houses to get completely out of debt. Doesn't that feel good? And you created a marvelous cash flow for yourself. You solved one problem and created another: a tax burden. If you want to alleviate the tax problem, you will reenter the real-estate market and buy approximately $500,000 worth of property in the next two to five years. You have become accustomed to buying two houses per year. Why not just keep it up until you own enough real estate to help you shelter the income from your free-and-clear properties?

But this time when you buy your yearly quota of properties, things will be quite different. You will no longer be in debt up to your eyeballs and taking what some might call inordinate risks. You will own ten free-and-clear properties, which, through wise estate planning, have been socked away into asset-protection entities (see chapter 17), far from the greedy reaches of malicious litigation. Your other properties, purchased only for tax shelter, will be kept outside these entities. If the world collapses around your ears, and you lose your tax-shelter properties to default, heaven forbid, you can retreat to your free-and-clear haven and wait for the storm to blow over.

Let me show you a chart of what this might look like:

You notice that your leverage line (debt-to-equity ratio) is very high in the beginning of stage 2 and decreases steadily throughout the holding period. In stage 4, since the goal is to eliminate debt, you sell ten properties and pay off the remaining ten. That puts you in a zero-leverage position in the eleventh year. Then, to avoid taxes, you continue your investment program for several years until you reach a zero tax position where your leverage line holds steady.

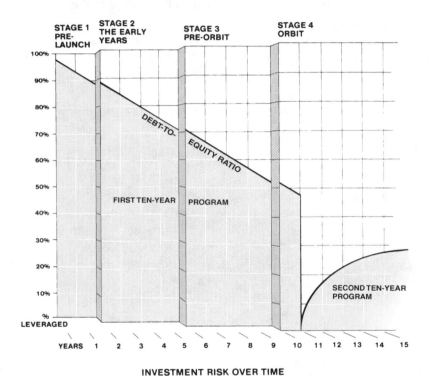

INVESTMENT RISK OVER TIME

You are now in permanent orbit with steady cash flow sheltered from taxes. Your net worth is shielded from inflation, with appreciating assets and increasing rents. A steady orbit, wouldn't you say?

At this point, you may decide to quit your job to devote more time to other interests. If you don't want to manage your properties personally, you can put them on automatic pilot by hiring, as I have done, a full-time manager on your own payroll. I have found that I retain much better control over my situation by hiring and training my own employee than I would by hiring an outside management company. With your own employee overseeing your "crops," your time is now free. You are what they call financially independent.

Plan 1, as described here, still relies heavily on real estate as not only wealth perpetuator, inflation protector, and tax shelter, but also as main cash-flow generator. Essentially, you are now in a defensive posture. You may not be significantly diversified into other investments, but you can always fall back on your insurance funds in time of trouble, if any. Your mortgageless assets are insulated in trusts. And you maintain a great degree of control over your investments.

Now, if you should want to venture into other risky areas, such as commodities, penny stocks, or selected business ventures, you are free to do so. It's fun to take some play money and see how far you can run with it. However, you would be wise to make a vow never to dip into your orbiting capital. If you should fail, you risk dropping out of orbit. Whenever you see someone lose great wealth, you can be sure that he made this fatal mistake. He gambled it all on one more roll of the dice—and rolled a seven.

Plan 2: Sell Your Real Estate with Nothing Down

Rather than selling your ten oldest properties for cash, you may wish to sell them instead for terms—nothing down, even. You won't have any trouble selling them. Your only problem will be qualifying your buyers. You will probably be able to ask higher prices than in plan 1, and you will definitely be able to spread out the tax consequences over a longer period of time, saving you tens of thousands of dollars. If you carry back your entire equity of $1,375,000 in the form of contracts or mortgages at, let's say, 8 percent for twenty-five years, you could earn as much as $10,000 per month—the same as in plan 1.

However, there is one major difference. In plan 1, 80 percent of your estate is in inflation-proof real estate. In plan 2, 60 percent of your estate is in depreciating notes and mortgages. Another 20 percent is in the form of ten highly leveraged single-family houses. And the rest is in insurance funds. You take a risk that your monthly cash flow will be slowly eroded by the power of inflation. If you retain your mortgages through the twenty-fifth year, the last mortgage payments, totaling $10,000, will be worth only $1,460 in today's dollars, factoring in an inflation rate of 8 percent. Terrible, isn't it?

Of course, you will have some inflation protection from your real-estate holdings. Your income-tax problems are only slightly different from those you have in plan 1. You will still need to shelter the $120,000 yearly interest income from your mortgages. In order to pay no taxes, you will need to buy more real estate, as in plan 1.

If you are worried about the effect of inflation on your wealth, you may also decide to buy an extra property or two per year. You can still hire a full-time manager, not only to manage but to find new properties for you to invest in. In essence, you reach a different kind of financial independence. Perhaps the only major disadvantage of plan 2 is the level of your overall leverage line. You will still own at least ten heavily mortgaged houses.

The reason I have included this alternative plan is to hedge against the probability that you will not be able to find ten cash buyers for your properties. The market may be soft. Mortgage money may be tight. If so, you can move your properties another way and still retire handsomely.

As I have tried to illustrate in these two plans, there are a number of viable routes for you to take. Instead of the alternatives I have outlined, you could be equally successful in many other investments. The goal is to perpetuate your wealth while generating a monthly cash flow.

Of course, this entire chapter has taken place in a vacuum. I have created an ideal world where all real estate appreciates in value and no problems exist. Perhaps you would be interested to learn what happens in the real world. Let me share with you what I have done with my own personal wealth—how I have planned for inflation and taxes, and how all of my automatic pilots function.

As of this writing, I have created at least four $1 million automatic pilots. The first of these consists, of course, of my real-estate holdings.

Most of the properties in my portfolio are free and clear of mortgages because I am in stage 4 of my real-estate wealth trajectory. I have sold most of my properties, and I have invested most of the cash in only a few properties. Of course, we live in a beautiful, brand-new house with fine furniture and totally free and clear of mortgage. Two foreign cars grace my garage, also totally paid for. The remaining investments include well-selected limited partnerships in real estate and investment-grade art. Our family trusts are already set up. I now work because I love to work, not because I have to work. Stage 4 is sweet.

All of my real-estate holdings are managed by partners who

receive a salary for managing plus a percentage of the ownership of each additional property they buy for me. Thus, they are managing "our" properties, not just my properties. As we shall see, this "ownership" incentive is critical to successful automatic pilots. With my real-estate holdings on automatic pilot, I can devote more of my time to the things I love to do, such as writing and speaking.

A few years ago, while in the latter stages of my real-estate wealth-building process, I decided to fulfill a lifelong ambition to write a book. In chapter 2, I shared with you some of the details of how I got it published. The book helped thousands of people, and its phenomenal success made me into a "bankable" author and thus created my second $1 million automatic pilot. Simon & Schuster, my publisher, prints, promotes, and markets my books. I cheer them on from the sidelines and receive a royalty for every book sold. And we both profit. In essence, the book is now on automatic pilot. Jillian Manus, my literary agent (the best in the world), makes sure that my new manuscripts are well received. And we both profit.

As you can see, when it comes to building automatic pilots, you need the best partners available. No stepping over dollars to pick up pennies. The best always produce much more than they cost.

My third automatic pilot is my seminar business. Several years ago, about the same time that I wrote my first book, I began teaching my system of investing in real estate in a two-day seminar. The original seminar grew from very humble beginnings to the point where we now have taught over two million students in every major city in the United States and Canada. I guess you could say I am president of my own university. The classes are taught by specially trained experts. I rarely teach my own seminar anymore. It too is on automatic pilot.

My fourth $1 million automatic pilot is in several other business ventures with excellent potential for growth and profit.

In order to set up successful automatic pilots, you need to hire the best. Share the profits with them so they can carry on the business for you without requiring your constant presence. It is only in this way that you can divorce yourself from day-to-day operations to spend time at your most important tasks.

I wouldn't want to give you the impression that your automatic-pilot businesses and the partners you bring in to run them are mere machines, robots, or servants. Your personal attention is required to lend overall direction to your portfolio. But direct day-to-day operational control can be delegated to others. You are, in a sense, only on *semi*automatic pilot. The old saying is still true: "The best fertilizer a farmer has is his own shadow." Business is competitive. Someone has to be minding the store at all times.

In order for an idea to be suitable for an automatic pilot, it must be able to be carried out by someone other than the boss. Let's look at one of the highest-paid professions and see if it qualifies. For instance, a surgeon cannot delegate his job. He is limited by the number of operations he can perform in a given time frame. The only way he can make more money is to raise his prices, and that has a limit. Although he may make buckets of money during his productive years, if he isn't preparing automatic pilots on the side, he will find himself in trouble.

The same goes for the mom-and-pop businesses that you see by the thousands in every city. These are generally not profitable enough to allow hiring a replacement for the boss. This is not an automatic pilot, it is just another job. It is not a route to freedom, it is a glorified prison.

Now, take the example of McDonald's. It's as if someone took a cookie cutter, stamped out thousands upon thousand of copies, and placed them around the world. Management was cloned, and now the residual profits flow to the originator of the idea for ever and ever.

The theory of automatic piloting creates the empire that never crumbles because only quality people run it. The more money they make for themselves, the more money you make. It is all embodied in the philosophy of win-win (chapter 8). I can't win unless you win—and if you win big, so do I.

Thus, every business I own purrs along on automatic pilot as I write these words. I created the wealth through "luck" and hard work. I set it into orbit and relegated the perpetuation of it to self-interested automatic pilots.

These are the principles of attaining and maintaining wealth. Now let's add some meat to the bones of these principles. Let's move on to the next chapter to add some detailed, nitty-gritty, how-to-do-it information.

PART THREE

Concentrating: Being in the Right Place at the Right Time

CHAPTER 6

Cookie Cutters:
Geese That Lay Golden Eggs

It has never been easier to make a fortune in real estate.

So what makes real estate tick?

First of all, the real-estate marketplace is an imperfect market. It's not like the stock, bond, or commodities markets—all perfect markets—where an investor merely has to open the *Wall Street Journal* to be able to calculate the profit or loss on his portfolio on any given day. A real-estate investor is never really sure what his property is worth. And to find out may take months of marketing. It is precisely this uncertainty that creates opportunity.

In addition, real estate is a very complex beast. There are intricacies that the average speculator rarely takes the time to learn. And when times get harsh, these quick-buck folks are the first to get burned. Stories abound about how everyone is losing his shirt. The amateurs head for the sidelines. That leaves the entire marketplace to the experts. The competition is gone. It is a veritable gold mine.

Finally, regardless of the times, real estate is a necessity. People need to live somewhere, in a house, an apartment building, a condominium, a townhouse, a trailer park. And the majority of newly formed families can't afford (or at least think they can't afford) to own their own home. That means they will always need a place to rent—which could be one of your properties.

Stick with what people have to have. Concentrate here. And leave the rest of the real-estate market to other experts. Become an expert in how to house people.

The late Russell H. Conwell, founder of Temple University and a gifted lecturer, used to tell the story of a wealthy man in ancient

Persia named Ali Hafed, who sold his farm and took the money to finance his search for a diamond mine. Shortly thereafter, the person who bought the farm from Hafed discovered a diamond in the stream behind the farmhouse. The diamonds from that very stream were used in the crown jewels of England and Russia.

Like the unobservant diamond investor, many of us have been off looking for diamonds when the best investment in the world is lying undiscovered in our very own backyard: the house we live in.

Why have we not recognized it until now?

A house, because of its sacred-cow status, has been generally regarded as a once-in-a-lifetime purchase. But the single-family house is an ideal wealth-building investment. Once you get the knack, houses are easy to understand, buy, and manage. (By the way, when I say *house,* I mean a detached single-family house or an attached condominium or townhouse.)

Since a single-family house is the basic building block of beginning wealth, let's explore in more detail what the ideal home should look like.

Target Property

There is a very narrow range of properties that are worthy of the term *investment grade.* I call this my target property. In my opinion, at this time an ideal target property should have the following description: a three-bedroom single-family detached house or condominium that is located in a stable neighborhood within a fifty-mile radius of your own home; priced at less than the median price in your city and worth at least 10 percent more than your cost; and can be bought with less than 10 percent down and terms that allow the buyer to rent out the home with little or no negative cash flow.

Now, why do I buy homes only in the bottom end of the price pyramid?

Because that is where all the demand is. Thus, lower-priced properties have the greatest potential for upward price pressure. When interest rates rise, people who own homes in the bottom third of the pyramid can't afford to sell and move up the ladder. They stay put, thereby causing a shortage of lower-priced housing.

Builders have not been building adequate quantities of economically priced houses. So the supply side of the supply/demand

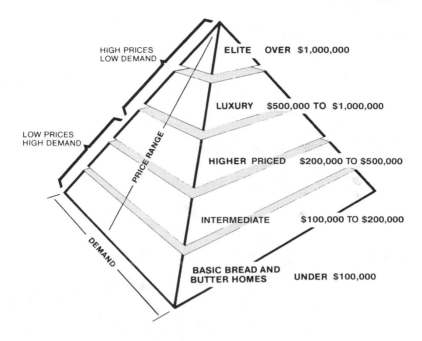

HIGH PRICES
LOW DEMAND

ELITE   OVER $1,000,000

LUXURY $500,000 TO $1,000,000

LOW PRICES
HIGH DEMAND

PRICE RANGE

HIGHER PRICED $200,000 TO $500,000

INTERMEDIATE $100,000 TO $200,000

DEMAND

BASIC BREAD AND
BUTTER HOMES   UNDER $100,000

PYRAMID OF PRICES FOR RENTAL HOMES

equation is always advantageous to real-estate investors. When the economy sputters, people can't afford higher-priced housing and fall down the price pyramid to buy houses they can afford. So regardless of the economy, there is always plenty of demand at the lower end of the price pyramid.

If you ever read in your newspaper that home prices are falling in your city, you had better check the figures. It usually means that the average price of houses is falling. What has happened is that greater quantities of lower-priced houses are selling while higher-priced houses are still sitting on the market. This brings down the average price but does not mean that all houses are declining in value. In actuality, the lower-priced house is increasing in value while higher-priced housing is falling.

While we're on the subject, let me tell you why I don't invest in higher-priced houses. Even though houses for the rich seem always to be in demand, it is very difficult to rent out a larger house for enough money to cover the mortgage payments. Therefore, it is wiser to stick with the cheaper property where rents and mortgage payments are more in line.

How to Find the Right House

Many investors have difficulty picturing what I mean by a lower-priced bread-and-butter house. Because much local media attention is focused on reporting information about the median-priced house, it is often assumed that this is your average bread-and-butter house. Not so!

What does *median* mean? If the median-priced house in your area is $200,000, this simply means that half of the houses are selling for more than $200,000, and half are selling for less. As an investor, you should be buying houses priced much less than the median. Basically, you want the simple, no-frills houses in a stable neighborhood.

How do you know what price range is right for your area?

If you have a friend who is a Realtor, ask him or her to let you browse through the local Multiple Listing Service (MLS) sold book. In most major cities, the Board of Realtors compiles information on all properties that have sold through the Multiple Listing Service during every three-month period. This is called the MLS sold book. If you don't know a Realtor, just drop in at any real-estate office and ask the secretary to let you thumb through the book or online listings. Tell her that you are just window shopping.

Generally, real-estate listings are organized by area, beginning with the lowest-priced properties and progressing to the highest-priced properties. You can tell by looking at the pictures the general condition of the neighborhoods. If you aren't familiar with your city, ask the Realtor which sections in the book have large numbers of middle-class houses in the lowest-priced category. What you want is a neighborhood of basic, no-frills homes. Some may be five or ten years old or older. It is hard to find newer houses in the lower price ranges. If you can find newer houses, so much the better. Condominiums and townhouses are OK.

Once you have identified the neighborhoods where your "target" bread-and-butter house is located, you should study the information given in the real-estate listings. It will tell you prices, mortgages, and terms. You will not be making any offers. You will be just assimilating information. The more you know about the market, the better prepared you will be.

Jot down the addresses of some houses that interest you. Take a drive out to look at them. Actually, what the neighborhood looks like is even more critical than what the house looks like. Try to choose houses in areas that you would be comfortable living in. Stay away from busy streets and commercial corners. Stable suburbs filled with hundreds of little houses all in a row are my favorite. Cul-de-sacs are also ideal. The most important feature of a neighborhood is pride of ownership. By this I mean the homes are well cared for, the lawns are mowed, the streets are clean. I am not thrilled with neighborhoods where debris lines the streets, old autos crumble on weedy vacant lots, and houses are deteriorating. Leave the upgrading of such neighborhoods to the experts. In a word, you are more interested in the look of the neighborhood than the age of the properties. Remember, you may be owning a property in this neighborhood for ten years or more.

As far as size, I am partial to three-bedroom houses. I have owned houses of all sizes, but I have had the best luck, in my area, with average-sized homes. Since the house is the Cadillac of rentals, people moving out of two-bedroom apartments like to move up to a larger place. This, however, may differ in your area. Do some checking with your local apartment owners' association before you decide what to buy.

Your goal in all of this looking is to establish what your local target property will look like.

Learning to be successful at real-estate investing is much like learning how to ride a bicycle. At first you are a little wobbly and unsure of your balance, but you soon get the knack of it. And once you master the art, you never forget, no matter how old you are. So when it comes to investing, learn to ride your investing bicycle close to home. Once you master it, you will be successful anywhere in the country.

If you live in one of the most expensive cities in the country, like San Francisco, Los Angeles, New York, or Washington, DC, you may be tempted to begin your investment program in other cities, like Phoenix, Oklahoma City, or Orlando, Florida, where prices are much lower. Don't be tempted. You can still find good prices in outlying suburbs at prices that will surprise you. So don't be misled by what you read in the newspapers about high prices. There are plenty of your kind of properties out there.

Now, what about terms? As we learned in earlier chapters, the leverage power of real estate is its most exciting feature. You want to be able to buy your properties with small down payments. I think that 10 percent down should be your upper limit. If possible, avoid using banks and S&Ls for the loans on the other 90 percent. Your best bet is to find sellers who are willing to finance the sale of their property at below-market interest rates. You're trying to find houses that can be rented out for enough to cover the mortgage payments.

How do you find such flexible, motivated sellers? According to our research, as many as 10 percent of the sellers in any given real-estate market are flexible, judging from the advertising in the classified section of the newspaper. Some sellers are not flexible on price but are willing to be flexible on terms—that is, to accept a small down payment and carry loans for the balance of the equity. Their need to sell is greater than their need for cash. On the other hand, some sellers are willing to reduce their price significantly to an all-cash buyer if you can come up with a lot of quick cash. In the next chapter, I'll show you an easy way to find both types of sellers.

The basic plan calls for you to buy at least one of these bread-and-butter houses each year for the next ten years.

Once you understand the basic plan, the next step is to choose your cookie cutter.

Cookie Cutters: Being in the Right Place at the Right Time

What is a cookie cutter?

It is a formula, a method that successful investors use over and over again to cut dough out of their particular investment marketplace. This is the characteristic of all wealthy people. They are experts in their chosen fields. They adapt their personalities to the circumstances. And they use these cookie cutters repeatedly.

There are at least eight different basic real-estate cookie cutters, each with its own benefits and detriments. Let's look at them one by one:

Cookie Cutter 1: Buy High, Sell Higher

Everyone knows the cardinal rule of investing: buy low, sell high. You buy a stock on a hot tip for $5 a share; six months later you sell it for $10 a share. Buy low, sell high. (And if you really like risks you can sell *short,* which in cookie-cutter language would be "Sell high, buy low.") But in reality, this basic buy low/sell high formula is a misnomer. You don't buy a stock low and sell it high. You buy it at market today and you wait until it goes up before selling it. You speculate that it will eventually go up in value. You don't buy it low at all. You buy it high and sell it higher. Buy high, sell higher.

The real-estate analogy to this is buying a house for $150,000, renting it out to cover the mortgage payments, and selling it several years later for $300,000.

What caused the house to double in value? Two things: inflation and demand for homes. But what happens when inflation slows down and rising interest rates dampen demand for housing? You guessed it: real estate doesn't go up in value. And that's the problem of investing for appreciation when there is none.

The wise investor learns to choose a cookie cutter that matches his future economic expectations. In an era of rapid appreciation, this cookie cutter works wonders. Millions of dollars were made by smart investors during the early 2000s. Wouldn't you like to have bought twenty single-family houses in 1995?

The chart on page 70 shows what has happened to the median price of single-family homes since the 1950s.

If you believe that property values will continue to escalate, then you should be stockpiling properties—buying with both hands. If you believe that we may have several years of stagnant real-estate prices, you may decide to use another cookie cutter.

Cookie Cutter 2: Buy Low, Sell High

The true buy low, sell high situation is when you can buy a product at wholesale and sell it at retail without having to wait for appreciation. Since real estate is an imperfect market, a savvy investor can literally buy a property and sell it the same day for a profit. I don't want to give you the impression that this is easy, but it is done all the time. It requires a keen sense of market value on the part of the investor coupled with nerve and the ability to market a property

MEDIAN PRICE FOR SINGLE-FAMILY HOME

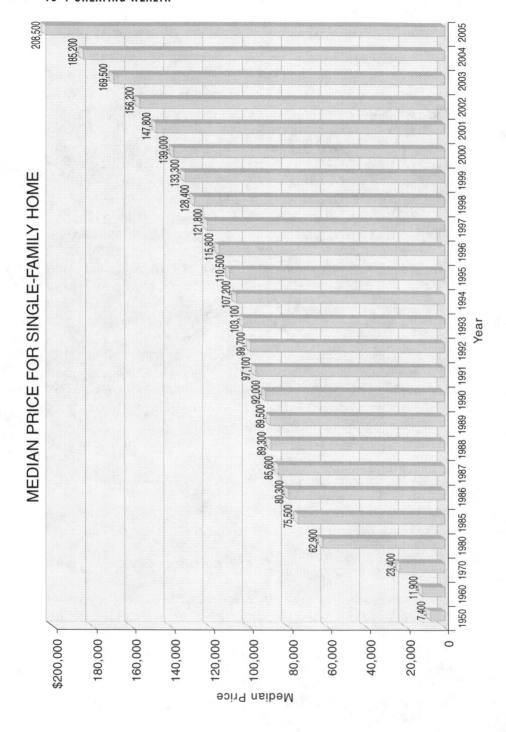

quickly. In one instance, I found a property priced below market and arranged to resell it to another investor at a $9,000 cash profit—even before I actually owned the property. I structured the transaction so that I signed the documents to buy the property in the morning and signed the documents to sell it at a profit that same afternoon.

An investor using this cookie cutter makes his profit on the way in. He is not a speculator, he is a businessman. Buying at wholesale and selling at retail. In full control. Not hoping for a dubious future profit but creating his profit immediately.

What are the disadvantages of the wholesale approach? Well, it takes more time and effort. The real-estate bargain hunter may have to dig through a hundred flexible sellers to find one that meets the criteria. And then when he does find the right deal, there is probably going to be a lot of cash involved. If you don't have a lot of cash, this can be a problem. (See chapters on leverage for solutions to this problem.)

Median Price of Single-Family Homes

You also need to know what you are doing. No guesswork here! What happens if you sink $20,000 into a property you *think* is priced 20 percent below the market and find out that the seller was flexible because he *knew* that a fertilizer factory was going to be built next door? Before you invest hard cash, you'd better ask some hard questions of local Realtors, other sellers in the area, city planning and zoning commissions, and others.

Sometimes you can pick up bargains without having to invest a lot of cash. For example, as a beginning investor many years ago, I added a perfect property to my portfolio. The seller responded to an ad I ran regularly in the newspaper. He indicated that he was very anxious to get rid of a duplex he owned. I began to explore the reasons for his high motivation.

There were three. He was moving. He didn't like to manage tenants. And last, and most important, he hadn't made his mortgage payment for three months and owed about $1,800. His property was appraised at $60,000 with loans of only $48,000—a $12,000 equity. I asked him what he wanted for his equity. He said he didn't want anything for his equity. He was sick of the unit and would sign over the property to me if I would just guarantee him that his payments would be brought current and kept that way.

"Do you mean you'll walk away from twelve thousand dollars if I just pay your back payments?" I asked.

He said, "Yes, but we must be able to get it done within a week. I don't want to own this property any longer than I have to."

Next week I owned a nice, fully rented property for less than $2,000 down. Now, I know that this entire transaction sounds too good to be true, but it actually happened. It is amazing what some sellers will do to get rid of their properties.

What was the return on my investment? Let's see: a $12,000 return on an investment of about $2,000 equals 600 percent—immediately. I didn't have to wait for the stock market to go up. I knew the day I bought this property that I would be $12,000 richer.

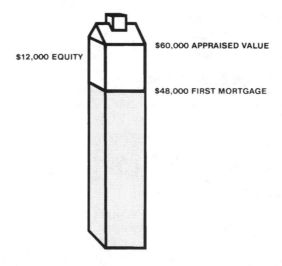

$12,000 EQUITY

$60,000 APPRAISED VALUE

$48,000 FIRST MORTGAGE

"Yes," you say, "but you didn't make a $12,000 cash profit. It was only on paper."

You have a point. But I'll take a $12,000 paper profit and a 600 percent return any day of the week when you compare it to what you can get from a money market fund.

Besides, how hard would it be to convert this profit into cash? I might not have been able to get the full $12,000 profit in cash in a slow market, but I almost guarantee you that I could have turned my $2,000 into $6,000 in a very short period of time.

I would have run an ad in the paper that would read something like this:

DESPERATE SELLER

Duplex fully rented in good condition. A bargain $6,000 below market with only $6,000 down. Hurry! Call Bob, 555-1234.

It might take three to six months to sell the property, but in the meantime, the tenants would continue to make the mortgage payments. All the time in the world to wait. And I would settle for a 300 percent return in six months. Wouldn't you?

I might even settle for a 200 percent return if it meant I could sell it faster. Better to get a fast nickel than a slow dime. Double your money in thirty to sixty days. And that's a lot better than waiting *seven years* to double your money in a "safe" investment!

To reap such profits, you need to make snap judgments born out of a fundamental understanding of values in your area. As one of my graduates said, "If you snooze, you lose."

If you are a good judge of value, I can say without question that you can make more money in one or two good wholesale purchases than you would make in an entire year at your job, perhaps doing something you hate.

But everything isn't all roses. There are risks. You could lose it all on a bad deal. That's why it pays to be careful.

I remember a conversation I had many years ago with Doug Casey, the author of the enormous best-sellers *Crisis Investing* and *Strategic Investing.* As you may know, Mr. Casey was opposed to investing in real estate, but he did pay me a kind of compliment. He said, "Bob, I like your way of buying real estate with little or no money down, because it limits your losses when the market collapses." I think you know what I thought about that; in hindsight, we now know that my real-estate investing advice was right on target despite the many naysayers in the past twenty years since *Creating Wealth* was first published. But Doug Casey had a good point. The more money you invest, the more you could lose under bad conditions. And that is one risk you take.

You also don't want to get sidetracked from your original "target" property. There are thousands of high-priced houses on the market.

Many sellers might consider a 10 percent discount for quick cash. But don't get tempted. You may just end up with the sellers' old problems; namely, a property with a large negative cash flow to pay. This approach may work in a fast-moving market, but in a slow-moving one it's murder. Even in your wholesale buying, stick with lower-priced properties.

You may ask, "How can I get my cash out when I need it?" This is the reason you always try to buy your wholesale properties at least 20 percent below the market. For instance, suppose you find a choice $200,000 home, which you can buy for $150,000 if you can come up with $25,000 to assume the existing $125,000 first mortgage. You buy it, invest your cash, and find out after three months that there is another great deal to be had across town if only you can get your hands on $25,000 cash. In most cities, there are finance companies that will lend up to 80 percent of the value of a property. You could feasibly borrow your $25,000 cash from your first property by using a hard-money second-mortgage company. It would be expensive, but wouldn't it be more expensive not to take advantage of a sure profit? Buy low, refinance high. It will ultimately pay off.

There are other advantages to discounting. You can generally buy properties below market and refinance with a low-interest-rate long-term mortgage. No messy second mortgages to pay to the seller. No balloons. And probably little or no negative cash flow.

If you are thus making profits "on the way in," you might be able to move your orbit date up by a few years or have more to spend if you continue the program for the full ten years.

You don't have to do it on the scale of the professionals. All you need is one or two properties a year.

Remember, by using this cookie cutter, you don't have to worry about what is going to happen to future appreciation. You made your money on the way in. If appreciation soars, and with it the value of your property, that's just more gravy. If not, you're safe. That's the best position to be in.

Cookie Cutter 3: Buy Low, Don't Sell

People who tell you that the game is over in real estate simply don't understand how versatile it is. If the game is over with appreciation, we just shift our emphasis to real estate's other benefits.

We don't stop buying. We just buy differently.

We turn into buy-and-hold bargain hunters.

How can you be a bargain hunter without somehow feeling that you are taking unfair advantage of a seller's predicament? There are a lot of good folks in this country who feel that this would violate their principles. But they are mistaken. There are plenty of win-win opportunities out there. Let me illustrate:

Suppose you get wind of a property for sale through a local finance company. It is a small three-bedroom house appraised at $150,000 and located in an outlying town where you would not normally invest. The finance company has repossessed the property from the original owner because he had failed to keep up the payments on his $25,000 second mortgage. The company has assumed the seller's original first mortgage of $100,000 and begun to make payments while trying to sell the property to recoup its losses. The company doesn't want the property. It is in the lending business, not the real-estate-management business. In fact, its operating regulations specifically prohibited holding more than a small percentage of its net worth in illiquid assets such as single-family houses. In talking with one of the company's executives, you learn that it is also company policy not to profit from its repossessions, only to recoup lost interest and legal fees. The bank offers to sell you the property for $130,000 if you will come up with the $30,000 necessary to pay it off.

Your rule is to never invest more than 10 percent down in a property unless you can buy it at least 20 percent below market. This home is worth $150,000 and priced at only 13 percent below appraisal at $130,000. A $20,000 paper profit on an investment of $30,000 is an immediate return of 66 percent. But that isn't quite good enough. You would need to buy it for $120,000 to meet your criteria. But that wasn't quite good enough for the finance company. On those terms, you would win, and the bank would lose. Win-lose. No go.

You ask for other alternatives. The bank counters with the following: "You buy the property at $130,000 and put only $10,000 down. We will check your credit, and if you qualify, we will make you a new second mortgage of $20,000 with payments for the next ten years." This looks good. A smaller down payment. A flexible seller. You decide to check further.

You place an ad in the local paper advertising the property for rent *before you buy it,* to test the rental market. Your phones ring off the hook. There is a rental shortage in this small town. You're in business. You accept the finance company's offer and now own a solid property with only a small investment.

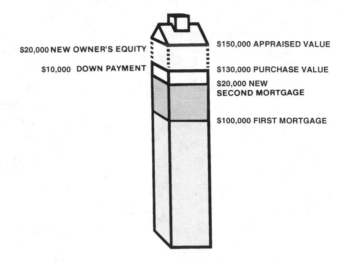

$20,000 NEW OWNER'S EQUITY

$10,000 DOWN PAYMENT

$150,000 APPRAISED VALUE

$130,000 PURCHASE VALUE

$20,000 NEW
SECOND MORTGAGE

$100,000 FIRST MORTGAGE

Was this win-win? The finance company got rid of a problem property, recouped its losses, and converted a bad loan into a brand-new loan with a strong customer.

Were you unscrupulous? Did you steal this property from the finance company? Of course not. You gave the company exactly what it wanted. And in the process, you got exactly what you wanted.

Your return on investment? An immediate $20,000 paper profit on an investment of $10,000—200 percent. Not to mention the tax benefits.

Let me be blunt: who cares if this property ever appreciates in value? You recoup your original investment shortly in tax benefits; have a built-in equity cushion; and are ready to experience a positive cash flow from this property, which will continue as long as you own it and keep it rented. In a few years, the second mortgage will be paid off, and your cash flow will significantly increase. When the first mortgage is finally paid off, this one simple property will be a source of cash flow to your heirs for generations, just like a producing oil well.

Do you get the picture? You don't need to sell this property to profit from your ownership of it. It is an automatic pilot. Why sell the goose that lays the golden eggs?

Cookie Cutter 4: Buy High, Fix Up Higher

This approach is as old as the hills. You have no doubt heard of it before. It is the fix-up routine. If you have seen me on any talk shows around the country, you'll know how I feel about improving property. I generally hold my hands up to the camera and say, "You don't see any calluses on my hands." And I mean it. I very rarely am involved in a fix-up project. I don't think I was built for it. I have a hard time distinguishing between a hammer and a tennis racket—which tells you how good I am at both.

Nonetheless, when I poll many of our seminars, I find that as many as half those present feel that they have the skills necessary to improve property. I shouldn't let my own biases steer you away from profit-making opportunities. And there are definite dollars to be made by locating run-down properties in improving neighborhoods, doing minor cosmetic face-lifting, and either selling or trading up to larger properties.

Perhaps the best-known of the fixer-uppers is William Nickerson, who wrote one of the greatest books ever on real-estate investing. *How I Turned $1,000 into Five Million in Real Estate,* published by Simon & Schuster, is still selling after more than forty years. His was one of the first books on real estate I ever read, and I must thank him for planting a seed in my mind.

Well, what are the disadvantages of this route to wealth? First of all, it takes more time and expertise. You need to know how to find the properties with the "right things wrong with them," as Albert Lowry, another fix-up expert, says. You try to find properties with only cosmetic problems such as paint, wallpaper, minor landscaping, carpets, and drapes.

You may improve a home immensely by redoing an outdated kitchen or converting a garage into an extra bedroom. The greatest dollar-for-dollar returns on your investment come in these areas.

You hope, by careful planning, to recoup $2 of profit for every $1 of improvement. Until you know the ropes, it is mostly guesswork. You are projecting profits. There is no guarantee. Your expertise grows with practice.

One of our graduates bought and improved thirty single-family houses in one year alone. This was his cookie cutter, and he was an expert at it.

If I were interested in this type of investment, I wouldn't make a move without finding a similar expert in my own community to counsel me for a couple of hours, regardless of the cost.

The benefits of the fix-up process are many. The greatest benefit is the fact that if you are prudent, you make immediate profits by improving a property. You don't have to wait for appreciation. You don't have to feel that you are speculating. You are actually making an economic improvement to your property and are enhancing the value of the neighborhood and your community.

The goal of a person using this cookie cutter would be to find and improve at least one property per year for at least the next ten years.

The difference between the wholesale buying approach and the fix-up approach is important. Using the fix-up alternative, you are finding market-valued property and fixing it up with cosmetic improvements. You fix the price up. When you buy wholesale, you find property owned by a flexible seller, and you negotiate the price down and buy significantly below current market prices.

With both plans, a lot of effort is expended. In one, the time is expended finding and negotiating with the right seller. In the other, the time is expended finding and improving the right property. In one, the profit you reap is called "brain equity." In the other, it is called "sweat equity."

But it doesn't take a lot of brains to figure out that with a minimum of sweat, either one of these approaches can take you to financial independence quickly.

You can use the fix-up cookie cutter in several variations to accomplish whatever goal you choose. If you want a monthly income stream from your investments, buy high, fix up higher, and keep your property—renting it out for a positive cash flow. This would also greatly increase your net worth. If you want immediate capital gain—chunks of cash—you could sell your property for a cash profit to repay you for all your efforts. Or you could also sell your property for little or no down payment (just enough to return your invested capital) and "carry the paper" with a steady monthly income for the next twenty-five years.

If you want an excellent book on the subject of this cookie-cutter variation, you must read *How to Build a Real Estate Money Machine* by Wade Cook. Mr. Cook's motto is: "If you will spend two years working as most people refuse to work, you will be able to spend the rest of your life in a manner which most people will never be able to afford."

His cookie-cutter program consisted of buying smaller properties, fixing them up immediately, and reselling them for enough down payment to recoup his initial investment. He would then carry his profit in the form of a secured note, with monthly payments coming in for the next twenty to twenty-five years. In a two-year period, he bought and sold forty-five properties, which brought him a monthly cash flow of about $4,500 per month. This sounds like a lot of work, and I'm sure that it is, but it is an alternative that works if you do.

Cookie Cutter 5: Buy High, Don't Sell

Back in the early 1980s, when interest rates were very high (16 percent) and the real-estate market was very soft, it was common to find advertisements in every major city in the country announcing properties for sale with zero-interest mortgages.

The buyer of the property put down a large down payment, made 60 to 120 equal monthly principal payments with zero interest, and ended up with a unit free and clear when the last payment was made.

Let me quote you some actual figures from an actual ad:

Announcing Our New Interest Rate:
0%
With Total Ownership in Six Years!
No Interest Paid Ever! No Balloons Ever!

That's right—now you can own a one- or two-bedroom condominium free and clear in six years! Here's how easy it is: pay just 20–40 percent down (depending on unit selected), make seventy-two monthly no-interest payments and in six short years you own it free and clear. No more payments! Sound like a great deal? It is! We are fighting back against today's high cost of home financing. For example:

0% mortgage		16% mortgage (today's rate)	
Sales price	$52,500	Sales price	$52,500
30% down	$15,750	30% down	$15,750
Mortgage balance	$36,750	Mortgage balance	$36,750
Monthly payment for six years	$510.41	Monthly payment for 30 years	$494.20
Total $ paid over six years	$36,750	Total $ paid over 30 years	$177,896
Total interest cost	0	Total interest costs	$141,146

The builder, desperate to unload some extra inventory, has agreed to zero interest. First, let's learn why such a program was so beneficial to the buyer at that time. Then we'll explore how the same idea could be adapted to our day and age of much lower interest rates. For illustration purposes, let's use a free-and-clear $180,000 property. Suppose the market is softening, and the seller needs to sell. You offer to pay $200,000, which is $20,000 more than the asking price, *if* the seller agrees to some very creative terms. You agree to pay a $32,000 cash down payment if the seller will carry a first mortgage of $168,000 at 0 percent interest with equal monthly payments of $2,000 for the next seven years.

The advantages of this offer to the seller are many. He receives a higher price, $200,000. He receives a large down payment of $32,000. His remaining $168,000 mortgage is paid off quickly at $2,000 per month for the next eighty-four months.

Why would you agree to such an offer? You've paid too much, had to make a large down payment, and may have negative cash flow on this property.

Here's why. Your return on investment is enormous! You'll be paying down your mortgage by $24,000 in the first year, which means you will gain $24,000 in equity each year. Your investment to obtain this equity was $32,000. Therefore, your return on investment is 75 percent. Of course, this figure needs to be adjusted downward because of overpaying for the property and perhaps having a negative cash flow for a few years. But even if we are conservative and assume no tax benefits and no appreciation, the average return on investment over the six years is over 30 percent. And the compounded rate of return is over 20 percent. And that is assuming no appreciation or tax benefits!

Clearly, this is not a get-rich-quick investment, but it gives a safe return on investment, produces a property free and clear of mortgages in six years, and will continue to produce cash flow virtually forever. A true money machine in a relatively short period of time.

Now, I realize that there aren't many people walking around with huge chunks of cash sitting in bank accounts for investments like these. But I thought that I would open your mind to some possibilities.

The first time I attempted such an investment strategy, I decided to take $20,000 from my pension and profit-sharing plan to see if I could earn a better rate of return on it. I contacted a local Realtor and told him to bring me the local MLS book. Together we selected ten properties in my target price range, below $75,000. Each property was free and clear, and the seller had indicated his or her desire to carry some financing with a large down payment. I had the Realtor offer each seller full price with $20,000 down and the balance of the seller's equity to be paid in 120 equal monthly payments at zero interest.

The Realtor thought I was crazy. He was certain that no one would ever accept my offer. He was almost right. Nine out of ten flatly rejected the offer. One finally agreed to my terms. I bought a $65,000 house with $20,000 down, with the remaining $45,000 paid off in equal payments of $375 per month for the next ten years at zero interest.

Now, how did the seller win by accepting my offer? He got a sale plus $20,000 cash so that he could move out of state to a new job. Then he received steady payments for the next ten years.

How did I win? My return on my $20,000 was significantly higher than I could get at a bank. Each year I owned the property, my loan was reduced by $4,500 ($375 x 12). That represented a return of over 20 percent on my invested dollars ($4,500 ÷ $20,000). Add to this the tax advantages, small appreciation, and positive cash flow, and I earned upward of 40 percent on my money. The home was paid for in ten years. I chose to use my profit-sharing funds in this way because it is a relatively safe way to get high rates of return. Needless to say, the Internal Revenue Service has fits over zero-interest loans. I had my accountant research the proper method for overcoming the current objections of the IRS. I suggest you do the same, since rules change constantly.

You may also consider using this approach when you are trying to liquidate difficult-to-sell properties. I had a woman come up to me recently in Philadelphia and relate a fascinating story. She had been reading a copy of this book while confined to a hospital bed. When she came to the section on zero-interest mortgages, the light bulb came on in her head. "That's it!" she exclaimed. She owned a small single-family home free and clear and she didn't want it. All efforts to sell it had proven fruitless. It had been listed for sale with a Realtor for months with no action. As soon as she read this book, she called up the newspaper and offered her house for sale with ZERO INTEREST FINANCING as the headline. As soon as her ad appeared, she was flooded with calls and sold her property a short time later. It's amazing what the right bit of knowledge can accomplish.

Cookie Cutter 6: Don't Buy

You heard me right. If you are afraid of what is going to happen to real estate in the future, don't buy it. I'm not being facetious. I really mean it. Instead of buying it and assuming all of the obligations of debt, why don't you specialize in option techniques? Don't buy, just option. Let me give you an example:

One of my seminar graduates related this story to me a few years ago. He and his wife located a highly motivated seller who had bought a house for his daughter in the Sun Belt. His daughter had died, and he was left with the job of selling the property from his home in New York. All he wanted was what he paid for it—$78,000—and to recoup his $25,000 down payment. My graduate checked into the value of the property and discovered that it was worth perhaps $70,000. Obviously, the man had overpaid.

He was now stuck with a vacant property two thousand miles from his home. Every month he had to make a mortgage payment of $471. And since his price was too high, no one was making him any offers. Lose-lose.

Our students analyzed the situation and made the following offer: instead of buying the unit, they would lease it from him for $400 per month with an option to buy it in four years for $78,000. This would mean that he would not even receive enough money from the lease payment to cover his mortgage payments.

Why did he accept it?

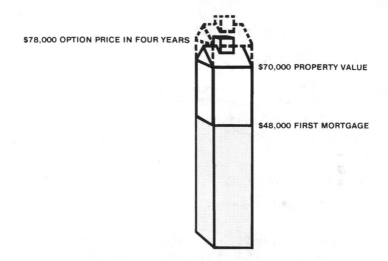

$78,000 OPTION PRICE IN FOUR YEARS

$70,000 PROPERTY VALUE

$48,000 FIRST MORTGAGE

First of all, he needed the tax shelter. If the property became a rental, it could be depreciated. The tax shelter would more than off-set the $71 monthly negative cash flow. (His accountant could show him how this single-family house would average a $2,000-plus write-off per year for the next four years.)

Then, of course, he would eliminate all problems with having to sell the unit in a slow real-estate market. This offer solved his immediate problems. And he readily accepted.

Why did our students like it?

They immediately rented out the property for $475 per month. Since their long-term lease payment is only $400 per month, they net $75 per month in the first year just for overseeing the manage-ment. In future years, with rent increases they could possibly net $100 to $200 per month from this one unit.

Now, what happens in four years? An option is not a guarantee to buy—it is just the right to buy at the negotiated price. If the prop-erty doesn't appreciate in value, they will not exercise their option to buy. The worst that could happen is that they lose the right to rent out this unit for a profit. In this instance, the seller could put the property back on the market.

A more likely solution would be to renegotiate the lease terms with the seller and extend the lease for another four years. Perhaps a $500 lease with an option to buy the house for $85,000.

If, on the other hand, the property did appreciate during the first four-year lease/option period, our students could sell the property and keep any profit over and above the locked-in $78,000 option price. This could feasibly amount to $10,000 or more.

Either way, they don't care if the property goes up or down in value. They win now or they win later. They just have to wait four years to see how much. Leasing a property with an option to buy in the future is an excellent strategy for cash-poor investors.

Cookie Cutter 7: Buy High, Sell High

How can you buy a property for $200,000, sell it for $200,000, and still make a profit?

It depends on the kind of profit you are trying to make. Sometimes you are not interested in making a capital gain. Perhaps you are more interested in positive cash flow. Well, how can you generate positive cash flow when you don't sell at a profit?

It all depends on the terms you can negotiate.

Let's suppose that you locate a motivated seller who doesn't want to discount his price but is willing to sell flexibly—with nothing down—and carry soft paper for his equity. It is a $200,000 free-and-clear home. The seller has $200,000 equity and is willing to carry his equity balance at 6 percent for twenty years with payments of at least $1,800 per month, including taxes and insurance.

It is a nothing-down deal. But you could rent it out for only about $1,500 per month, and that would mean $300 to $400 monthly negative cash flow. Not so hot.

Is there another way to profit from this situation?

Suppose you put it back on the market, again for nothing down to attract more buyers. You are offering bargain terms: nothing down and a wraparound contract for the entire $200,000 balance at only 7 percent for thirty years. No assumption problems. No balloons. No stringent qualifying, although you will, of course, do some checking. You're not looking for an investor, you're looking for a house user. Someone who wants a house and likes fabulous terms.

In essence, you'll be earning a 1 percent spread on the loan for the next twenty years, which could earn you a hassle-free cash flow of about $170 per month. Do this ten times, and you'll fatten your retirement income. One of my students did this hundreds of times for a huge monthly cash flow!

This cookie cutter works because you don't look for bargains in prices; you concentrate on finding bargains in terms. And then you take some of the cream off the top and sell the same property at the same price (more if you can get it) but with a higher interest rate, which is still a market bargain.

Now, this may sound like a lot of work to generate some cash flow. After all, you have to find a seller *and* a buyer in order to pull this off. But it is a viable cookie cutter that hundreds of people are using profitably right this very second.

Become an expert. Learn the ropes. Learn the pitfalls. And then you too can join the profit makers.

Cookie Cutter 8: Buy High, Sell Low

The best of all possible worlds would be to buy high and sell low and still make money. If this were possible in the stock market, there'd be millionaires on every street corner. Well, you may not be able to do it in the stock market, but you can do it in real estate.

That's right. Since real estate is such a flexible beast, you can even sell it for less than you paid for it and come out ahead.

"Now, wait just a cotton-pickin' minute," you say. "Do you mean to tell me that you can buy a property for, say, $180,000, sell it for $144,000, and still make a profit?"

That's exactly what I'm saying. A $10,000 *cash* profit!

But you're going to have to wait a few pages to find out how to do it. This chapter is getting a bit long, so I have explained this powerful cookie cutter at the end of chapter 12, on discounted mortgages. Don't miss it. It's one of the most exciting formulas in this entire book.

So there you have them. Eight specific cookie-cutter formulas. Each plan has its advantages and disadvantages. Some are easier to use in times of rapid appreciation, others are more profitable when times are bad. Some cookie cutters work best in areas where prices are low, others are more suitable for cities such as San Francisco and Los Angeles, where prices are high. In other words, there is no inappropriate time or place to be investing in real estate, only an inappropriate strategy.

Now let's look at exactly what you need to know before you buy.

CHAPTER 7

The Lazy Man's Method: Making the Opportunities Come to You

So you're ready to make your move. A whole sea of potential single-family houses (alias golden-egg layers) is spread before you. You have chosen your cookie cutter. You can hardly wait to buy your first property. What now?

Before you run off half-cocked to get half-hocked, let me share with you the secret of buying property successfully. If you learn this secret well, buying will be fun and easy. If you don't, you will end up like so much wreckage on the shoreline of the real-estate market, discouraged and frustrated.

This is the secret:

Don't waste your time with inflexible sellers.

Now, that didn't seem so mystically secret, did it? It's just plain common sense. But if it's so obvious to everyone, why is it so universally unheeded?

Most real-estate investors spend their time looking for the right property. And then they try to discover the seller's flexibility through a written offer. I try to do the opposite. I don't even care what a property looks like until I know that the seller will accept an offer that fits within my narrow financing parameters:

1. I will pay full price for a property if the seller is willing to accept terms that include a down payment of less than 5 percent and excellent seller financing.

Or:

2. If the seller wants a large cash down payment, he must accept a reduced price for his property. I don't get really

excited until the price is reduced a minimum of 10 to 20 percent from a current appraisal value.

Once I have a preliminary indication that the seller is willing to consider such an offer, then I look at the property to see if it also fits within my narrow property parameters, which include:

1. An excellent neighborhood
2. A property in good to excellent condition

Now, how do you find sellers who will be so flexible in selling their excellent properties? There is a hard way and an easy way. Let's cover the easy way first.

The normal approach is to look for flexible sellers by canvassing all Realtors and calling all ads in the classified section of the newspaper. This is the hard way. My modus operandi is to place less emphasis on looking for flexible sellers and to place more emphasis on having them look for me. In order to save time and to attract a more qualified seller, we place our own newspaper ad. It reads something like this:

> FULL PRICE. We will pay full price for your property if you are willing to sell on flexible terms (little or no money down). Call Spencer. 555-1235.

The ad is placed in the real-estate section of the classified ads. This section is normally filled with other ads looking to attract the wholesale all-cash seller. By running the full-price ad, you are essentially going the opposite direction of most of the ads. From a weekend paper, we may get four to ten calls during the week. This may not sound like a lot, but remember, you need only one property per year.

Out of as few as twenty calls in a month, at least half are curiosity seekers: "What are you guys trying to do?" "Can you tell me about your program?" Of the remaining calls, perhaps only two or three have potential. You may find only one excellent property every other month that you can get excited about.

The best part of the telephone ad is the fact that the sellers who call have prequalified themselves. They know that they will consider a flexible deal or they would not call. This takes a lot of the negotiation out of the process. You only need to describe your "target property" and the kind of terms you are looking for, and the rest is in the seller's hands. If your terms are too strict, he will try to sell elsewhere. If he feels that it fits his situation, then the rest is easy. You make arrangements to view the property and to write up the offer.

Now, this may sound too simple for some—and newspaper response may vary from state to state—but this is how I do my personal buying. Since my time is limited, I would rather spend the money on a regular newspaper ad than spend the time searching elsewhere. The ad costs also vary according to the size of the newspaper. It is certainly worth the investment, even if you run your ad only once per month.

One of my students took this simple idea and expanded upon it. His genius idea was to place a version of my ad in the *Wall Street Journal.* Sellers from all over the world wrote and offered to sell him, by latest count, over $200 million worth of property, all with little or no money down! And he purchased several million dollars' worth of the choicest properties. See what one idea can do?

Two recent graduates of my "Nothing Down Seminar," a father and son from Oregon, ran the following ad in their local paper:

**"I buy and sell houses.
Please call Lyle at ___."**

Notice the differences between their ad and mine? They experimented and got better results in their area using boldface type and double spacing. (I encourage you to come up with your own ad, one that works even better.) This father and son bought over $800,000 worth of property and increased their combined net worth by $500,000. All from using this one simple idea!

Since many of you still wouldn't feel confident about recognizing a really good deal over the telephone, let me share with you a simple scoring system I use to help me spot the good deals from the mediocre. Notice the property-selection grid on the following page.

I ask questions in each of these five areas to determine a rating for each category. In each category, a poor rating merits a score of 1. An average rating merits a score of 2. And an excellent rating merits a score of 3. I assign a *poor, average,* or *excellent* score to each category by circling the appropriate circle on each line. Then I add up

·PROPERTY SELECTION GRID·

		POOR	AVERAGE	EXCELLENT
1	SELLER'S MOTIVATION AND FLEXIBILITY	**① POINT** Won't budge on price or terms. "Take it or leave it." Doesn't need to sell. Not anxious at all. In the driver's seat.	**② POINTS** Might consider a small discount in price. Needs cash for new house or property. Needs cash for bills, etc. May carry small second or contract but leery of unusual deals.	**③ POINTS** Needs cash for pressing items, i.e. behind in payments, etc. Or, doesn't need cash at all . . . has tax, management, transfer, time problems, or divorce, retiree, or investor looking for a solution without major need for cash. Flexible in price or terms.
2	LOCATION	**⓪ NEVER** No pride of ownership. Junk and debris in streets. High crime. No appealing shopping close by. Declining neighborhoods. Abandoned buildings and boarded up properties. Close to major streets, industrial areas, or commercial zones (across the street). Far from employment centers or commuter accessibility.	**② POINTS** May be clean older neighborhoods. Close to shopping, churches, schools, etc. but not very appealing. Working class tenants, neat, established. May be poor location on the upswing with pioneer fixer-uppers. Nicer inner-city neighborhoods.	**③ POINTS** Easy accessibility to all necessary amenities and transportation. Middle class, suburban neighborhoods. Not on busy streets. Cul-de-sacs ideal. Properties nearby very similar in price. Good foliage and landscaping except in brand new subdivisions. Only high class inner-city locations.
3	FINANCING	**① POINT** More than 15% down. Seller needs lots of cash and wants all of his equity. Or property will have heavy negative cash flows for more than two years. Or, there will be a large balloon payment due in less than three years from date of purchase. **Consider only if price is excellent.**	**② POINTS** Financing required from an institution with up to 15% down of buyer's money. Credit checks. Institutional, secured loans for part of the down payment (high interest, high monthly payments). Seller carries small amounts. Cash required from buyer. Balloons due in less than 5 years.	**③ POINTS** Less than 5% of buyer cash involved. Seller carries most of the financing at lower than market rates with no balloons in less than 7 years. No negative cash flows projected beyond the first year. Contract sales, no credit checks.
4	PRICE	**① POINT** 10% or more above the reasonable market price. **Consider only if financing is excellent.**	**② POINTS** Within + or − 5% of market price.	**③ POINTS** At least 10% or more below market price.
5	PROPERTY CONDITION	**① POINT** **Consider only if price is excellent.** Needs major cosmetic and structural improvements. At least 10% of purchase price will need to be spent immediately to make unit rentable. Improvements do not significantly improve the rent roll because of quality of tenants and location. Improvements not to increase value more than 10% above purchase price. Usually associated with poor locations. Possible to find this property in excellent locations where prices are so high that improvements do not increase value but just make units acceptable to renters. Viewed as making a larger down payment (for improvements) and receiving an averaged priced property.	**② POINTS** This is the true fixer-upper. Cosmetic improvements would be nice but not immediately necessary. Costs not to exceed 5% of the purchase price. Cosmetic improvements immediately affect the value upwards and make the property more desirable, saleable, and attractive. Not much structural work (if any) is necessary . . . only paint, landscaping, drapes, and other inexpensive improvements. This type of property should not be bought if the buyer does not have the time or mental capacity to undertake supervision of improvements. This property can prove to be the most profitable in the short run. The worst house in the best neighborhood.	**③ POINTS** Newer property or older property with recent renovation. No problems, clean inside and out . . . good landscaping. New components to replace major items. May have been a recent fixer-upper project which is being sold by a don't wanter at an excellent price. No work necessary before renter moves in. Solid property with a hassle factor of zero. Quick closing, quick rent-up, quick cash flow.

- Analyze and assign a point value to each factor of a property.
- If in doubt about a point value always pick the lower number.
- Add up the numbers and total.
- The lowest acceptable score is 9, the highest possible is 15.
- Greater fools always buy property in the 9, 10, 11 range.
- Great investors always buy property in the 12, 13, 14, 15 range.

TOTAL SCORE

the total points. A property that scores below 9 is a no-go property; I wouldn't buy it under any circumstances. A property scoring 9 through 11 is a speculative, borderline deal. I am very wary of these properties and rarely buy them. I get really excited when I find a property that scores in the 12 to 15 range. This means that I have a green light and can consider the purchase seriously.

This has taken a lot of the guesswork out of my own investing. Rather than agonize over a particular property, I can reduce the decision to a simple score. If it doesn't score high enough, I have a rational reason to say no. This takes the emotion out of the buying and replaces it with analytical skills. And it helps immensely when you have a persistent seller or Realtor breathing down your neck.

Let me walk you through some of the actual calls that we have received in response to our newspaper ad. I'll assign a score to each property, and you'll be able to see for yourself why we eventually ended up buying the property we did. We are now leaving the realm of theory and entering reality. The information you will read on the next few properties is realistic. Only the names and dialogue have been slightly altered.

SELLER: I'm calling about your ad in the paper. I'm interested in selling my property. Can you tell me what you are looking for?

BUYER: We like to buy properties from flexible sellers. We will pay full price for your property as determined by a bona fide appraisal done by an FHA [Federal Housing Administration] or VA [Veterans Affairs] appraiser. We will pay for the appraisal. Can you tell me a bit about your property?

SELLER: It used to be a commercial building. I converted it into two rental units of two bedrooms each. The work is about 80 percent completed. It still needs paint, carpet, exterior stucco, and cabinets. I ran out of money and am looking for a buyer who can finish the job to make a good profit. I'm willing to sell for $225,000 in as-is condition. It will take about $20,000 to complete the work and should be worth about $300,000 when finished.

BUYER: What about the loans?

SELLER: There is a thirty-year mortgage for $200,000, with monthly payments of $1,200.

BUYER: What about the location?

SELLER: It's pretty good.

BUYER: You say you're flexible. What price and terms are you considering?

SELLER: I'm willing to sell for $225,000. I'd like you to refinance. I suppose I'd be flexible on the down payment. You can have the lion's share of the profits.

BUYER: I'll need the property address and your own name and number. I'll check out the location and call you back for a more in-depth inspection if I like what I see from the outside.

I thank the seller for the information and proceed to do the analysis. The analysis grid will be filled out line by line. The first line is the seller's flexibility.

Seller's Flexibility

Judging from this brief information, how would you score this person's flexibility? Would you say that he is motivated? What motivates him? Obviously, he needs more money to complete his fix-up job. Until the property is put back in shape, he has to pay the mortgage ($1,200 per month), with no rent to offset it. Until he gets more money, his negative cash flow will continue to eat him alive. He is probably fed up with the project and will consider any offer to get it off his back. I would say that he is extremely motivated and deserves an excellent rating: a 3.

Location

Until we have seen the property, we won't know what the location is like. We'll assume that the seller is correct when he says that the location is "pretty good." We'll score it average—a 2—and reserve final judgment until we have seen it.

Financing

Our parameters are strict. If the down payment required is more than 10 percent, we will require a concession of at least 10 percent off the appraisal price. In this case, we will invest up to $25,000 up front for the seller's down payment plus at least another $20,000 to fix up the property. Based on preliminary discussions, our total cash investment in this property could be $45,000. In order to conform to our guidelines, then, the $245,000 cost of our property ($225,000 price plus $20,000 in improvements) must be less than 90 percent of the new appraised price. The seller tells us that the property should be worth about $300,000 when improved, and 90 percent of $300,000 is $270,000. Our cost will be $245,000. Therefore this property falls within our parameters.

This property has mortgage payments of $1,200 per month. Will I be able to rent out each unit for enough money to cover this payment? The seller said that each side of the duplex could be rented out for $600. That totals $1,200. In other words, each month this property will break even. But that doesn't include vacancies or expenses like taxes and insurance! The expenses will be at least 20 to 25 percent of the projected rents (and could go higher), or at least $240 per month. So, realistically, the total negative cash flow will be $300 if we can keep the property rented out every day of the year. My $45,000 investment will cost me $300 a month until I can raise the rents to cover the negative.

Now that you have done this preliminary pencil pushing, let's give this property a score in the financing category. Here are the definitions:

- *Poor financing* means more than 15 percent down (down payment includes cash to seller plus any costs necessary to bring the unit up to rentable condition). Or the property will have a heavy negative cash flow for more than two years.
- *Average financing* means a small negative cash flow.
- *Excellent financing* means positive or break-even cash flow potential within twelve months of ownership and/or a down payment of less than 5 percent of the sales price.

Obviously, this property scores a 1, because of the high negative cash flow and the large down payment.

Price

Poor price means as much as 10 percent above market.
Average price means at or near the market price.
Excellent price means at least 10 percent below the market price.

Our property scores a 3, since when the work is done it will be worth $300,000 on a cost of $245,000.

Condition

> *Poor* means needs major fix-up.
> *Average* means needs 5 percent of the purchase price to get in rentable condition.
> *Excellent* means needs less than $1,000 to get in rentable condition.

Our property needs extensive work and hence scores a 1.
   Let's add up the scores:

> Flexibility: 3
> Location: 2
> Financing: 1
> Price: 3
> Condition: 1
> Total: 10

Decision

This is a speculative investment. Has possibility but requires too much sweat equity to recoup the profit. Better keep looking. *No go.*
   Let's go look at the property just to make sure. The property is, as the seller said, in a "pretty good" neighborhood. But the condition of the property, from the outside, is pretty rough. It is obviously going to take more than $20,000 to get this building into shape. We check with a neighboring rental unit to see what two-bedroom units are going for. The consensus is that $500 is top dollar. We ask people what they think of the old commercial building's being converted to rental units. They say that it had been condemned. They recommend that we make sure all the work done is able to meet code. All of this just confirms our no-go decision.
   This scoring system shows us where the weak spots are with the property. Sometimes you can upgrade a property's score by further checking or negotiating. Suppose, for instance, that the property was in an excellent location. The location category would then have scored 3 instead of 2. And this would have raised the total property

score to 11. Still borderline, but more interesting. Could it be possible to eliminate the negative cash flow and the large down payment? Probably not. Since the property is marginal, we pass and look for something else to buy.

It may seem that this system is very strict. In fact, it might be strict enough to prohibit me from buying a property that has potential. This is the chance that I take. I would rather miss a few good ones than let a few bad ones in the door.

The system is also skewed toward the flexibility of the seller. This shows my bias toward dealing only with motivated sellers. It is also skewed against fixing up properties. (I give a score of 1 to properties needing major improvement.) This is to remind me that a deal must be really good before I get involved with a renovation project. The seller of the property above probably wishes he had never started his renovation project. I'll try to learn from his mistakes.

You should be getting the hang of this by now. Let's try another one:

> SELLER: I noticed your ad in the paper. What are you guys looking for, anyway?
>
> BUYER: Do you have a property for sale?
>
> SELLER: Not really. I'm just interested in your approach.
>
> BUYER: I've got another call coming in. Could you call back in about five years?

Of course, you would never be this rude, but be prepared for a lot of curiosity seekers. Maybe half your calls will be like this. You have to sift through a lot of gravel to find the golden nugget.

Let's take another call:

> SELLER: Is this the person running the ad in the paper?
>
> BUYER: Yes, it is. Do you have a property you would like to sell?
>
> SELLER: I sure do. It's a four-bedroom home located up in a [community about fifty miles away], which is a suburb of a [a major city]. We have owned it for about three years. It's too far away from home to manage effectively, so we let it run down a bit. Our tenants just moved out, leaving a mess. Quite frankly, I just don't have the energy to go clean it up. My husband, who is a doctor, tells me to just get rid of it. He noticed your ad and thought that if you would pay us full

PROPERTY ANALYSIS FORM

NAME _____ PHONE _____
ADDRESS OF PROPOSED
PROPERTY TO PURCHASE _____

BEDROOMS ____ # BATHROOMS ____ # STORIES ____ BASEMENT ____   ASKING PRICE _____

GARAGE ____ CARPORT ____ LOT SIZE ____ CONDITION _____   FHA APPRAISAL _____

DETAILED INFORMATION

1ST MORTGAGE _____ MONTHLY PAYMENT _____

2ND MORTGAGE _____ MONTHLY PAYMENT _____

3RD MORTGAGE _____ MONTHLY PAYMENT _____

TOTAL MORTGAGES _____   TOTAL MONTHLY PAYMENTS _____

ESTIMATE OF MONTHLY EXPENSES

TAXES _____

INSURANCE _____

MAINTENANCE _____

MANAGEMENT _____

TOTAL MONTHLY EXPENSES _____

TOTAL PROPERTY OUTGO _____

ESTIMATED RENT _____

NET INCOME OR NEGATIVE _____

COMMENTS AND ADDITIONAL INFORMATION

_____
_____
_____
_____
_____
_____
_____
_____

POINT SYSTEM FOR PROPERTY SELECTION	POOR	AVERAGE	EXCELLENT	
SELLER'S MOTIVATION AND FLEXIBILITY	1	2	3	
LOCATION	0	2	3	
FINANCING	1	2	3	
PRICE	1	2	3	
PROPERTY CONDITION	1	2	3	TOTAL SCORE _____

* Since the first edition of *Creating Wealth* many readers have written wanting to be able to purchase blank copies of the forms found in this chapter and throughout the book. To fill this need, I have created a packet of blank forms which can be obtained for $5.00 by writing 5072 North 300 West, Provo, UT 84604 or by calling 1-801-852-8700 and asking for information regarding the forms packet.

price for it, we would be glad to carry our profit in the form of a note.

BUYER: How much do you think it is worth?

SELLER: We feel that it's worth about $175,000.

BUYER: Can you tell me about the financing?

SELLER: It has a loan of $125,000.

BUYER: How much have you been renting the property for?

SELLER: About $1,000 per month. I'm sure that if you made it presentable, you could get $1,100, easy.

BUYER: What is the location like?

SELLER: It is a quiet neighborhood of three-bedroom homes. It's pretty good, actually.

BUYER: How much money do you think it will take to get it into shape?

SELLER: I don't dare guess. Maybe $2,000.

BUYER: You have about $50,000 equity in the property. We like to buy properties for as little cash as possible. Is a nothing-down offer a possibility, or do you need some cash?

SELLER: I wouldn't sell for nothing down. It's just the principle. Maybe we would consider $5,000. I'll talk to my husband. He's more flexible than I am.

BUYER: What about monthly payments? If we make you large monthly payments on the balance of your equity, we would have a heavy negative cash flow. It would be best for us not to make payments for about five years. But at the end of five years, we would pay you your $45,000 balance in full with 7 percent accrued interest. Would this be a problem?

SELLER: I don't think so. But I'll have to check with my husband.

BUYER: Thanks for calling. Let me have your name and number and the address of the property, and I'll go look at it and call you back.

As you follow this dialogue, you see that I am asking questions in each of the five areas of analysis. I jump around some, but I am gathering information and filling in the sheet you see on the preceding page.

Let's analyze the information:

What about the seller's flexibility? I'd give her a 3, wouldn't you?

What about location? We'll assume a 2 and look at it later.

What about financing? The $5,000 down sounds great, but we

also have to consider our fix-up costs of $2,000. That totals $7,000, or 3 percent of cost. This seems to fit in our retail or full-price guideline. What about the mortgage? A new loan of $125,000 would have monthly payments of about $800, and the house could be rented out for about $1,100.

What about other expenses? After taxes, insurance, and repairs, our average negative should be less than $100 per month. This could be solved with aggressive management in twelve months or less. The seller seems to feel that she and her husband may accept no payment on their second mortgage. A balloon of the entire equity will be due in five years. According to the financing scoring system, a property with this kind of financing scores a 2.

What about price? We have agreed to pay full price for the property. This will be determined by having an FHA or VA appraiser inspect and appraise the property. You can find a good appraiser listed under "Real Estate Appraisals" in the yellow pages. When you call, ask if the company does appraisals for FHA or VA. If it doesn't, keep on calling. Or you might just call up any savings and loan association (yellow pages under "Real Estate Loans") and ask one of the loan officers to recommend a very conservative FHA or VA appraiser. Anyone interested can go to https://entp.hud.gov/ idapp/html/apprlook.cfm, type in their city or zip code and see an online list of credited appraisers in their area. As for locating a VA appraiser, anyone (buyer, seller, real estate personnel, or lender) can request a VA appraisal by completing VA Form 26-1805, Request for Determination of Reasonable Value. The completed form can then be mailed to the Loan Guaranty Division at the nearest VA office for processing, or one can request an appraisal by telephoning the Loan Guaranty Division for assignment of an appraiser. The local VA office may be contacted for information concerning its assignment procedures. The appraiser will send a bill for his or her services to the requester according to a fee schedule approved by VA. The cost of an appraisal should be a few hundred dollars. Government-approved appraisers are generally more conservative in their appraisals, and because of the strict guidelines for government-backed loans, they are trained to notice special property problems. You will use this appraisal as a guideline for your further negotiations with the seller. But you don't order the appraisal until you have agreed upon terms in writing with the seller. If the appraisal comes in too low, or with too many problems, either you or the seller has the option of backing out of the deal.

We will assume that this property is priced right on the market. The score is then a 2.

What about condition? The seller indicates that it will take little or no money to bring the property into rentable condition. This is a 3 in score.

Let's add up the scores:

> Seller's flexibility: 3
> Location: 2
> Financing: 2
> Price: 2
> Condition: 3
> Total: 12

Decision

In our preliminary analysis, we have a go. Let's go look at the property. Everything is as the seller said. A call to the seller reveals that the terms as discussed on the phone will be agreeable. We set a closing date.

You may have wondered why the doctor and his wife were willing to accept such flexible terms. Was it win-win? Well, obviously it was good for me. But what about them? Their main motivation was to get rid of an albatross. They didn't need the cash, because of their financial status. They didn't need the monthly income—in fact, the monthly interest income would have been a detriment to them taxwise. Under this plan, they receive a small down payment and no monthly payments for five years, and thus no taxable consequence at all for at least five years. They were happy with the deal. In fact, at the closing, they expressed their gratitude that we were taking the problem off their hands.

Now, what about the balloon payment due in five years? Rather than deal with this now, I will cover it in more detail in chapter 10. Let me just say that I rarely buy a property with a balloon payment unless I have a fabulous deal and a plan for paying off the obligation when it comes due.

Let's take another call:

SELLER: Hi. Your ad intrigued me. Can you tell me about your-self?

BUYER: Sure. My name is Bob, and I buy real estate. What's your name? [You get the drift. Small talk usually helps to loosen up the seller who is a bit skeptical. When you feel comfortable, ask if he has a property for sale.]

SELLER: Yes, I do. My home is worth $450,000. It's a totally self-sufficient home in excellent condition. The property is only two years old and sits on almost twenty acres of ground. We are very flexible. We don't need much cash.

BUYER: Where is it located?

SELLER: About a forty-five-minute drive south of town in a beau-tiful recreational subdivision in the mountains.

BUYER: Thanks so much for calling. I'm sure that you have a great property that will eventually sell, but we only buy properties in a lower price range, and we don't invest in recreational property. Good luck.

Remember not to be tempted out of your target price range. And a slow economy will hit marginal recreational areas the hardest. Even if this was a well-located property in the city, it is still out of your price range. Can you see yourself trying to rent this property without a negative cash flow? You don't want to end up in that seller's shoes, do you? Let's take another call:

SELLER: Hello, I'm calling about your ad.

BUYER: Yes, do you have a property for sale?

SELLER: Yes. Can you tell me about yourself? Why are you buy-ing properties?

BUYER: We're investors. What is your property like?

SELLER: It's a house priced at $250,900. We have a first mortgage of about $182,000 at 7 percent. Our equity is about $60,000.

BUYER: Are you flexible?

SELLER: Well, I've got a job offer in another city. I think it would be a good change for me. I noticed your low-down-payment ad in the paper and thought I would see what you are offering.

BUYER: Well, we like to buy properties with small down pay-ments, or we can also pay a larger down payment in cash if the seller is willing to discount the price of the property by at least 15 to 20 percent. I know that this sounds like a lot, but many sellers would rather have cash and a sure sale immediately than leave their properties on the market.

SELLER: I know that we'd need at least $20,000 out of our property if we were to move. We'd have to buy a new home and all. The 20 percent discount might be a possibility. How much would that be?

BUYER: We would base the price on an appraisal done by an FHA or VA appraiser. We would deduct 20 percent from the price of this appraisal to come up with the final sales price. You say that it's now priced at $250,900. Is that what it's worth?

SELLER: We think it's worth about $250,000 based upon what other houses have sold for recently in our neighborhood.

BUYER: Well, if the appraisal comes in at $250,000, our cash offer to you would be $200,000. How does that sound?

SELLER: Well, I'd have to discuss it with my wife. It might be worth it to sell now and move on to bigger and better things.

BUYER: Give me your name and number and the address of the property. I'll drive by and look at the neighborhood. In the meantime, you check with your wife. You're under no obligation to sell. Our policy is that if you should happen to change your mind, even after you have signed the papers, we will let you back out of the deal anytime right up to the closing. And we'll put that in writing. We want you to feel that this is the right decision for you at this time in your life. If you find a better deal, you are free to take it.

You'll notice the last comment I made. The last thing you want to do is to take advantage of people in a time of stress. We let them have the freedom to change their minds up to the last minute. It doesn't do any good to have hard feelings. These people will end up being friends over the years. Once sellers realize that you operate under a win-win philosophy, they refer friends and relatives. I bought a four-unit building from a referral who'd heard of our fair reputation and offered his building to me for nothing down. The word spreads. Cast your bread on the waters, and you always get back a sandwich.

Now let's analyze the above property:

Seller's flexibility: 3
Location: We'll guess 2 and drive by later to confirm.

Financing: If the price is $200,000 and the mortgages total $180,000, that leaves a seller's equity of $20,000. This will have to be paid in cash. You can plan on a little negative cash flow. Maybe more. Judging from this information, the financing score is 1.

Price: 3

Condition: We'll assume it is average (2) and readjust after our on-site inspection.

The total is: 3 + 2 + 1 + 3 + 2 = 11

This is a borderline score. How could we improve it? If, in our on-site inspection, the condition or location turns out to be excellent, we may have an adjustment. There is not much you can do to the financing. You will need a large cash down payment, and even then, you'll have to contend with negative cash flow.

Our on-site inspection revealed that the condition was excellent. It was now scored at 12, and an offer to purchase was made based on a favorable appraisal. The appraisal came in at $235,000; 80 percent of this amount would have meant a sales price of $188,000. The sellers decided that as much as $10,000 cash for their equity would not be sufficient. We parted company. We spent $300 on the appraisal and lost some time. Our guidelines, because they are strict, cause us to lose a good deal or two. But they protect us from the bad ones.

Let's take another call:

SELLER: Can you tell me about your ad in the paper?

BUYER: Do you have a property for sale?

SELLER: Yes, it was listed for $210,000. The listing has just expired after three months of no action. I have a first mortgage that is not assumable for $180,000. My equity is about $30,000.

BUYER: How flexible are you?

SELLER: I have a building lot that I want to build a new home on. I figure I'll need most of my cash out of this house to be able to finish it, plus my other savings. It's a great little home. A good investment.

BUYER: If you need cash, are you willing to discount the price?

SELLER: No, I want full price. And I need the cash too.

BUYER: It doesn't seem to me that you are all that flexible.

SELLER: Well, I thought I might see what you were looking for.

You notice here a conversation with a seller who is really not flexible. He is not motivated. He'll just wait it out to get his price and terms. As I said before, there is usually no use talking with inflexible sellers. Inflexible sellers are just fishing for a sucker. Don't take the bait. They'll just pick your brains and say no thanks. I want to find a motivated seller. Then the negotiation is easy.

Just for fun, let's score this property anyway:

Seller's flexibility: 1
Location: assume 2
Financing: 1 (either way, you would have lots of cash down
    or a high negative cash flow.)
Price: 2
Condition: assume 2
Total: 8

No go. Let's try one more call:

SELLER: I'm calling about your newspaper ad.
BUYER: Hello. Do you have a property for sale?
SELLER: Yes, a duplex. It's worth about $275,000.
BUYER: Where is it located? And what are the outstanding loans?
SELLER: I don't know if I want to share all of this information
    with you over the phone.
BUYER: If I don't know this information, I won't be able to make
    you an offer.
SELLER: I'll call back later.

If the seller is not motivated enough to give you the information you need on the telephone, he is not a motivated seller. Keep looking.

These examples give you a brief idea of how to find a high-scoring property from a flexible seller.

If you aren't running your own newspaper ad, the next best source of flexible sellers is your local newspaper. How many motivated sellers are there in a weekend newspaper?

As the chart on the next page shows, as many as 10 percent of all ads indicate some flexibility on the part of the seller. Maybe only 2 percent to 5 percent are seriously motivated—willing to be extremely flexible. This is the group we zero in on. The chart outlines the various kinds of flexible sellers and some clues to use in spotting their ads.

It is rare that you will find a seller who says blatantly, "Nothing down," or "Low down payment." But when you find such clues, you'd better call. Maybe one in a hundred ads is this obvious. Most ads have only one clue. They will say, "seller will carry," or "owner financing," or "flexible." These ads usually mean that if you make a large down payment, the seller will carry some of his equity in the form of a note and mortgage. This doesn't fit in our parameters. We need sellers who are much more flexible. I usually find the best success with ads that have more than one clue in them. I bought a property in Washington, DC, while I was there doing some PR for my first book. The ad read something like this:

> Two-bedroom condominium. Good location. Low down payment. Assumable VA loan. By owner.

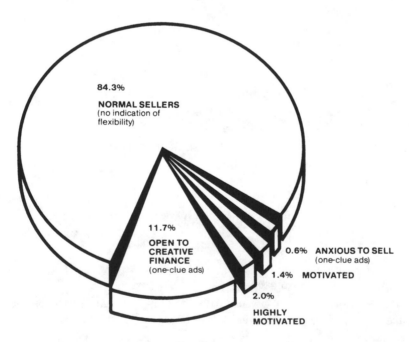

84.3%

NORMAL SELLERS
(no indication of flexibility)

11.7%

OPEN TO CREATIVE FINANCE
(one-clue ads)

0.6% **ANXIOUS TO SELL**
(one-clue ads)

1.4% **MOTIVATED**

2.0%

HIGHLY MOTIVATED

Figures based on an analysis of nearly 230,000 *Homes/Condos For Sale* ads in 9 major newspapers.

CHANCES OF FINDING A MOTIVATED SELLER THROUGH NEWSPAPER ADS

Chances of Finding a Motivated Seller through Newspaper Ads

The clue here is obvious: low down payment. This is rare. You can tell by the size of the ad if the seller is flexible or not. Large ads that go on for pages about the amenities of the property are not what you are looking for. In reality, I don't care to know the quality of the carpets, what the landscaping is like, or whether it has a garbage disposal. I want to know if this seller is motivated or not. You can usually spot the motivated sellers' ads. They get right to the heart of the matter: the financing.

This seller was motivated.

As I recall, it was about eight-thirty at night. The next morning I was scheduled to appear on a television show. I thought it would spice things up a bit if I could say that I had bought something the night before with nothing down. That would shut the skeptics up.

I called and found the seller home. He said he didn't need a lot of cash. He had purchased another property, which he was planning on moving into shortly. He just wanted to move this one to get rid of the monthly mortgage payment. I could sense that I had a hot one. I told him that I would be right out and asked for directions. I caught a cab and headed for the property. I had one problem: no paperwork to consummate a deal. As we were driving along the freeway, I noticed a large real-estate company that still had its lights on. I asked the cab driver to stop, and we found a late-working agent who gave me an offer-to-purchase form. I was now ready to roll. I took careful note of the neighborhood as we drove up to the condominium project. The neighborhoods we passed through were great. At the project, I knocked on the door of another unit, which had a For Sale sign out front. The owner confirmed that the going prices were similar to the price the seller was asking. While the cab driver waited, I visited with the seller of the advertised unit. Sure enough, he was flexible, and within less than an hour I had a signed contract to purchase his unit with a very low down payment. The actual cash for the down payment would be easily raised from the first tenant to rent the unit; the first and last months' rent plus a healthy deposit.

As I was leaving, I asked the seller what he was doing the next morning. He asked why. I told him that I would be discussing this exact purchase on television. I gave him a copy of my book and rec-

FINDING AND DEALING WITH MOTIVATED SELLERS

TYPES OF MOTIVATED SELLERS	PROBLEMS OR CIRCUMSTANCES	NEWSPAPERS	MLS BOOK	REALTORS	COURTHOUSE	PROPERTY RENTAL CO	EXCHANGERS	DRIVE AROUND LOOKING AT PROPERTIES	SUCCESSFUL INVESTORS	CLUES AND KEY WORDS TO LOOK FOR	KEY MOTIVATORS: PLACE EMPHASIS IN NEGOTIATIONS
NEED SOME CASH BUT NOT ALL	Flexible seller	❯	❯	❯			❯			Will carry second, paper, OWC, wraparound, mortgage, owner will finance, consider second, contract sale, no qualifying, low loan/high equity, seller doesn't need to have his money for several months, even longer but wants to sell now, needs cash for small consumer items that could be obtained with a credit card (not ours). Debts to be paid off.	Stress the ability to get him the cash he needs for his minor problems but that it will be necessary to carry some paper. Stress honesty and ability to close. Credibility is all important.
DON'T CARE ABOUT CASH	Management problems	❯		❯	❯		❯			Mgt. problems, negative cash flow, high loan/low equity	Stress quick closings so that seller can rid himself of problems quickly. "We could arrange to have this problem out of your hair in 24 hours."
	Transfer/out of state	❯						❯		Transfer, out of state, moving, date for move is very close	Stress quick closings plus saving commissions if property does not sell fast. Seller won't have to leave wife and list with Realtor. He can use your note as down payment to buy house in new city. "You don't need any more stress at a time like this!"
	Behind in payments	❯			❯					Behind in payments, motivated seller	Stress credit rating and how important it is to save it. Stress ability to pay back payments but that is all. (You can get the money from a partner later, if you're worried about the money)
	Fixer-upper	❯		❯			❯	❯	❯	Fixer-upper, handy-man special, needs work, property not rented out because it needs work	Stress his problem property and how nice it will be when he has the headache out of his hair. "Life is too short to worry about this"
	Time problems, too busy	❯		❯		❯	❯			Other interests—going on long vacation, promotion to new job	Stress quick closings. Stress importance of time and how precious it is how it's not worth wasting on something you can't stand.
	Sickness/ health	❯				❯	❯			Too much to handle, seller in hospital, other family members handling investment	Stress quick closing. Stress cash flow to help with medical bills.
DON'T NEED CASH	Divorce	❯		❯	❯					Single owner, divorce	Stress starting a new life … how important it is to cut your losses and run with your winners. Stress psychological freedom that will come when this "curse" is removed from his neck.
	Retirees	❯		❯		❯	❯			Time to relax, retirement near, needs cash flow to supplement pension	Stress cash flow to aid retirement and tax savings for no down payment sales. "Why pay all that money to the government when you could use it for a better retirement."
	Already bought new property	❯		❯		❯	❯			Option to buy, buy or rent, rent to own, vacant	Stress how he doesn't need any cash. Your payments will coincide with his so that he is not at a disadvantage. Offer to pay the same interest rate he has on his new loan…or higher.
	Investor, builder	❯		❯			❯		❯	Interest in % return, will consider trade, need to sell out subdivision to clear bank loans, slow moving projects	Stress the amount Uncle Sam will take of his profits if he gets cash. Offer to pay him more than he would earn at the highest local "paper" certificate return. Stress security. Remember "greed."
	Wealthy owners	❯		❯		❯	❯		❯	Don't need cash	Stress no necessity of cash. Stress profit. Stress that you are an honest, hard-working individual who is trustworthy but cash poor. "How did you get your first break?" Act like a beginner, let him "counsel you." Try sympathy.
DON'T WANT CASH	Tax problems	❯	❯	❯			❯			Willing to accept cash chunks in different years, exchange only	Stress tax consequences—the best way to avoid this is to sell with little or no money down. Offer to bend over backwards to help him with his tax planning.

ommended that he watch if he could. The cab driver drove me back to my hotel. It was almost midnight. The taxi fare wasn't cheap.

The next morning, I described to the television audience how I had gone about buying this unit. I showed them the exact ad in the paper as well as the exact paperwork that I had used to buy the unit. Then I told them that an ideal buying program would be to buy at least one property per year for the next ten years. As a parting note, I told the seller, on the air, that in all fairness, he should not sell his property to me. He should instead keep it and rent it out for the long run. It would be the first property in his investment portfolio. In essence, I gave the property back to him—on the air.

Before I got on the airplane to leave Washington, I placed a phone call to this seller. Sure enough, he had stayed home from work (he was an accountant) to see the show. He agreed with me that he would be better off keeping the property. We parted friends.

But the reason this situation was possible is that I knew how to read the clues in the newspaper. I have bought many properties this way—looking for clues, searching for high motivation, negotiating with flexible sellers.

When you are calling ads in the paper, you can't get discouraged. You will get twenty no's before you get a maybe. You will get several maybe's before you find a yes. The only path to the yes's is through the no's. The no's will hurt less and less after a while. You will get callused. You are looking for sellers who are so motivated to sell that they will welcome you with open arms. Believe me, they are out there, and you are the answer to their prayers. The motivated seller has a need to sell greater than his need for cash, or a need for cash greater than his need to sell for full price. Either way, you solve people's problems, and they solve yours.

And that is what win-win is all about.

The third source of flexible sellers is through a Realtor. Working with Realtors is both easy and hard. It is easy because the Realtor does most all of the work for you: the looking, the screening, the negotiating, the paperwork. The hard part comes at the beginning, when you tell the Realtor that you are a bargain hunter with very narrow buying parameters. And if you mention that you want to put little or no money down, watch out! An uncreative Realtor will tell you categorically that it cannot be done.

Not to worry. I've been doing this a long time and have bought a couple million dollars' worth of property this way. It does work. In fact, the graduates of my nationwide seminar bought over $1 billion dollars' worth of property with little or no money down in a period of twelve months. Check out their stories at www.millionaire-halloffame.com. I don't listen to skeptics anymore. I just show them this Web site. That settles it. When a skeptic tells you it can't be done, he usually means that he doesn't know how to do it. Or he may mean that he feels it is immoral or unethical. The skeptical Realtor may mean that he doesn't want to do it because it means little or no commission or that it may not be the best thing for his client. I respect all of these objections, but they are unfounded. There is nothing illegal or immoral about solving problems in a mutually beneficial way. We'll go into more detail about win-win in chapter 8.

To end our discussion of Realtors, you would be much better off dealing with a creative Realtor—one who understands creative financing.

Once you find a creative Realtor, you will soon realize that he or she is worth a king's ransom. Tell your Realtor of your goal, whether it be one or ten properties a year, and turn your Realtor loose on the market.

Now, let's advance to the least understood part of buying property.

CHAPTER 8

The Win-Win Philosophy:
How to Achieve Win-Win Wealth
in a Win-Lose World

The ideal that all wealth is acquired through stealing is
popular in prisons and at Harvard.
> —GEORGE GILDER, Wealth and Poverty

Everybody knows that all businessmen are crooks. And those that
aren't crooked are bumbling idiots or buffoons out to make a buck.

At least that is the prevailing attitude.

It is common to think that we live in a win-lose world where the
only success is achieved at the expense of others, where the only
way to climb up is to push someone else down. In a nationwide
survey we conducted, we asked people to respond to the following
statement: "People who become wealthy take unfair advantage of
others."

The responses were: strongly agree, 10 percent; agree, 30 percent; disagree, 40 percent; strongly disagree, 20 percent.

Where does even 40 percent of the population get the idea that
wealthy people are crooked?!

There are many culprits. Let's look at a few of them.

The Media Institute, a nonprofit research institution in Washington, DC, released a study entitled "Crooks, Conmen and Clowns:
Businessmen in TV Entertainment." This survey of two hundred
episodes from the top fifty entertainment programs found that two
out of three TV businessmen were portrayed as foolish, greedy, or
criminal. Over half of all corporate chiefs were shown committing
illegal acts ranging from fraud to murder.

Is it any wonder, then, that the average person, watching an average of seven hours of television per day, begins to believe sooner or later that capitalism is a win-lose game? It would be almost a miracle if he thought otherwise. On every channel, in virtually every time slot from the early morning news broadcasts through the morning talk shows to the afternoon soaps and into prime time, everywhere you turn, businessmen and businesswomen are generally seen creating wealth at the expense of others in some illegal or immoral way. Now you know why they call it television "programming."

The same holds true for the print media. And who can blame them? Which of the following headlines do you think would sell the most newspapers?

"Prominent Businessman Bilks Little Old Lady out of Life Savings" or "Thousands of Local Business People Work Late to Bring Home the Bacon"

The nature of the news is to report the spectacular, the unusual, the exception to the rule. Unfortunately, with widespread exposure, the exception to the rule appears to look more like the rule.

It is in politics where the win-lose myth tends to be most deeply ensconced. There is, for example, a certain type of self-styled crusading, welfare-state liberal politician who wages a righteous campaign against the thieving upper class. He draws attention to the glaring inequities. And since the poor and middle classes far outnumber the rich, he has little trouble gaining a constituency.

Thus, many politicians mistake wealth as the prime cause of poverty. The struggling masses yearning to be free are held captive by a powerful, crooked, rich elite. But as George Gilder says, "Rather than wealth causing poverty, it is far more true to say that what causes poverty is the widespread belief that wealth does."

Any reasonable person should recognize that you don't have to steal from the poor to get rich. You don't even have to steal from the rich—although this would seem more politically acceptable. You don't have to steal at all.

Wealth doesn't have to be win-lose. Or even lose-lose. It can be and ought to be win-win.

What is the win-win philosophy? It is modern jargon for an ancient saying: "Do unto others as you would have them do unto you." The wisdom in this hasn't changed one iota in twenty centuries.* The skeptics laugh and say that when it comes to economics, this Golden Rule should be changed to read, "He who has the gold makes the rules." This is true to a degree, but he who obtains much gold does so much less often by stealing it than by working and sacrificing for it. The truly successful capitalist lives the economic golden rule by providing unto others what he, himself, would like to be provided with: namely, a quality product at the right price.

Those who try to obtain their wealth by cheating the customer may seem to win in the short run. But in the long run, a win-lose situation generally becomes lose-lose. Win-win is not a short-term technique, strategy, or method—it is a long-term philosophy. I am deeply indebted to Stephen R. Covey, author of the phenomenal best-seller *The 7 Habits of Highly Effective People,* for first introducing me to the win-win concept.

What are the principles of this philosophy? There are at least six. I'll couch them in the context of the investment world so that the principles are clear.

Principle 1: If Both Parties Can't Win, Don't Play

The win-win investor is as gentle as a lamb but as shrewd as a fox. He doesn't want to take advantage of anyone, nor does he want to be taken advantage of. He would no more steal his wealth than have it stolen from him. He doesn't want to win by making someone else lose.

Therefore, the first rule of the win-win game is to steer clear of situations in which either party is bound to lose.

Now, this may sound obvious, but I have seen many a foolish real-estate investor enter into win-lose transactions in which the seller took advantage of a buyer's greed, stupidity, lack of careful analysis and planning, or naïveté. And vice versa.

A win-win negotiator needs to have a predetermined idea of

*Obviously my own religious views have been kept to a minimum in this book, but for those so inclined, I have a prepared speech entitled "God and Money" available for those who specifically request it by writing me at the Enlightened Millionaire Institute, 5072 North 300 West, Provo, Utah 84604, or by calling 1-800-345-3648.

what winning and losing mean. Then when he is in a negotiating setting, he will know his own limits and boundaries. In this way, he will be less likely to lose. If you are a real-estate investor, your goal may be to buy one or two good "target" properties per year on good terms. Finding and buying these properties constitutes a "winning" year. If you run into a seller who is trying to sell an over-priced, run-down property for all cash, your instinct should tell you that something is amiss. If the seller gets everything he wants, and you get nothing, that's win-lose. As the saying goes, "One more good deal like that, and I'm out of business!"

According to the nineteenth-century writer and philosopher Ralph Waldo Emerson, "Every man takes care that his neighbor shall not cheat him. But a day comes when he begins to care that he not cheat his neighbor. Then all goes well. He has changed his mar-ket-cart into a chariot of the sun."

Principle 2: Since the Essence of Win-Win Is Mutual Problem-Solving, Don't Negotiate with People Who Don't Have Problems They Are Motivated to Solve

In other words, the more flexible the seller, the easier it will be to find suitable alternative solutions to the problems of both parties. Inflexible sellers are not motivated to search for solutions. Maybe only one in ten real-estate sellers could be classified as a true flex-ible seller—the classic motivated seller. Look for the motivated seller. He will be more likely to work out prices and terms that are realistic and beneficial for both parties.

Let's try to buy a property from a seller, to show you what I mean:

BUYER: Hello, my name is Bob Allen. I'm interested in your ad in the paper, in which you indicated some flexibility in the sale of your property. Can you tell me about it?

SELLER: Well, this is a rental property I bought about three years ago. I have an appraisal showing that it is worth $225,000. I have a mortgage of $175,000. My equity is $50,000. I need $30,000 cash. I would consider being flexible with the remaining $20,000 of my equity. [Where is his problem? Could it have to do with the cash he needs? Let's find out.]

BUYER: Excuse me for asking, but would you mind sharing with me what you plan on doing with the $30,000 cash down payment? It might shed some light on how to solve your selling problem. [See how we start to bring in the idea of problem solving.]

SELLER: I took out a personal unsecured loan at my bank for $30,000 about two years ago to help out my business in a pinch. The loan is coming due, and I know that my banker would roll it over again, but my wife and I have decided that we would like to be out from under the burden of this debt. We have decided to sell this rental unit and take the proceeds to pay off the bank loan before it comes due in three weeks. We never did like the management hassles anyway.

BUYER: So your problem is you want to pay off a bank loan. If I could take this loan off your back so that you would be relieved of the responsibility and liability on this loan, would you consider less cash down?

SELLER: You mean, you would take the loan out of my name and assume it?

BUYER: Yes.

SELLER: That might work. What do you have in mind?

BUYER: Well, I don't have a lot of cash for a down payment. But I do have an excellent credit rating and can afford higher monthly payments. I think I could assume your loan. I would try to get a five-year loan with monthly payments to the bank. As for the rest of your equity, would you accept $2,000 cash now and $10,000 in three years?

SELLER: Yes, if you could solve my problem with my banker, I suppose I could be a little flexible with you on the down payment.

What made this negotiation possible? Each party had a problem to solve. The buyer had little money for a down payment. The seller wanted to get out of debt and was motivated to act by an upcoming deadline. The win-win solution was to have the buyer assume the seller's loan. The seller gets rid of the debt. The banker gains a new customer and has an old loan paid off. The buyer buys a property with a small down payment. Win-win-win.

If the seller had little or no motivation to sell or act quickly, the conversation might have gone something like this:

BUYER: Hello, I noticed your ad in the paper. Can you tell me something about your property?

SELLER: Yes. I have it priced at $225,000, and I need all of my $50,000 equity in cash.

BUYER: I know that this is none of my business, but could you tell me what you plan to do with the proceeds from the down payment you are asking for? I might have some other ways of solving your cash problem.

SELLER: First of all, I don't have a cash problem. And second of all, as you said, it isn't any of your business anyway.

This person is not a motivated seller. Your conversation should end in the next ten seconds or so.

Do you get the drift? When you deal only with people who have pressing problems that need solving, you will find a friendlier reception. If you enter with the spirit of problem solving, the barriers will slowly come down, and you can begin to negotiate as partners instead of as adversaries. That leads us to the next principle.

Principle 3: Make Friends with the Seller—He Will Be More Apt to Enter into Problem Solving with a Friend Than with an Enemy

A win-win negotiator tries to build an atmosphere of trust, honesty, and understanding. It is only in this atmosphere that true problems are revealed and alternative solutions can be explored.

Creating this atmosphere is not easy. Generally, most people you negotiate with will look upon you as an adversary. They have been well trained by the world to see every situation involving money as win-lose. This should not offend you. On the contrary, it should be your challenge to make every party in a transaction feel comfortable—to diffuse the tension that is always present in discussions about money.

Fear is a powerful emotion. I try my best to dispel the seller's fears about me by making small talk about the property. I may notice something of interest and suspend active negotiation in order to pursue it. All of this talk gives me important information about the seller and his motivations. I am trying to be his friend, whether I buy his property or not. I may ask tough questions, but I will always try to preface them with a statement that clarifies why I am asking the question or detoxifies the question so that it is not so blunt. "Mr. Seller, I'm not trying to be overly critical, but the appliances in this unit don't seem to be in very good condition."

There is a saying when it comes to negotiating: "The stronger the tactics, the greater the resistance." Why? Because trust is destroyed when strong tactics are used, and resistance is the by-product. When trust is destroyed, the parties in a negotiation become adversaries. And adversaries don't have much incentive to help each other.

In the final analysis, why would anyone sell a property to a stranger with little or no money down? That's just the point! When the seller is finished negotiating with me, I am no longer a stranger. I am a friend. I have been helpful, not abrasive. I have tried to solve problems, not intimidate. I am part of the solution instead of part of the problem. I have been sensitive, not bullheaded.

All of this may sound like so much sappy, utopian mush when viewed in the context of the seeming ugliness of the world of competition, but I have learned that win-win is much more effective and satisfying than "winning through intimidation." "Getting to the other guy before he gets to you" is just another way of saying win-lose. In a win-win transaction, even if the deal is not consummated, this temporary "failure" can result in a new friendship that may bear fruit many years hence.

The story is told of an African farmer who asked his neighbors to help him in his harvest. He asked each neighbor to bring a basket for carrying the grain out of the fields. Some brought large baskets, others small ones. At the end of the day, as they carried in the last load, the farmer announced that each helper would be able to keep the final load as a token of gratitude for the help he or she had rendered. Those with the largest baskets were able to bring the largest amounts home, those with the smallest baskets only small amounts. In other words, you get out of any situation what you put into it. You reap what you sow. Even in negotiation.

Principle 4: You Can't Solve a Problem Unless You Understand It

How do you begin to understand problems? There are three simple rules:

Rule 1: listen.
Rule 2: listen.
Rule 3: listen.

It is the duty of the win-win negotiator to seek to understand the motivations of the party he is negotiating with. Let me illustrate:

A clergyman goes to his superior and asks a simple question: "Father, may I smoke while I'm praying?"

Since this doesn't seem appropriate, the superior counsels against it.

After thinking about it, the clergyman again approaches his superior with a similar request: "Father, may I pray while I'm smoking?"

"Of course, my son. You should have a prayer in your heart always."

Isn't this the same question? This win-win negotiator took time to think through the motivations of his superior. Once he understood the problem, the negotiation went rather smoothly. It was just a matter of searching for appropriate alternatives.

Principle 5: Once You Understand the Problem, Search for Alternative Win-Win Solutions

I think this is best illustrated with an example. Many years ago, I bought a single-family house as an investment. The owners had been trying to sell for several months. The property had a price tag of $55,000 with an underlying loan of about $15,000. They had only one firm offer of $48,000 with $5,000 down and the balance of $43,000 to be on a contract with monthly payments over the next thirty years. The owners didn't like the offer because it didn't give them much cash and tied up their equity for thirty years. About this time, my property-acquisition team became aware of their property and made some inquiries. The owners told us that they had sold the property but were very unhappy with the terms of the current offer to buy their property. For them it was a win-lose transaction. We began to do some problem solving. We learned that this couple had lived in this house for over twenty years. They wanted to sell because they had recently made an offer to buy a beautiful condominium across town and needed a down payment of $7,000 cash. After Realtor's commissions and closing costs, they would be lucky to have $1,000 from the sale of their house. This would mean that they would have to dip into bank savings to make the down payment on their new condominium, leaving very little money for furniture and drapes.

Their problem was that they needed an offer that would give them more cash at closing plus the balance of their equity in less than thirty years. They were motivated and flexible. And they were impressed by our desire to help them solve their problem.

Now, our goal was to buy properties with as little cash down as possible. We had to find a solution that would give the seller lots of cash at the closing but require little or no cash out of our pockets.

With these problems in mind, we sat down and structured an offer beneficial to both parties—a win-win solution. We suggested that the seller go down to his savings and loan association and obtain a new first mortgage against his property for $35,000. Since his old loan was a low-interest-rate loan through FHA, the bank should be more than happy to refinance his old loan and make him a new, higher-balance loan at a market interest rate. With a new $35,000 loan paying off the old $15,000 loan, there would be $20,000 in cash proceeds that could go directly to the seller. We agreed to assume the seller's new loan. (Since it was an FHA loan, it was completely assumable with very little red tape; in the 1970s and 1980s it was much easier to assume existing mortgages.) We offered a sales price of $52,000 instead of the previous offer of $48,000, and we agreed to pay the balance of the seller's equity ($17,000) in five years at 11 percent interest with no monthly payments.

The offer looked something like this:

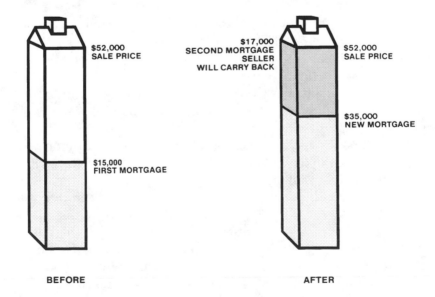

The sellers would receive $20,000 cash at closing less closing costs plus a note for $17,000 due in five years (with a one-year extension if necessary). When this was compared with the previous offer of $5,000 cash at closing plus monthly payments over thirty years, the sellers were ecstatic to accept our offer. But they had some questions.

"Why should we refinance our own home? Why don't you do it?" We explained that there would be fewer questions asked and much less red tape involved if they refinanced their home than if we, as investors, tried to do it. And this would make for a quicker closing.

Then they asked, "But if we refinance, we have to pay all the closing costs. And that can be expensive." We explained that they were receiving a higher price from us for this very reason. But to make it fairer, we agreed to pay half the closing costs if the sellers would pay our half of the closing costs with the cash from the new loan and lend us this amount to be repaid in five years at 11 percent interest. They felt that this would be fair.

Then they asked, "Why can't you make us monthly payments like the other offer?" We explained that we were investors and would be renting out this home. The payments on the new $35,000 loan would be almost $500 per month, and it would be difficult to rent out the house for more than this. Any additional payments would have to come out of our pocket in negative cash flow. And if the negative cash flow was too great, it would not be in our best interests to go through with the deal (win-lose). Most sellers are more receptive to creative deals when they know why the offer is different from more conventional financing methods. Studies have proved that people respond better to requests when there is a reason included, even if the reason given is a poor one. Let the seller be part of solving your problem as much as you help him solve his. That is the essence of win-win.

The sellers were also concerned about the future balloon payment. "Where will you get the money in five years to pay the balloon payment?" We showed them that with only minimal appreciation, the property would increase in value enough over the five-year period to allow us to refinance it and completely pay off the sellers.

The sellers agreed to our offer because they could see that all involved would benefit. They obtained a new loan and with the proceeds were able to move into their new condominium and have plenty of cash left over after closing costs and commissions to furnish it. They were thrilled. The Realtor earned a commission. The bank made a new loan and got rid of an old one. And we were able to buy a beautiful single-family investment house with absolutely no money out of our pockets. And little or no negative cash flow. That's win-win-win-*win.*

It is amazing what you can accomplish when you seek to understand problems and are committed to solving them for others.

Sometimes a seller needs just a little guidance in brainstorming alternative solutions to a pressing problem. One seller of a four-unit apartment building I bought was very leery of an offer we had given him. He was sick of managing, he didn't need cash, he liked the fact that our offer would give him a steady cash flow, but he didn't like the fact that we weren't putting any of our money into the deal. He balked. His main concern was security. "What will happen to me if you default on your loan to me? I could really be left holding the bag."

You've got to admit that he had a valid concern. Once we understood that his problem was security and not cash, we agreed to give him extra collateral to secure his loan. I had $50,000 worth of notes secured by a property I had sold a few years back. The notes weren't doing me any good except as a source of monthly income. I agreed to let him use these notes as additional collateral for the sale. If I defaulted on my payments to him, he would have the right not only to foreclose and repossess his building but to confiscate my additional collateral. This seemed to solve his security hang-ups, and we were able to buy this property without a cash down payment—just collateral. Win-win.

Principle 6: Optimism Is the Root of Persistence

Searching for creative solutions to people's problems is not easy. There will be many times when you will be tempted to give up. You should be motivated by the knowledge that when a seller tells you no, he may simply mean that he doesn't understand. This is the time for patience.

"Mr. Seller, let me understand this. You say you won't accept my offer because you don't like the 'low-down' part. But you told me earlier that you didn't need a lot of cash. Could you help me understand where I went wrong?" (In other words, "What's bugging you?")

When a financial adviser tells his client not to accept your deal, he may simply mean that he doesn't know how to put it together. You need to educate all parties involved to the benefits of the transaction. This takes time and effort. But that is the stuff of which successful negotiations are made.

When you are practicing the win-win philosophy, you can proceed with optimism. You can't hurt anyone by trying to solve his problems. And if you can't solve your own problems (buying a property), you will have at least shed some light on a seller's problem—which may help him with the next seller. By treating a seller with respect, no matter how he treats you, you always come out a long-term winner. And that is reason enough for you to persist.

One final thought: You can't win unless you put these ideas into practice. And if you lose, so do all of the sellers out there who need your help. And that's not win-win.

The ball is in your court.

CHAPTER 9

Leverage: I Love Debt!

By now the story is famous.

In January 1981 the *Los Angeles Times* challenged me to live up to my advertising claim: "Send me to any city. Take away my wallet. Give me $100 for living expenses. And in seventy-two hours I'll buy an excellent piece of property using none of my own money."

I had made this boast in many of the newspaper advertisements announcing my first book, *Nothing Down,* subtitled *A Proven Program That Shows You How to Buy Real Estate with Little or No Money Down.* This claim, being rather bold and seemingly impossible, raised a few eyebrows. In fact, my first call came from people in Ralph Nader's organization. They'd seen my ad in the *Wall Street Journal* and, being concerned about truth in advertising, inquired whether or not I would be amenable to a formal challenge. I told them to get a copy of my book, study it, and get back to me with a written challenge. They never called back.

A few months later, the *Los Angeles Times* called, made a formal challenge—and I accepted.

At six in the morning on January 10, 1981, I met a *Times* reporter at a hotel in Los Angeles. We had previously agreed that I would not know where they were sending me to until the morning of the challenge. That morning, the reporter announced for the first time that they were sending me to San Francisco. He would accompany me every step of the way to verify the results. And he let me know that if I failed, his paper would let the whole world know that I was a fraud. We boarded a Pacific Southwest Airlines flight bound for San Francisco, arriving a little after 8:00 AM. Near the baggage-claim area, he ceremoniously handed me my $100 spending money, and I handed him my wallet. I was now on my own in a strange city with nothing but $100 in my pocket and less than three days to make good on my claim. My entire future hung in the balance.

Now, before I go into the details of what happened, I would like you to step into my shoes for a moment. Imagine what it feels like to be totally and completely broke (maybe the feeling is not all that foreign to you). You are almost penniless, with no job, no credit, no financial statement to speak of. I have taken away all of your crutches, all of the security blankets that you have carefully wrapped around yourself over the years. And in this most desperate financial situation. I'm going to teach you the most profound and simple lesson: *Wealth does not reside in material possessions. Wealth resides in the mind. Wealth is not a thing, it is a thought.*

While all the world is hoarding things in a vain scramble for security, the rare person of wealth is calm. He is not attached to his possessions. They are the mere trappings of wealth, frail counterfeits, the appearance but not the substance of wealth.

When the winds blow and the rains descend, he is not long shaken by financial collapse or catastrophe. It is only the poverty minded that jump out of windows when they lose everything. The wealthy person cannot lose his wealth. His wealth is infinitely portable, for it resides in his head and his heart. Therein lies his only security.

I accepted the *Los Angeles Times* challenge because I wanted to prove that, armed with only what I had in my head, I could go into any city and start again on the road to wealth by acquiring at least one piece of excellent real estate without using any of my own money.

Was I successful?

The headline on the front page of the *Times* financial section on February 1, 1981, read: "Buying Homes without Cash: Boastful Investor Accepts *Times* Challenge—and Wins."

The article went on to describe how in fifty-seven hours I signed agreements to purchase not one but seven properties with a total value of $722,715. I eventually closed on four of them. My goal had been to find and tie up as many properties as I could so that no one could ever claim that it had been a fluke, a stroke of luck, or that it had been rigged in any way. When the dust settled, I still had $20 of the original $100 spending money in my pocket. With a reporter at my side as witness, I had managed to survive in the San Francisco area for two nights and three days on $80 cash and no credit

cards (if you think that is easy, try it sometime) as well as locate and
negotiate with six separate real-estate owners and come to terms to
buy their properties without having any assets of my own. If you
would like a special report including the details of the challenge,
write me at the Enlightened Millionaire Institute, 5072 North 300
West, Provo, Utah 84604 or by calling 1-800-345-3648.

I was able to do this because I understood the power of the principle of leverage. This principle is one of the elementary lessons in
physics. With a lever and a fulcrum, it is possible for a person to
move large objects that would be impossible to move by hand.
The Greek scientist Archimedes, who discovered this principle,
said, "Give me a place to stand, and I will move the earth." In the
financial world, leverage means using borrowed assets to magnify a
person's small efforts into a large result. In chapter 3, I showed you
how a small investment in the stock market with the proper use of
borrowed money could produce a much larger rate of return.

The use of leverage in a financial sense is often associated with
the letters OPM—other people's money. But this is only part of the
power of leverage. There are at least eight major areas or resources
that a wealth seeker can draw upon to increase his or her wealth:

Financial resources	Nonfinancial resources
Cash	Time
Credit	Knowledge
Financial statement (equity)	People
Steady income	Courage

It is not necessary to possess any of the above resources in order
to amass material wealth. The only prerequisite is a strong desire.
Everything else can be borrowed. This was the knowledge I possessed as I stood in San Francisco with only $100 in my pocket.
Firmly embedded in my mind were the nine simple words of the
wealth seeker's motto: "If I don't have it, I can get it!"

The only real assets I possessed during the *Los Angeles Times*
challenge were time (seventy-two hours), courage, and the knowledge of how to use leverage. I knew that if I needed cash to take
advantage of a bargain property, I could always find someone with
cash who would be delighted to participate with me in a win-win
purchase. The yellow pages are full of wealthy professionals who

are flush with all the necessary financial resources but are miserably lacking in time, courage, and knowledge. I could show them marvelous ways of obtaining a badly needed tax shelter and much higher rates of return in well-selected investment real estate, without having to invest a lot of cash.

I knew that if I didn't have the necessary credit to complete a transaction, I could always borrow someone else's creditworthiness. In other words, whatever I lacked, someone would possess.

To illustrate this point, I often ask my seminar students the following question: "How many of you would be my fifty–fifty partner if I could find you an excellent piece of real estate, priced at least $100,000 below market, which could be bought with nothing down, no negative cash flow, no balloon payments, and no management hassles—and all that would be required of you would be to cosign with me to obtain a mortgage?" Over half the people in the room raise their hands. Then I say, "For those of you who didn't raise your hands because you felt you couldn't qualify for a loan, this should have been a powerful lesson. Remember, if you don't have it, someone does. And that someone is probably sitting right here in this room. Rather than spending years improving your financial resources, your time would be better spent improving your nonfinancial resources, such as learning how to find and finance bargains. Once you have found a bargain, it will be easy to find a partner who will share the profits with you."

You see, if you don't have the necessary ingredients to put together a deal, someone does.

Let me illustrate:

One of my early seminar graduates had few financial assets. Of the eight major wealth resources, he was strong in only one—he had lots of time because he had no job. He met an attorney who was specializing in foreclosure properties. The attorney's problems were just the opposite. He had money, credit, and knowledge, but he lacked the time to find and negotiate the bargains. Our graduate offered to be the "finder" if the attorney would show him what to do, handle the paperwork, and come up with the necessary cash. On their first deal, they made a $40,000 cash profit, which they split fifty-fifty. And in the next few years they made more than $500,000 working together. Neither one would have been successful without the other. And that is the essence of win-win leveraging.

Remember the motto: "If I don't have it, I can get it!"

Sometimes all you need to start your snowball rolling down the hill is the knowledge of how to find the right kind of flexible seller for whom a lot of cash and credit are not high priorities—and how to show this seller several win-win ways to sell to you with nothing down.

As difficult as this may seem, it is fairly simple once you learn what to do. Recently I was challenged by a San Diego CBS affiliate TV station to prove how easy it is to buy real estate with nothing down. Although I had already amply proved my point with the *Los Angeles Times* challenge, I agreed to do it one more time—except this time I was going to be filmed in the act.

One Tuesday morning at ten thirty, I strolled off the airplane in San Diego. The TV reporter, a beautiful woman, and her camera crew met me at the jetway. Outside the airport, they filmed me giving up my wallet and receiving only $100 in cash. Once again, I was broke with a challenge to fulfill, but this time I didn't have seventy-two hours. My plane was going to leave in less than *seven* hours, and I had promised my wife that I would be home for supper.

Since the time was short, we immediately made our way to a nearby motel, where I rented an inexpensive room for $18, bought a paper for 25¢, and started reading through the classified section under "Homes for Sale." I was looking for a clue in the ads that would indicate to me that the seller didn't need a lot of cash. The most obvious ad read:

No money down, 2 BR condo. Assumable loan. Agt.

After calling on several other ads with no success, I called on the ad above. The agent was trying to sell this condominium for his client. He indicated that his seller didn't need any cash and that any commissions involved wouldn't have to be in cash either. All they wanted was a solid buyer who could assume management responsibilities. They would accept my IOU secured by the property. I made an appointment to look at the property in about two hours. Since it was time for lunch, I treated the TV people to lunch, using part of my $100 cash. Afterward we drove to the unit, found the agent, inspected the unit, and sat down beside the condominium pool to write up the offer. All this time, the cameras were rolling. By three that afternoon, less than four and a half hours after stepping off the plane, I signed the offer to purchase a nicely located two-bedroom condominium. I gave the agent $1 as a deposit to bind the contract. The camera crew drove me back to the airport, and I was home that evening. Two weeks later, the offer was formally closed, and I assumed the legal ownership of the unit. I didn't even need to find a renter, since the current renters agreed to stay on. In the time I owned this unit, it appreciated nicely in value.

If I truly had been broke, this unit would have been the first stepping-stone in my rise to wealth. I didn't need a lot of money to start with, just the knowledge of how to find bargains. Or to say it a different way, what a person lacks in financial resources, he can generally compensate for by acquiring the right kind of knowledge.

Suppose you possess some specialized knowledge—perhaps you know of an excellent real-estate bargain, or you know the whereabouts of an abandoned gold mine, or you have invented an engine that runs on water instead of gasoline—and you want to know how to turn that idea into money. What do you do next?

The first step is to determine what ingredients are essential to success, and if you don't possess them, find them. (If you don't have it, someone does!)

Wealth is in the mind.

Some people look out over the lights of a big city and say, "Look at this big, ugly city. It is overpopulated and polluted. I will never have enough money to buy a ticket out of here. This is my prison. I will live and die in this dungeon."

Others look out on the same scene and see an entirely different sight. They say to themselves, "Look at this big, beautiful city. Full of opportunity. Bargains in every direction. Within a ten-mile radius of this spot are enough below-market properties to make me a millionaire several times over. And I will be able to take the money and buy a ticket to anywhere in the world."

Remember, when you are low, and don't have two dimes to rub together, there is always a way.

"If you don't have it, you can get it!"

CHAPTER 10

Overcoming the Three Major Problems That Leverage Creates

Leverage is debt. Debt is bondage. Bondage is the antithesis of freedom or independence. For a wealth seeker, isn't that a catch-22? The answer is yes and no. Yes in the short run, no in the long run.

Ironically, long-term financial independence is rarely attained without going into short-term debt. But let me emphasize that this short-term debt must be carefully acquired and prudently managed, or nothing but financial ruin can result.

In the last chapter we saw the enormous potential of being in debt. Debt is the lifeblood of the successful wealth builder. This chapter will alert us to the pitfalls of imprudent leveraging.

There are three major problems that leverage creates. When faced with these problems, unwise investors make a host of major mistakes. If you are serious about your financial independence, you will avoid these mistakes as you avoid jumping out of an airplane without a parachute.

Major Problem 1: Debt Creates Family Tension

I wonder how many divorces are the direct or indirect result of money pressures. I think you know the answer. Our consumer-oriented society places a high priority on instant gratification. Buy now, pay later. Indulge now, suffer later.

Any couple who is serious about investing should be in agreement about the word *investment.* Investment is just a nice way of saying *sacrifice.* Sacrifice is the opposite of instant gratification. It means sow now, reap later. Sacrifice now, enjoy the fruits later.

It takes a strong couple to make the commitment to invest

together, to sacrifice for the future. The greatest mistake couples make is not spending time exploring the pressures that go with seeking financial independence. Developing a successful marriage is hard enough without adding to it the burden of trying to achieve financial independence. And either one of these goals is extremely difficult without full spousal agreement and support. Without a mutual recognition of what you really want, and what it will take, the whole investment process is on a shaky foundation. No serious wealth seeker can afford to take this risk.

One of the greatest destroyers of wealth is divorce.

Major Problem 2: It's Easy to Borrow Money but Not as Easy to Pay It Back

A beginning businessman borrows money from a bank to start a business. His hope is that the profits from the business will be adequate to repay the bank debt. If the business is unsuccessful, the bank steps in and sells off the company's assets to satisfy the debt.

The real-estate investor is a small-business person who acquires property using leverage with the hope that the property acquired will be rented out for enough income to cover the mortgage payments and expenses. At least, that is the theory. In practice, it is not easy to obtain a positive cash flow. In fact, one of my colleagues told me about an investor friend who had gotten caught up in the speculative fever of buying real estate. He rushed out and eagerly bought twenty single-family houses within a very short period of time. Unfortunately, each one of them had a negative cash flow, as the rents he collected were not enough to pay the mortgage payments. Within a year, he was forced to bail out and lose a lot of money, time, and pride, not to mention the damage to his credit rating. The two-edged sword of leverage had sliced his financial picture to ribbons.

How much more prudent it would have been for him to devote that same energy and enthusiasm to looking for perhaps one or two properties priced well below the market and bearing more favorable mortgage terms. It is easy to buy real estate with little or no money down. The hard part is having the patience to wait until the right investment comes along.

Whenever people called about our "Real Estate Wanted" ad (see chapter 7), and we asked them the reason they were selling their property, the usual answer was: "We can't afford the payments." Or "We have a balloon payment coming due, and we can't come up with the lump sum necessary to pay it off."

These are the two most common mistakes people make when they invest in real estate. They forget that they will have to pay the debt off someday and buy real estate imprudently, with heavy negative cash flows and short-term balloon mortgages.

So what is the answer? For negative cash flows, I have six solutions.

First of all, if "alligators" scare you, don't buy them. (An alligator is slang for a property with a negative cash flow.) Keep shopping until you find bargains. Or negotiate with sellers who are willing to sell and carry their own financing at below-market rates. While I was on a radio talk show in Columbus, Ohio, a while back, I received a hostile call from a listener. He told me that I was crazy to think that such deals still exist in today's marketplace.

The very next caller told us how he had just purchased a duplex in a good location from a seller who accepted nothing down and a first mortgage at 6 percent on the entire purchase price. And this was at a time when bank mortgage rates were much higher. Needless to say, there was a positive cash flow.

How does one fall into deals like this? You must be out there "falling." Suppose you had to call one hundred flexible sellers to buy one property that would net you $5,000 in the first twelve months of ownership. How much would each rejection be worth to you? Every time someone said no, it would be worth $50 ($5,000 divided by 100) to you. So rather than getting discouraged at rejection, you can look at it another way. Every rejection is valuable to those who persist.

The second solution to negative cash flows is to lower the price of your target property or to raise the number of units in your target property.

In single-family houses, select the cheapest three-bedroom house available in a respectable neighborhood within a fifty-mile radius of your own home. Ideally, the price should be below median price. The higher the price, the higher the negative cash flow. In cities where home prices are double the national average (like Los Angeles, San Francisco, Washington, DC, and Honolulu), the solution may be to look farther out in the suburbs. If you don't have any attachment to your present city, the prices are excellent in Orlando,

Florida; Oklahoma City; and Atlanta, just to name a few. The goal is to invest in the cheapest house in a respectable neighborhood.

As for apartment buildings, it is normal to expect better cash flows from larger properties. The more units, the better the cash flow. The reason for this is that the enormous demand for smaller units has tended to drive up the prices and therefore affect the cash flows. If you want more information on buying apartment buildings, I refer you to my first book, *Nothing Down.*

The third solution to negative cash flows is to improve management. This sounds obvious, but it deserves a mention. A conservative investor trying to avoid a monthly negative cash flow often forgets that the problem is usually temporary. With a few years of rent raises, a tight management policy, and a firm fist with expenses, it is possible to create a positive cash flow that will last a lifetime.

The fourth solution is the use of partners. We learned in the last chapter that if you don't have it, someone else does. In other words, if you can't handle a negative cash-flow problem, someone else can and would love to help you for a percentage of the future profit. If you have located an excellent property with little or no down payment, but you are not financially strong enough to carry the negative cash flow, look for a friend, business associate, or family member who needs a tax shelter and may be willing to participate. Make him or her your fifty–fifty partner. Half a pie is better than no pie at all.

In fact, if you own a property now with a negative cash flow that is straining your budget, you may consider this as an alternative. Don't sell 100 percent of your property just to solve the problem. Sell a half interest in it for little or no down payment and have your new partner agree to pay the negative cash flow.

I used this technique to handle a property I had bought in Miami.

While there to do some media appearances, I found myself with a free evening. As is my custom, I bought a local newspaper and started to scan the classified section for good real-estate buys. I came across an ad with some good clues in it: a low-down-payment, fully furnished, one-bedroom condo, rent or buy, owner agent, $35,900. I couldn't believe the price, and although I expected it to be in a bad neighborhood, I called anyway.

The seller was sophisticated and recognized that I also knew the ropes. She mentioned that this unit had just become vacant and that since it was a distance from other properties she and her husband owned, they had decided to sell it. They didn't need a lot of down payment. I asked her what her definition of "low down payment" was. She said, "$5,000." I told her that my definition of low down payment was only $1,000. She agreed to accept my definition. I drove out to look at the property, using the five-point system of analysis explained in chapter 7. I was impressed. The seller met me, and we signed up the deal immediately and drove to find her husband, who was an attorney. We agreed that I would give them $100 to tie up the property plus another $900 at the closing, which was, as I remember, about three weeks off. The payments were to be $425 per month including taxes, insurance, principal, and interest at 12 percent for thirty years. No balloon mortgage or other lump-sum payments. I was told that the unit had been rented out previously at $375 per month. If I could find a tenant, I would have at least a $50 negative cash flow. In addition, I would be a long-distance landlord. I decided that I had a problem.

I advertised to find a partner who would share the negative cash flow with me and handle the management problems in exchange for half ownership. A typical ad might read:

> Nothing down to qualified person. I will deed half ownership to you in beautiful one-bedroom condo if you make the monthly payments of $425 per month. I'll make the down payment, you make the monthly payments. Why rent when you can buy? Call Bob.

Or something to that effect. I located a partner who was happy to become part owner for a small negative cash flow per month. She took care of all details.

Why was I willing to give away half interest for nothing down? Because the very first tenant that my partner found to rent the unit paid me first and last month's rent and a deposit for a total of $1,150—more than enough to reimburse me for the $1,000 I had spent to buy the unit. The closing costs were negligible, since the seller was a real-estate broker and waived any commission, while her attorney-husband drew up the closing documents at no charge. I had therefore bought the unit for nothing down. With nothing invested in it, I could afford to bring in a partner to reduce my future negative cash outlays and to relieve me of the headache of managing a property from two thousand miles away. This was a perfect win-win solution for both of us.

As in the example above, equity sharing is a process of bringing together (1) buyers who have adequate monthly income but inadequate down payments with (2) investors who have adequate down payments but who hate negative cash flows and management. These partners pool their resources and share profits. It's a perfect solution to many of today's real-estate financing problems.

The fifth solution is to make larger down payments. In any major market, there are thousands of properties for sale. If you specialize in bargain hunting, you would search for distressed sellers in need of cash who are willing to discount their price substantially. For example, suppose you locate a $275,000 property. The seller is willing to reduce his price considerably for a quick cash settlement. You offer him $25,000 cash for his $50,000 equity, and he accepts. By using a large down payment and negotiating a discounted price, you increase probability that you'll be able to rent out this home for a break-even or positive cash flow.

"Fine," you say, "but what if I don't have the cash to buy these bargains?" That's when it's time to remember the motto of a leverage-loving investor: "If you don't have it, you can get it!"

If you know how to find the bargains, you are halfway there. The last half is to find someone who wants to participate in the profit with you. Find a partner. Show him or her the benefits of owning a bargain-priced property that generates monthly cash flow and equity buildup as well as tax benefits. Your partner will have no management hassles, since that is your responsibility.

The sixth solution to negative cash flows is the balloon mortgage. A balloon mortgage is an agreement to pay off an amount due in a future lump sum. Unfortunately, this eliminates the current negative cash flow but creates an equal or greater problem in the future. In essence, it is a way of delaying the day of reckoning. But let me first tell of the benefits; we'll get to the detriments later.

Remember the example in chapter 7 of a home owned by a doctor and his wife? The balloon technique was used to solve a negative cash flow. Now, here's what you do with the balloon mortgage when it comes due. First let me refresh your memory. The situation was as follows:

The property was priced at $175,000. The sellers had $50,000 in equity. They agreed to accept a $5,000 down payment and to carry back the balance of their equity ($45,000) in the form of a second mortgage secured by the property. The payments on the new first mortgage totaled about $1,100, including principal, interest, taxes, and insurance. We knew that we could rent the property out for only $1,000. The problem was obvious: if we agreed to make any payments at all on the seller's second mortgage, there would be a heavy negative cash flow. And that meant that we would have to feed the alligator as much as $500 per month.

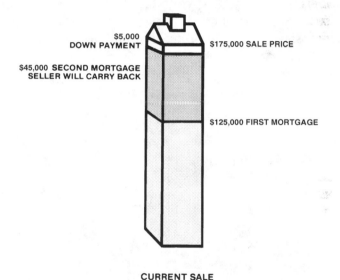

$5,000 DOWN PAYMENT

$175,000 SALE PRICE

$45,000 SECOND MORTGAGE SELLER WILL CARRY BACK

$125,000 FIRST MORTGAGE

CURRENT SALE

What alternatives do we have? One alternative is to make the monthly payments and suffer the negative cash flow for a period of years while attempting to increase the rents. This is an expensive solution, but feasible. A less painful solution is to offer the seller a no-monthly-payment mortgage with a balloon of accrued interest and principal in five years. If there are no monthly payments to make on the second mortgage to the seller, it would be possible to have a monthly break-even or positive cash flow immediately. The seller agrees to this alternative, and the deal is done.

In essence, the seller receives his equity plus interest in one lump sum in the future. Could this possibly be win-win?

For the doctor it is a perfect way to get out of a poorly managed property, to lock in a management-free fixed return of 7 percent per year for at least five years, and (the most important consideration) to receive no interest payments for five years—a perfect tax-planning tool for a high-income investor.

For you, the low down payment and the no-monthly-payment balloon provide you with access to a well-located investment property for a small initial investment and no negative cash flow for at least five years. In fact, with increasing rents over the next sixty months, you could expect to reap several thousand dollars' worth of positive cash flow. Not to mention the tax benefits.

But where is the catch? If you are not paying regular monthly payments, the piper will have to be paid sooner or later. The following diagram shows what the situation will look like in five years:

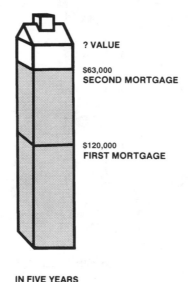

? VALUE

$63,000
SECOND MORTGAGE

$120,000
FIRST MORTGAGE

IN FIVE YEARS

The loan balance on the existing first mortgage will be paid down to about $120,000. But the second mortgage will have grown to $63,000, which is the original $45,000 mortgage plus accrued interest of $18,000. These two mortgages add up to almost $10,000 more than the original purchase price of $175,000. The second-mortgage amount of $63,000 will be due in five years in one balloon payment. One lump sum. This is the problem with balloon mortgages—they are fine until the day of reckoning comes. And then, watch out.

So a balloon payment is the sixth solution to negative cash flows, but sometimes the medicine is worse than the disease. We now have to examine some ways to solve the balloon-payment problem. Let's look at the example again:

The property will have appreciated, and although we are not certain of the future, even a 3.5 percent appreciation rate will allow us to sell the property and pay off the mortgages without any loss. If rates of appreciation are as high as 10 percent, the property could be worth as much as $275,000. If this is the case, what alternatives are open to you in five years?

As I see it, you have six alternatives to the balloon problem.

First of all, you could refinance the property. By putting a new second mortgage on the property, you could pay off the old second mortgage. The new monthly payments will be steep, but rents will have increased over this time to reduce the potential negative cash flow.

As a second alternative, you could refinance another property that you had bought in the meantime. Remember, you have experienced a nice positive cash flow from the original property, which would have enabled you to buy other property.

As a third alternative, you could sell another property in your portfolio to pay off the balloon mortgage.

As a fourth alternative, you could sell the subject property to satisfy the balloon mortgage. Let's dwell on this a moment. Suppose the market is bad in five years. Suppose money is tight, and properties aren't moving. How could you arrange to sell the property in such a way as to give you a profit and pay off your mortgage obligations? In my experience, any property advertised as "nothing down" always draws more prospective buyers. There are many more buyers in a given marketplace with the ability to make monthly payments but no down payment than there are those with adequate down payment but no monthly income. Try to attract this group. Advertise your property for sale for $200,000 with no down payment, qualify the buyer, and have him refinance your property as an owner occupant. You agree to carry your equity in the form of a second mortgage so that the new buyer doesn't need any cash for a down payment. The new buyer pays off the original first mortgage and the ballooning second mortgage with a new first mortgage, and you take a second mortgage for your profit. In our example, your paper profit would be about $15,000 after closing costs plus all of the tax and positive cash-flow benefits (see illustration on page 136).

Even in the worst situation, there would be potential for profit.

You could convert this dormant paper profit into a cash profit by selling your second mortgage at a discount. Suppose a 50 percent discount, and you still end up with more than a $10,000 cash profit in addition to all of the other benefits.

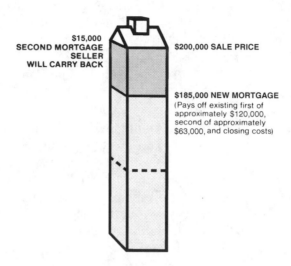

$15,000
SECOND MORTGAGE
SELLER
WILL CARRY BACK

$200,000 SALE PRICE

$185,000 NEW MORTGAGE
(Pays off existing first of approximately $120,000, second of approximately $63,000, and closing costs)

As a fifth alternative, I could renegotiate with the seller. Perhaps he would be amenable to a higher interest rate, or a monthly payment, or an extension of the balloon with the payment of a nonrefundable fee of $1,000. About a year before the note is due, it is worth trying to talk the seller into a renegotiation of the terms. It is always worth a try. Many times the private mortgage holder will renegotiate an extension if he feels that his mortgage may be in jeopardy. This is the alternative that I used several years ago. Two years before a note was due, I offered the mortgage holder $13,000 cash for the note, which had a balance of over $26,000. He accepted it. You never know what you can get until you ask.

A sixth alternative is to give the property back to the seller. Repossession is never an attractive alternative, but it isn't sudden death, either. In the above example, I doubt if the doctor would be overly upset if you let him repossess his property. He would regain control of a more valuable property that he could resell for extra profit. Foreclosure is the last alternative, but it is a possibility.

Obviously, you must feel that the future profit potential is great enough for you to accept the risk of a balloon mortgage. Be very careful before you accept the risk.

The following safeguards should be used anytime you decide to eliminate a negative cash flow by using the temporary solution of a balloon mortgage:

1. Use balloon mortgages only as a last resort. If a seller is willing to accept longer-term solutions, don't discourage him. If you can't afford to make monthly payments on all the mortgages, a better alternative would be to defer mortgage payments for a period of time—let's say five years—with a monthly payment to amortize the balance over the next ten years.
2. Never buy a property with a balloon payment less than five years away except under extremely rare circumstances.
3. If you do use balloon mortgages, do so only with the seller's written permission to allow you to extend the balloon payment for at least another twelve months upon the payment of a nonrefundable fee—perhaps $500 or $1,000.
4. At least twelve months before the balloon is due, begin to arrange new financing to solve the problem. Don't procrastinate.

With these precautions, you should be able to eliminate many of the present creative financing problems.

Now we come to the last major problem that leverage creates.

Major Problem 3: Leverage Increases the Danger of Losing Control of Your Financial Empire

As one of my students stated: "If you're not careful, it's the pyramid theory on the way up and the domino theory on the way down."

We proved that many fools are soon parted from their money because they lose control. They overextend. They miscalculate. They project high profits and low expenses. In reality, the best policy is just the opposite—to be overly pessimistic about future profits and future expenses. And if there still remains a profit, it is worth the risk. Around my company, we have what we call the Allen rule. After we have prepared our most reasonable projection of expenses and income from the sale of a product, we either double the expenses or halve the revenues. If the product is still profitable, we run with it. This wouldn't hold true for many products, but we use this as a starting point. It causes us to look at profit differently.

I also try to do this same thing in my real-estate investing. I try to pretend that the property I buy will never appreciate in value. In this way, I wring out of my system the last ounce of speculative fever, which lurks in the soul of every human being. I am optimistic about the future of real estate, but I sprinkle this optimism with a healthy dose of pessimism. If I pretend that real-estate values will not spiral upward as in the past, it changes the way I look at negative cash flows and balloon mortgages. I avoid any property that doesn't meet my strict guidelines.

I don't want to have to count on inflation to bail me out. Even with zero real-estate price growth, I want to win—and win big.

In summary, then, leverage is a double-edged sword. It creates mental and marital pressure. It creates obligations that have to be repaid. And there is always the temptation to go in over your head. But these detriments shouldn't stop you. You don't stay off the freeways because there is a chance that some drunken idiot might run you off the road. No. You use the freeways because they are the fastest route, a marvelous modern convenience. You accept the minimal risks involved and do your best to be careful.

Leverage is a marvelous tool—to be used wisely. To repeat, no one becomes wealthy without it.

Don't be afraid. Just be careful.

CHAPTER 11

I Hate Real Estate!

That's right. I hate real estate.

I liken it to fishing. I love to fish in the cold alpine lakes of the Canadian Rockies, where I fished as a young boy. The air is clear and crisp. The hike up to the lake is invigorating. I love to cast in my line and wait for a hungry fish to bite. It is a challenge, a battle of wits and reflexes, and exciting to land a fighting rainbow trout.

But as soon as I get the fish on the shore, the thrill is gone. I hate the whole dreary process of killing it, cleaning it, and then carrying it down the trail to my car. But most of all, I hate to eat it. I've come to hate the taste of fish. I spent two years in Tahiti as a Mormon missionary, and I've had enough fish for a lifetime or two.

In other words, all the fun is in the chase. And so it is with real estate. I love to buy it. It's fun and exciting. But once I sign the final closing documents, it's all downhill for me. I hate the paperwork, the record keeping, the mortgage payments—the endless little details that can drive an antidetail person like me up the wall.

The worst part of all is dealing with tenants. It's no fun to collect rents. It's no fun to clean up after a tenant moves out in the middle of the night without paying rent. It's no fun fixing broken windows and taking care of minor or major repairs. There always seem to be surprises in the rental business, and for some reason the surprises are all bad. It will be a cold day in Hades when you hear some good news, like a thank-you from a tenant.

If I hate all these hassles, why do I buy so much real estate? Because the good points far outweigh the bad ones. Real estate is a vehicle that takes a person to wealth. And it shelters precious income from the tax collector better than any other kind of shelter. I buy real estate because I want to. I have to. And with a workable management system, even the bad things about real-estate management can be minimized. When your neighbor tells you horror stories about his real-estate experience, you can be sure that he was doing something wrong. He didn't have a system.

For the first few years, I did all of my own managing. I didn't have a system. And everything seemed to go wrong. So I tried professional management companies. I assumed that they would take care of my property like professionals. I learned a sad lesson quickly. Most professional management companies are professional *mis*management companies. The only way to find the few good companies in your marketplace is to ask around. And when you try your luck with one company, you still should follow two basic rules.

First, don't ever believe a word the management company says, or anything you read in the monthly reports it gives you. Question every number. Require receipts for all expenditures. Don't let the company spend more than $500 without your OK. In other words, don't assume that just because you have turned over the management to someone else, it will be good management. Make the company prove itself to you over a long period of time. Ask it about vacancies, since every vacant day costs you money. Look at the ads it runs to attract new tenants. What about deposits? Stay on top of the situation. You are only a small part in a large number of units the company has to manage. If you don't squeak, you won't get greased.

Second, inspect your properties at least once every month. It doesn't have to be an elaborate inspection. Just walk through and see if the unit is vacant or rented. And see if the tenant is the kind of person you want living in your property. It takes only fifteen minutes or less to see the inside of a property. The inspection can be a regular day of the month, so the tenant can prepare. You can learn a lot about your management company from your tenants. Take the criticism with a grain of salt—all tenants complain—but notice the trends. If all your tenants complain about the same thing, this could be a red flag.

In general, management companies, if well selected and watched over, can be much help to an extremely busy investor. Look in the yellow pages under "Real Estate Management" to find out more about companies in your area. Just don't forget the two rules.

As you grow larger, you may wish to take the route I took. I hired my own manager. I deliberately chose someone who was good with his hands, since I'm not. And I gave him the education he needed by sending him all over the country to attend seminars on property management. He became an expert through experience and education.

He not only did my management, but also partnered with me in buying properties. We became a team. He was not just an employee, he was a partner. Since he owned the properties he managed, the quality of the management was better. I liked the feeling of having my management in-house because I now had more control over what happened to my wealth. With this area of my portfolio on automatic pilot, I could devote energies to other areas with more peace of mind.

Until you have acquired experience managing rental properties, or until you can afford to hire your own automatic pilot, you may wish to follow the management system in this chapter and continue to learn through experience and education.

Tenant Selection

The key to any good management system is finding good tenants. If you fill your properties with good tenants, managing will be a snap. Too many cash-flow-conscious owners are impatient and want to rent to the first warm body that answers the ad in the paper. There's no better way to get a lousy tenant. There are two kinds of vacancies: one where the property is empty and another where the property is occupied by a deadbeat who won't pay the rent. Which would you rather have? A few lost days of rent to find the right tenant will repay you well.

How do you select good tenants? Common sense. Take an application from every prospective tenant like the one reproduced here.

You notice that the form asks questions like those any banker would ask. Credit references. Job information. Present and previous addresses. Like a banker, you will be lending something; one of your precious properties. Lend only to those worthy of your trust. If the tenant refuses to fill out your application, he is not your kind of tenant.

The tenant fills out the application and leaves a small deposit. The local apartment owners' association can usually help with inexpensive credit checks. Make calls to verify employment. Call the manager of the unit where the applicant is presently residing. A call to previous landlords may prove fruitful. A past landlord is usually more open than a present landlord. The present manager might

APPLICATION TO RENT*
TENANT'S PERSONAL AND CREDIT INFORMATION

PERSONAL DATA

	SOCIAL SECURITY NO.
NAME _____ BIRTHDATE _____	DRIVERS LICENSE NO.
	SOCIAL SECURITY NO.
NAME OF CO-TENANT _____ BIRTHDATE _____	DRIVERS LICENSE NO.

PRESENT ADDRESS _____ PHONE _____

HOW LONG AT PRESENT ADDRESS _____ LANDLORD OR AGENT _____ PHONE _____

HOW LONG AT PREVIOUS ADDRESS _____ LANDLORD OR AGENT _____ PHONE _____

NO. OF OCCUPANTS: RELATIONSHIPS: _____

AGES: _____ PETS _____

CAR MAKE _____ YEAR ____ MODEL _____ COLOR _____ LICENSE NUMBER _____

OCCUPATION

OCCUPATION	PRESENT OCCUPATION*	PRIOR OCCUPATION*	CO-TENANT'S OCCUPATION
OCCUPATION			
EMPLOYER			
SELF-EMPLOYED			
BUSINESS ADDRESS			
PHONE			
POSITION HELD			
HOW LONG			
NAME AND TITLE OF SUPERIOR			
TYPE OF BUSINESS			
MONTHLY GROSS INCOME			

*IF EMPLOYED OR SELF-EMPLOYED LESS THAN TWO YEARS, GIVE SAME INFORMATION ON PRIOR OCCUPATION.

REFERENCES

BANK REFERENCE _____ ADDRESS _____ PHONE _____

CREDIT REFERENCE	ADDRESS	PURPOSE OF CREDIT	HIGHEST AMOUNT OWED	OPEN OR DATE CLOSED

IN CASE OF EMERGENCY, PLEASE NOTIFY	ADDRESS	PHONE	RELATIONSHIP

NEAREST RELATIVE	ADDRESS	PHONE	RELATIONSHIP

HAVE YOU EVER FILED A PETITION IN BANKRUPTCY? _____ HAVE YOU EVER BEEN EVICTED FROM ANY TENANCY? _____

HAVE YOU EVER WILLFULLY AND INTENTIONALLY REFUSED TO PAY ANY RENT WHEN DUE? _____

I DECLARE THE FOREGOING TO BE TRUE UNDER PENALTY OF PERJURY

I AGREE THAT LANDLORD MAY TERMINATE ANY AGREEMENT ENTERED INTO IN RELIANCE ON ANY MISSTATEMENT MADE ABOVE.

APPLICANT _____ APPLICANT _____

DATE _____ DATE _____

_____

_____

* See note at bottom of page 96.

well be tempted to lie to the pope if he thought he could get rid of a bad tenant.

All of this takes time, but only an hour or so. You should check out each item on the application and inform the prospective tenant of your decision within a day or two. If there are several applicants, choose the most qualified one. If you invest the time at this point, it will save you hours of grief later.

Even after this thorough check, a bad apple or two will slip through. Don't be discouraged. An occasional mistake is inevitable.

Deposit—A Must

How much of a security and cleaning deposit you can require depends on your rental market. Try to get the first and last months' rent and a security/cleaning deposit equal to at least half a month's rent. The more the tenant has to lose, the more likely he is to take care of your property. At the very least, you need the first month's rent plus a deposit equal to one month's rent. The deposit is never to be applied to rent. You want the tenant to understand that if he doesn't pay the rent on time, for any reason, you will proceed to evict him, keeping the deposit as security that the rent will be collected. There are always minor repairs to make when a tenant moves out, and you don't want the tenant to have the security deposit applied to rent, or you may have to take care of the tenant's unpaid utility bills out of your own pocket. For this very reason, return a tenant's security deposit fifteen to thirty days *after* he vacates. I learned this lesson the hard way. Learn from my stupidity.

Property Inspection

You should inspect the property before, during, and after a tenant's stay. The tenant should be present each time. Before he moves in, walk through and fill out a property-inspection form like the one reproduced on the next page. This protects both of you if a dispute should arise concerning who is responsible for damage. It will save you many a trip to small claims court.

During the tenant's stay, make regular inspections, perhaps around rent-collection time. One of our tenants recently skipped town, leaving the unit vacant. We were waiting for him to send in the rent check. After about two weeks, when it didn't arrive, we

INVENTORY AND INSPECTION LIST

NAME _____ PHONE _____

ADDRESS _____

	CHECK-IN	NEW	GOOD	COMMENTS	CHECK-OUT	CONDITION	CHARGES
GENERAL							
CARPET							
DRAPES							
WINDOWS							
DOORS							
SCREENS							
LIGHT FIXTURES							
MAILBOX KEYS							
DOOR KEYS							
LIVING ROOM							
WALLS							
CEILING							
CARPET							
DINING ROOM							
WALLS							
CEILING							
CARPET							
KITCHEN							
WALLS							
CEILING							
CARPET OR VINYL							
CABINETS							
RANGE							
REFRIGERATOR							
VENT HOOD							
DISHWASHER							
DISPOSAL							
COUNTER TOP							
HALL							
WALLS							
CEILING							
CARPET							
BEDROOM NO. 1							
WALLS							
CEILING							
CARPET							
BEDROOM NO. 2							
WALLS							
CEILING							
CARPET							
BEDROOM NO. 3							
WALLS							
CEILING							
CARPET							
BATH NO. 1							
WALLS							
CEILING							
FLOOR							
FORMICA							
CABINETS							
MEDICINE CABINET							
FIXTURES							
TUB							
BATH NO. 2							
WALLS							
CEILING							
FLOOR							
FORMICA							
CABINETS							
MEDICINE CABINET							
FIXTURES							
TUB							

I, and/or we, accept the aforementioned CHECK-IN-LIST as a part of the Rental Agreement and agree that it is an accurate account of the condition of said premises.

CLEANING CHARGE _____

RENT DUE _____

TOTAL CHARGES TO RESIDENT _____

RESIDENT _____ DATE _____

AMOUNT OF DEPOSIT _____

AGENT _____ DATE _____

AMOUNT OF REFUND, IF ANY _____

REMARKS _____

_____

_____

went to see why. The tenant was long gone. And we will never collect. If we had inspected this property closer to rent day, we could have rerented the property and salvaged at least part of the loss.

Of course, when a tenant moves out, you reinspect the property with the tenant, using the original property-inspection form. Any new damage is either repaired by the tenant or comes out of the security deposit.

Discount Rent Program

As for the payment of rent, we use the discount rent system. I first heard of this from Jack Miller and John Schaub. They taught a nationwide seminar on real-estate investing entitled "Making It Big on Little Deals." If either of these speakers makes an appearance in your area, don't miss it. Their seminar together was excellent! We've added our own refinements to the Miller-Schaub formula. We try to advertise our properties for a little more than what we hope to eventually get. Suppose we have a home with a monthly payment of $1,000, which would rent for about this same amount. We advertise it for rent at $1,100. A prospective tenant would be told that the rent would be $100 less than advertised upon two conditions:

First, rent is due on time. Part of the discount is for prompt payment. If the rent is late, the discount doesn't apply. Explain that this is a strict rule that can't be bent. Spend some time educating your prospective tenants concerning your rental philosophy. There are only three things that we need in life: food, shelter, and clothing. In your book, shelter is the most important. It comes before the motorcycle payment, the encyclopedia payment, or a vacation. To avoid hard feelings, your discount plan rewards those who are smart enough to pay rent on time. (This sounds better than having a late penalty for late rent. And it works better, too.) You catch more flies with honey than with vinegar.

Second, the tenant will do all minor repairs and will pay up to $50 in cost of materials per month. All major items will be taken care of by you. You explain tactfully that you are very busy and don't have the time or the knowledge to fix small problems. You are willing to lower his rent if he takes this burden off your shoulders. In this way, he will save a few dollars, and you can save some time. Win-win.

This program works very well. It cuts small repairs to a minimum

LEASE-RENTAL AGREEMENT

In consideration of the agreements of the Tenant(s), known as: _____ ,
the Owner, hereby rents them the dwelling located at _____
for the period commencing on the _____ day of _____ , 20_____ , and monthly
thereafter until the first day of _____ , 20_____ , at which time this Agreement is terminated.
Tenant(s), in consideration of Owners permitting them to occupy the above property, hereby agree(s)
to the following terms: The sum of $_____ (_____ dollars), evidenced by
_____ , as a deposit receipt, which upon acceptance of this rental agreement,
the Owner of the said premises, hereinafter referred to as Owner, shall apply said deposit as follows:

	Received	Payable Prior to
Rent for the period from _____ to _____	$ _____	$ _____
Security Deposit _____	$ _____	$ _____
Last Months prepaid rent_____	$ _____	$ _____
Key deposit _____	$ _____	$ _____
Cleaning charge _____	$ _____	$ _____
TOTAL _____	$ _____	$ _____

In the event that this agreement is not accepted by the Owner or his authorized agent, within
_____ days, the total deposit received shall be refunded. Tenant hereby offers to rent from the
Owner the premises situated in the city of _____ , County of _____ , State of
_____ , described as
_____ , described as
upon the following Terms and Conditions:

TERM The term hereof shall commence in _____ , 20 _____ , (check one of the following
alternatives):
- ☐ Until _____ , 20 _____ .
- ☐ Either shall terminate the same by giving the other party _____ days written notice delivered
  by certified mail, provided that Tenant agrees not to terminate prior to the expiration of
  _____ months. _____
_____

RENT Rent shall be $_____ per month, payable in advance, upon the 5th day of each
calendar month to Owner or his authorized agent, at the following address: _____
_____
or at such other places as may designate by Owner from time to time.
DISCOUNT RENT CLAUSE There is a $_____ discount off the above stated rent if the rent is received by
5:00 p.m. on the first day of the month.

CLAUSE The Owner shall reserve the right to increase the rent upon a 30 day notice. The Tenant will
reserve the right to approve or reject this proposal. Upon rejection or approval the Owner will make a
decision.

UTILITIES Tenant shall be responsible for the payment of all utilities and services, except: _____
_____ which shall be paid by the Owner.

USE The premises shall be used as a residence by the undersigned Tenants with no more than
_____ adults and _____ children, and for no other purpose, without prior written consent of the
Owner. Occupancy by guests staying over _____ days will be in violation of this provision.

PETS No pets shall be brought on the premises without prior written consent of the Owner.

HOUSE RULES In the event that the premises are a portion of the building containing more than one
unit, Tenant agrees to abide by any and all house rules, whether promulgated before or after the
execution hereof, including but not limited to, rules with respect to noise, odors, disposal of refuse, pets,
parking, and use of common areas. Tenant shall not have a waterbed on the premises without prior
written consent of the Owner. This will be an ammended section of the contract.

ORDINANCES AND STATUTES Tenant shall comply with all statutes, ordinances and requirements of all
municipal, state and federal authorities now in force, or which may hereafter be in force pertaining to the
use of the premises.

ASSIGNMENT AND SUBLETTING Tenant shall not assign this agreement or sublet any portion of the
premises.

MAINTENANCE, REPAIRS OR ALTERATIONS Tenant acknowledges that the premises are in good order
and repair, unless otherwise indicated herein. Owner may at any time give Tenant a written inventory of
furniture and furnishings on the premises; and Tenant shall be deemed to have possession of all said
furniture and furnishings in good condition and repair, unless he objects hereto in writing within five days
after receipt of such inventory. Tenant shall at his own expense, and at all times, maintain the premises in
a clean and sanitary manner including all equipment, appliances, furniture and furnishings therein and
shall surrender the same, at termination hereof, in as good condition as received, normal wear and tear
excepted. Tenant shall be responsible for damages caused by his negligence and that of his family, or
invitees, or guests. Tenant shall not paint, paper or otherwise redecorate or make alterations to the
premises without the prior written consent of the Owner. Tenant shall irrigate and maintain any
surrounding grounds, including lawns and shrubbery, and keep the same clear of rubbish or weeds if such
grounds are a part of the premises and are exclusively for the use of the Tenant. _____
_____
_____
_____

RIGHT OF ENTRY FOR MONTHLY INSPECTION   The Owner may enter the property only with prior consent of the Tenant, or with 24 hours written notice to any Tenant in the apartment to be entered. The Owner may enter the premises only during reasonable hours and for the purpose of inspecting the premises, making necessary or agreed repairs, decorations, alterations or improvements, supplying necessary or agreed services, or exhibiting the dwelling unit to prospective or actual purchasers, mortgagees, Tenants, workmen or contractors. The Owner shall be deemed to have given said 24 hours written notice by posting a notice in a noticeable place stating such intent to enter at least 24 hours before the intended entry. The Tenant shall be deemed to have given consent to the above said notice if no verbal or written objection, which objection must be reasonable, is made to the Owner before the intended entry. However, in the event of an emergency constituting a danger to life, health or property, the Owner may enter the property at any given time without the consent of or notice to the Tenant. The Owner shall have the right to enter the property at any given time upon request for repairs.

INDEMNIFICATION   Owner shall not be liable for any damage or injury to the Tenant, or any other person, or to any property, occurring on the premises, or any part thereof, or in common areas thereof, unless such damage is the proximate result of the negligence or unlawful act of the Owner, his agents, or his employees. Tenant agrees to hold Owner harmless for any claims from damages no matter how caused, except for injury or damages for which Owner is legally responsible.

POSSESSION   If Owner is unable to deliver possession of the premises at the commencement hereof, Owner shall not be liable for any damages caused thereby, nor shall this agreement be void or voidable, but Tenant shall not be liable for any rent until possession is delivered. Tenant may terminate this agreement if possession is not delivered within _____ days of the commencement of the term hereof.

DEFAULT   If Tenant shall fail to pay rent when due, or perform any term hereof, after not less than (3) days written notice of such default given in a manner required by the law, the Owner, at his option, may terminate all rights of Tenant hereunder, unless Tenant, within said time, shall cure such default. If Tenant abandons or vacates the property, while default of the payment of rent, Owner may consider any property left on the premises to be abandoned and may dispose of the same in any manner allowed by law. In the event the Owner reasonably believes that such abandoned property has no value, it may be discarded. All property on the premises is hereby subject to a lien in favor of Owner for payment of all sums due hereunder, to the maximum extent allowed by law.

In the event of a default by Tenant, Owner may elect to (a) continue the lease in effect and enforce all his rights and remedies hereunder, including the right to recover the rent as it comes due, or (b) at any time, terminate all of Tenants rights hereunder and recover from Tenant all damages he may incur by reason of the breach of the lease, including the cost of recovering the premises, and including the worth at the time of such termination, or at the time of an award if suit be instituted to enforce this provision, of the amount by which the unpaid rent for the balance of the term exceeds the amount of such rental loss which the Tenant proves could be reasonably avoided.

SECURITY   The security deposit set forth, if any, shall secure the performance of Tenant's obligations hereunder. Owner may, but shall not be obligated to, apply all or portions of said deposit on account of Tenant's obligations hereunder. Any balance remaining upon termination shall be returned to Tenant. Tenant shall not have the right to apply the Security Deposit in payment of the last month's rent, unless prior written consent has been given by the Owner.

DEPOSIT REFUNDS   The balance of all deposits shall be refunded 30 days from the date possession is delivered to Owner or his authorized agent, or end of contract, together with a statement showing any changes made against such deposits by Owner.

ATTORNEY'S FEES   In any legal action to enforce the terms hereof or relating to the demised premises, the prevailing party shall be entitled to all costs incurred in connection with such action, including a reasonable attorney's fee.

WAIVER   No failure of Owner to enforce any term hereof shall be deemed a waiver, nor shall any acceptance of a partial payment of rent be deemed a waiver of Owner's right to the full amount thereof.

NOTICES   Any notice which either party may or is required to give, may be given by mailing the same, postage paid, to Tenant at the premises, or to Owner at the address shown below or at such other places as may be designated by the parties from time to time.

HOLDING OVER   Any holding over after expiration hereof, with the consent of Owner, shall be construed as a month-to-month tenancy in accordance with the terms hereof, as applicable.

TIME   Time is of the essence of this agreement.

ADDITIONAL TERMS AND CONDITIONS

ENTIRE AGREEMENT   The foregoing constitutes the entire agreement between the parties and may be modified only by a writing signed by both parties. The following Exhibit, if any, has been made a part of this agreement before the parties' execution hereof:

THE UNDERSIGNED TENANT HEREBY ACKNOWLEDGES RECEIPT OF A COPY HEREOF.

Date _____

_____ Agent   _____ Tenant
_____ Address/Phone   _____ Tenant
By _____   _____ Address/Phone

and saves hours of detail work. Tenants like it because everyone is trying to save a buck here and there. I have even gone so far in some cases as to promise the tenant that I won't raise the rent for two years if he promises not to call me—ever. I'm really not trying to make a killing from my rental cash flow. In most instances, I just want to break even and let the property increase in value.

Using the discount rent system goes a long way toward cutting turnover. And turnover is what kills a landlord. Every time a tenant moves out, you have to clean, repair, and repaint. A house portfolio that is constantly turning over because of a poor management system is hemorrhaging money—all of your profit. If you can get your tenants to cooperate with you by letting you know thirty days before they vacate, you have time to find a new tenant and cut "down time" to a minimum.

I have included one of our lease forms that includes the discount rent program. Before you implement it, check your local rental laws. They vary from state to state. My form may not be legal for use in your area.

Utilities

It is our policy to have the tenant pay all utilities. This way he deals directly with the utility company and bears the brunt of all increases. He can swear at them and not at me. In our single-family-house rentals, we expect our tenants to take care of the yard also. We offer to cut the lawn for them for a $20 fee every two weeks, but they usually decline (good). A neighbor's kid will cut the lawn weekly for half that. If we find during our inspection that the lawn is going uncared-for, we leave a written notice, a warning. If we find after two weeks that the problem still exists, we cut it ourselves and deduct $20 from the security deposit. We haven't had to deduct anything yet.

I like to compare this management system with the Ten Commandments given to the Israelites. The Lord promised that if the Israelites kept the commandments, they would go to heaven. If they broke them, they might end up in a less comfortable spot. If my tenant keeps my management commandments, we have a heavenly relationship. If not, all hell breaks loose.

Now, all of this may seem rather harsh or strict. But listen to the voice of experience. I tried to be more lenient at first and ended up listening to every sob story in the book. Once your tenants discover that you will be lenient, then rent is no longer a priority. Anyone else whose collection tactics are stronger will get the money that should be going to you. If you would like to try another system, be my guest. We'll compare notes in a year or two.

I am not saying that you shouldn't be charitable when the occasion permits, but I always prefer to be lenient with a faithful renter who has earned my trust than with one who is trying to see how far he can push me. After all, you have a payment that you have to make to your friendly banker. If your payment is late, there goes your credit rating. It doesn't hurt to explain that to your tenants.

With a strict set of rules like this, you will find less misunderstanding in your managing. Whenever you stray from these basics, you will live to regret it. I remember on one occasion my management company rented to a paraplegic veteran. Perhaps out of a sense of duty or pity or both, the manager did not require a deposit. One month later, he went to collect the rent and received a sad story about a late disability check. The same thing happened the next month. Finally, the manager realized that he had been the victim of a rental scam. Eviction notices were filed. Four months' rent went down the drain. Someone broke one of the commandments, and I paid the bill. I later learned that this person lived almost rent free this way. He would move into a home belonging to a lenient landlord and would not pay rent until evicted. Then he would move on to the next sucker. Now you see why I always stick to the rules.

Good managing is an art. It takes time to develop your own style. I suggest that you read a good book on the subject before you get your feet wet. *Landlording* by Leigh Robinson is an excellent work with really useful advice. Happy landlording!

PART FOUR

Perpetuating Wealth: Spreading the Risk

CHAPTER 12

The Coming Enormous Profits in Discounted Mortgages

Let me share a secret with you. Like most of the secrets of the world, this one is as plain as the nose on your face. The best part about this secret is that although it is well known, it is little used. That is why it is so powerful.

The secret is this:

Some people would rather have less money now than more money later.

This simple sentence may not seem important to you now, but as you learn to use it, you will discover its money-making potential.

Let me illustrate. Every day, in every city and town in America, the following scene is reenacted over and over again:

A seller—let's call him Mr. Seller—decides to sell his house. Mr. Seller puts a $200,000 price tag on the property. There is a $140,000 first mortgage. Ideally, he would like to have his $60,000 equity in cash. He lists it with a Realtor and waits for an offer. A few months later, the offer arrives. The buyer offers a $30,000 cash down payment and asks the seller to carry the balance of his equity in the form of a $30,000 second mortgage secured by the home. There will be a monthly payment on this mortgage of $364 for the next ten years at 8 percent interest. (See the diagram on page 154.)

Mr. Seller mulls over the offer. "It is full price. That's good. The buyer seems established, with a good job and excellent references, and puts a large amount down. That should make me feel comfortable. I would rather have all cash, but I really don't need all of my cash. The buyer's offer would guarantee me monthly payments for the next ten years, bearing an excellent rate of interest. Maybe I should accept it."

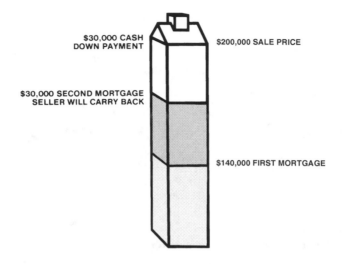

$30,000 CASH DOWN PAYMENT

$200,000 SALE PRICE

$30,000 SECOND MORTGAGE SELLER WILL CARRY BACK

$140,000 FIRST MORTGAGE

And so he accepts it, pockets the $30,000 cash less closing costs, and begins to get accustomed to a regular monthly check.

Two years go by.

Mr. Seller receives a flyer in the mail advertising a once-in-a-lifetime around-the-world cruise. Everything is first class. It sounds interesting. He is getting on in years and would like to go on one more fling. The price tag is $15,000. That's a lot of money, but the more he thinks about it, the more he wants it. There is only one problem. He doesn't have $15,000. He has spent his proceeds from his house sale two years' previous. All he has is a note with a remaining balance of about $26,500 bearing an 8 percent interest rate and payments of $364.

He checks around. He discovers that he could borrow $15,000 from his banker using the note as collateral (this is called *hypothecating*), but he doesn't like the idea of being in debt to anyone. He notices an ad in the paper, which says, "We buy mortgages at a discount." He calls, talks to Mr. Investor, and finds that Mr. Investor will pay $18,300 in cash immediately for the $26,500 note.

He mulls it over. "Which would I rather have: monthly payments for the next eight years and no trip, or $18,300 now and a trip?" If he doesn't take the trip now, he may not have the opportunity again. Mr. Seller decides to take the cash. The last I heard, he was in Hong Kong, having the time of his life.

What about Mr. Investor? Who in his right mind would invest

18,300 hard-earned dollars in a depreciating piece of paper with monthly payments attached? How can he win?

Actually, there are three ways he could win. Let's examine each.

Probably the worst that could happen is that Mr. Investor continues to receive the regular monthly check of $364 for the entire eight years until the note is paid in full. But even this worst alternative is not all that bad. Over the life of the loan, he will receive another ninety-six payments of $364, or $34,944. This is an overall yield of 18 percent on his invested cash. Not too shabby! Beats any money market fund.

Another possible scenario is that the person who is making the monthly mortgage payments will cease making his payments. Mr. Investor will then be forced to step in and foreclose on the property to protect his investment. None of this sounds very exciting, but let's look at the situation a little more closely. Let's see what this mortgage is secured by.

He has a second mortgage against a prime piece of real estate that is worth, by this time, at least $210,000. There is at least $70,000 worth of equity above the first mortgage. Do you think Mr. Investor would have any trouble selling the property for enough money to just recoup his $18,300 cash investment? I doubt it. That would mean selling a $210,000 property for about $160,000. And if Mr. Investor sold the home for $175,000 cash, he would almost double his money. If he was really greedy, he could triple or almost quadruple his money. You can see by this that Mr. Investor might actually hope that the mortgage goes into default, regardless of the legal hassles involved.

The third and most likely of the three eventualities is that the property securing the mortgage will be sold before the eight years expires. Every year 20 percent of all Americans move. There is a turnover of the entire population every five years. Let's suppose that the sale occurs two years after Mr. Investor buys the discounted note and mortgage. If the new buyer gets a new loan, it would pay off all underlying loans at full face value. The balance of Mr. Investor's second mortgage would be about $22,000. At closing, he gets a check for $22,000 cash, not to mention the $8,736 in monthly payments he received during the two years before the house was sold. In other words, he invested $18,300 and received back over $30,000 worth of benefits in a two-year period. That's over 30 percent return per year.

In other words, Mr. Investor only has to wait to see which way he wins. In the worst case, he receives 18 percent on his money, and in the best case, over 100 percent or more. All with fabulous security.

But this is not all. A savvy investor can easily learn how to buy these discounted mortgages for nothing down (none of the investor's money) and then trade them at full face value to flexible real-estate owners for immediate profit. This fancy stuff will come later, however. For now, let's return to the basics.

I can hear your questions:

"All right, Bob, so how do I find these thousands of anxious mortgage holders who will agree to deep discounts in their notes for the privilege of my cash—supposing I have the cash?"

In the early 1970s, less than one sale in ten involved seller financing like the case described above. Sellers were very reluctant to "carry paper." Mortgage money was cheap and plentiful, so most sales involved bank financing, with the seller receiving all his equity in cash. Still, with such a relatively small amount of seller financing, there were plenty of excellent loans to buy at a discount for the investor who was willing to shop.

Starting with the skyrocketing interest rates in 1979 and the early 1980s, and the ensuing tight mortgage markets throughout most of the eighties, sellers soon learned that they would have to resort to seller financing if they wanted to sell their properties. This started the era of creative financing. With the era of creative financing came an absolute deluge of "private" mortgage holders. In 1981 more than half of all real-estate transactions involved seller financing. The next year this percentage increased to over 70 percent. In the early years of the twenty-first century, with the deluge of low-interest-rate mortgages, private seller financing was involved in less than 10 percent of all sales. But there is still a large amount of existing and newly created privately held mortgages from which to profit. In future years, as the mortgage market tightens and loosens, there will always be a market for the techniques explained in this chapter. Creative financing is here to stay. The market and potential for buying discounted mortgages is perpetual.

The goal is to find deeply discounted mortgages secured by excellent property in excellent locations. How do you find these "motivated mortgage holders" who want less cash now rather than more cash later?

There are five major sources of these kinds of loans:

1. The newspaper
2. Mortgage brokers
3. Realtors and exchangers
4. Referrals
5. The county courthouse

The Newspaper

Finding motivated mortgage holders is much like finding motivated real-estate sellers. The cheapest and most productive source is your local daily newspaper.

For starters, turn to the classified section or Web site of any major newspaper. On any given Sunday, there are many ads such as:

> Selling your TD?
> For fast action, check our discounts.
> Phone for quotes. Bkr.
> Top dollar on 2nd TD purchases. Fast funding.
> We buy seasoned TDs with good equity.

Directly below this heading is another one entitled "Trust deeds/sale," with ads such as these:

> 2nd TD on duplex property in Long Beach—discounted to yield 16%. By owner. $27,000 TD $9,000 discount. Pays 13% int. Due 3 years. Bkr.

You may be having trouble catching the lingo: "TD," "discounted to yield," "seasoned," and so on. A TD is a trust deed. Let's cover what this means.

Suppose I own a free-and-clear $200,000 home. I need some cash, so I go to my banker to borrow $20,000, using my home as security. The banker checks my credit and agrees to lend me the money. Before he gives me the check, he makes me sign two documents. One is a note stating that I will pay back the money at a certain percent interest, so much a month for so many years. The other document I sign is a collateral agreement. If I should happen to be delinquent in the monthly payments, the collateral agreement gives the banker the right to repossess my property and sell it at auction for enough to recoup his money plus costs. This collateral agreement is referred to as a mortgage or a trust deed. The major difference between a mortgage and a trust deed is the length of time it takes to actually foreclose on a property. Trust deeds generally take between three and four months. Mortgages can take a year or longer. For this reason, in most states the use of trust deeds is becoming more common.

Although mortgages and trust deeds have their differences, they accomplish the same purpose. For the purpose of this chapter, you should know that insiders refer to both mortgages and trust deeds as "paper" or "notes." All four—mortgages, trust deeds, paper, and notes—are basically interchangeable. For this chapter, I will use the word *mortgage.*

For right now, it's important to know that there are people out there who want to sell mortgages and trust deeds. These people constitute your market. There are also people out there who advertise to buy these same mortgages and trust deeds. These people are your competition.

You will notice that many of the ads in the "Mortgages for Sale" column are run by mortgage brokers (Bkr). You will notice that some of the same mortgage brokers run ads in the "Mortgages Wanted" column. The discounted-mortgage business is analogous to the real-estate selling business, only on a much smaller scale. If you want to sell a mortgage, you can go to a mortgage broker and list it with him. He will advertise it and try to sell it for you for a fee. If you want to buy a mortgage at a discount, you could also go to this same mortgage broker, and he could arrange to sell you one based on your particular circumstances. A beginning investor would probably want to deal with a reputable mortgage broker. But once you gain experience, you may want to start looking for loans to buy directly from the seller.

The simplest way to find out about the market in your area is to call your competition (these loan brokers) and find out their parameters. Respond to the ads in your local newspaper. If there aren't any, you're in luck. You have a virgin marketplace, and as soon as you start running your ad, you'll be the only game in town. If there are lots of ads, you're also in luck. People don't run regular ads in the paper unless they make money from them.

Suppose you sold a house a few years back and are receiving monthly payments on a $10,000 second mortgage. Call your soon-to-be competitors and ask them what it is worth in cash. Ask them the guidelines they use to determine the amount of discount and how they determine whether or not a loan is properly collateralized. All of this calling won't cost you a cent. It will just build your confidence and add to your store of knowledge about the ins and outs of the local mortgage business.

Once you feel a bit more comfortable, you may try responding to some of the ads in your paper in the "Mortgages for Sale" column. When you call, tell the mortgage holder that you have some cash to invest and would like to learn more about the loan he has for sale and the property securing it. You are just gathering information here. No need to make any commitments. Just say that you are shopping for the best deal and have several you are deciding among. You may even go so far as to ask for the property address so that you can inspect the neighborhood. Even if you don't have any cash to invest, it won't hurt to pretend that you do. I'll be showing you where to get it in a minute.

All of this homework is to give you practice in what it feels like to respond to ads—both those for buyers and those for mortgage sellers. This will come in handy later as you begin to empathize with those who may call in response to your ads.

Other Sources of Discounted Mortgages

Real-estate brokers are another excellent source of discounted mortgages. They would be familiar with sellers who had sold their property using seller financing. Often, the best way to locate such sellers is to ask the Realtor you have dealt with in the past to let you look through old copies of the MLS sold listings.

To find mortgage holders who might consider discounting for cash, start researching in MLS sold books that are two and three years old. Often you can tell from the information whether or not the seller participated in the financing of the transaction. Like a detective, you begin to track down these sellers. Once you find them, a short telephone call will tell you whether or not they are interested in selling their paper at a discount.

As you become more expert in this field, you will want to establish a referral system so that you have access to a constant stream of potential deals. You may want to start your referral process by visiting with top real-estate brokers, real-estate exchangers, accountants, bankers, and attorneys in your area. Explain your parameters to them and leave them your card. As they learn that you are a serious, fair investor, they will begin to use you more and more as a source of cash for their mortgage-holding clients who need cash. A full-time mortgage investor relies heavily on a network of satisfied referral sources.

Some full-time investors also spend a lot of time at the county courthouse. Every mortgage in your county will eventually be recorded at your local county courthouse. It will list the name of the borrower and the lender. By searching through these recorded mortgages regularly, you will find those mortgages that are in the names of private lenders. You may wish to send each of these mortgage holders a letter stating that you are a cash investor in discounted mortgages. If the mortgage holder is interested, he will call to learn about your deal.

How you use these five sources of discounted mortgages depends upon how much time you intend to spend in this investment area. If you are a small-time investor, you probably won't have to look further than your local newspaper, either by calling a local mortgage broker or by placing your own ad. If you plan on being a full-time investor, you will probably want to have the maximum exposure and keep your fingers in as many pies as possible.

Suppose you have $10,000 cash to invest and would like to get it working for you. Now that you know where to find a discounted mortgage, what is the next step?

How to Analyze a Mortgage

A potential mortgage seller responds to your newspaper ad. He has a mortgage that he would like to sell at a discount. It is a $20,000 second mortgage with monthly payments of $191 with interest at 8 percent for fifteen years. He would rather have $15,000 for it now in a lump sum than $20,000 parceled out in monthly installments plus interest for almost fifteen years.

You ask for some more information.

The loan is secured by a single-family house worth approximately $200,000. There is an underlying first mortgage of $120,000. You tell him that you will take a look at the location of the property and call him back.

Before you buy this mortgage, you should conduct analysis in two specific areas:

1. The physical aspects of the collateral
2. The financial aspects of the note

Let's take them one at a time.

Analysis 1: Inspect the Collateral

Every time you buy a mortgage, you should pretend that you just bought the property securing that mortgage—because if the mortgage ever goes bad, you'll have to foreclose on the property to protect your investment. For that reason, you never want to buy a mortgage that is secured by a lousy piece of property. You may own it someday.

The best security for a mortgage is a single-family house in the lower price ranges. You should be very wary about buying mortgages secured by any other type of property. Especially avoid commercial specific-use buildings, recreational property, and personal property. If you stick with owner-occupied single-family houses in the lower price ranges, you will significantly reduce your risks.

Since you have the address, your first step is to drive out and check the location and neighborhood. You will probably not be able to look inside the home, since the person you are buying the mortgage from no longer lives in this property. Your objective is to determine if the property is in a neighborhood that is stable or increasing in value, and also to come away with a rough idea of what the subject property is worth in its present condition. In the back of your mind, you will be asking yourself, "Would I like to own this property?"

If the property is in a slovenly condition, you can almost be sure that the person paying the mortgage will also be slovenly in his monthly payments. These two problems seem to go hand in hand.

Suppose that you are reasonably comfortable with the collateral. The next step is to check out the financial aspects of the loan.

Analysis 2: Study the Financial Aspects

There are three simple ratios that you will want to determine. The first is the ratio of total loans to value. In our example, the first loan is $120,000 and the second loan is $20,000. The value, according to your rough drive-by appraisal is closer to $190,000 than $200,000, as the seller indicated. *The loan-to-value* (LTV) *ratio* would then be:

Loans/Value = $140,000/$190,000 = 74 percent

The smaller the percentage of loans to value, the better. This ratio should never go above 75 percent in a soft real-estate market or 85 percent in an extremely fast-moving real-estate market. In this way, you will always have a cushion of equity to protect you should you ever have to foreclose.

The second ratio is called the *equity-to-debt ratio.* In our example, this ratio is determined by dividing the equity in the property above the loan for sale ($190,000 - 140,000 = $50,000) by the amount of the total debt ($140,000):

Equity/Debt = $50,000/$140,000 = 36 percent

The higher the percentage of equity to debt, the better secured you are. You should be very careful in buying a mortgage with an equity-to-debt ratio lower than 25 percent.

The next ratio is the *discount-to-debt ratio.* In our example, the seller of the mortgage has a $20,000 second mortgage, which he will discount $5,000 for $15,000 cash. The debt amount in this ratio is the amount of mortgages in front of the discounted mortgage. This would refer to the $120,000 first mortgage. This ratio would then be:

Discount/Debt = $5,000/$120,000 = 4.2 percent

This percentage should not fall below 10 percent. This ratio is an indication of the amount of exposure you have. *Exposure* is another word for the risk you are taking in buying a mortgage. The amount of profit in the discount may not be worth the effort and risk necessary to bring the underlying loans current and pay foreclosure costs.

For example, suppose someone had a $2,000 second mortgage that he would be willing to discount for $1,000 (a healthy 50 percent discount). Should you jump at it? It would depend on the exposure. Suppose this same second mortgage was secured by a $150,000 property with an existing $140,000 loan. If this loan goes into default, it may cost you more than your $1,000 discount to solve the problem. The discount-to-debt ratio foretells this problem. In this latter example, the ratio is:

Discount/Debt = $1,000/$140,000 = less than 1 percent

All three of these ratios serve as basic green-light or red-light signals. If you get green lights on all three, you can proceed. In our example, we got green lights in only two of our ratios. This indicates a risk that may be too great. You might need to proceed if the next signal is positive.

Another signal which is important is the payer's payment record on the note. The ideal is, of course, to find a payer who pays regularly each and every month, with no slow pays or skipped payments. He would be a great credit risk. If you plan on reselling the note or using it as a down payment on real estate, it is wise to have an almost impeccable payment history. If the payment record is made up of constant skipped payments, this is a sign that trouble may be ahead. If you are investing in a mortgage to hold for the long term in your own portfolio, you will have to determine whether or not you want the risk of owning a note with a poor payment history. You may end up owning the collateral someday through foreclosure. Do you really want to own that particular piece of property?

If your analysis produces green lights in all areas, there is still one item left to check: determining the yield on the note or mortgage. In our example, the $20,000 note is discounted $5,000. Is this good or bad? It all depends on the monthly payment, the interest rate, and any early balloon payments. Determining the yield can be either easy or difficult. We could wade through three chapters of detailed explanation—the hard way. Or I can tell you how to do it the easy way, which is what I have done. Buy a cheap calculator and learn how to use it. Using my calculator, I simply enter in the figures concerning the existing note, plus a figure equal to what I want to have my money earning, and presto, the calculator does all the work for me. It even can determine the yields when there are tricky balloon payments involved.

Suppose I decide that I don't want to invest any of my money unless it earns me at least 15 percent annually. My calculator tells me that if 15 percent is my bottom line, I would have to buy the sample $20,000 note for no more than $13,656.20. That's almost a 32 percent discount off the face value. If I can't get a return of at least 15 percent, I will let my competitors take the risk. Since in our example the note holder is only willing to sell it for $15,000, we're going to have to decide whether or not a 13 percent rate of return is adequate.

The market for first and second mortgages is much like the market for homes; it depends on supply and demand. The greater the supply of notes, the lower the prices offered, and vice versa. In today's market, notes are generally discounted to yield a sophisticated investor 12 percent to 16 percent on his invested dollar. A savvy investor buys a note with a 24 percent yield and resells it to another investor at a lower yield and pockets the cash difference as a profit.

Buying Mortgages and Making Profit with Nothing Down

Let's see how this would work.

Assume that you received a call from the mortgage holder of our sample $20,000 mortgage. If the note holder is willing to sell it for $15,000, my calculator tells me that this note yields 13.14 percent. I tell the note holder that I'd like to check it out. Since I have no cash, I call up an investor friend of mine who likes to invest in mortgages but doesn't like the hassle of finding them. He is more than happy to let me do the shopping and take some of the profit. His bottom line is a 12 percent yield on his invested dollar. My calculator tells me that our sample note would have to sell for $15,925 in order to yield 12 percent.

But I can buy it for $15,000!

I tell my friend to give me $15,925, and I will get him the note he wants. He gives me the cash, and I buy the note for $15,000 and pocket the $925 as my profit. How much of my own cash did I invest in this note?

None!

I found a willing buyer and a willing seller, and put them together for a neat profit. In essence, you are buying your notes at wholesale (16 percent yields) and reselling them at retail (10 to 15 percent yields). If you can resell this same note to yield only 10 percent, the note is now worth $17,786. If you can buy it for $15,000 and sell it for $17,786, you earn a $2,786 profit with nothing but some time invested.

I must caution you that if this idea turns you on as much as it does me, you should check your state laws governing the sale, solicitation, and resale of notes. If you do it as a business, you may need a securities license, and the notes may be deemed a security and be subject to registration with the Securities and Exchange Commission (SEC).

There are some win-win ways of manipulating notes to everyone's benefit. Using our sample $20,000 note again, suppose you arrange to buy the note for $15,000 cash, but before you do, call the payer of the mortgage and make him an offer he can't refuse. Tell him that you are planning to buy his mortgage and that if the paperwork goes through, he will soon start sending his monthly payments to you. You remind him that his payment goes for almost the next fifteen years (180 months) and that over the years he will be paying almost $35,000 in principal and interest ($191 x 180 months = $34,380) on his original $20,000 loan. You tell him that if he agrees to double his monthly payment to you from $191 to $382, you will cut his interest rate from 8 percent to 5 percent. This will pay off his loan in five years and will save him in interest over the other loan ($382 x 60 months = $22,920 as opposed to $34,380). This sounds very enticing.

But why in the world would I want to do such a thing?

Because a $20,000 note with payments of $382 per month and 5 percent interest is worth more than a note with payments of $191 per month and 8 percent interest. Sounds incredible, doesn't it? My calculator tells me that the original note at 8 percent interest discounted to yield 16 percent should cost me no more than $13,014. But the second note at 5 percent discounted the same is worth $15,560, or $2,556 more!

I could call up my favorite investor and offer him 14 percent on his money and still pocket a good amount of cash. Everybody wins. The note's seller gets the $15,000 he wanted. The payer on the mortgage gets a better interest rate and a shorter term—and that means big savings over the years. My investor buys a note with a 14 percent yield instead of the usual 12 percent. (Depending on the circumstances, this 14 percent could go much higher.) And I pocket a healthy profit because of my knowledge of the intricacies of the mortgage market.

Are there any other ways to take advantage of the exciting possibilities with discounted mortgages when you don't have lots of cash? Maybe even no cash?

If you have a good relationship with your banker, he may provide the cash to buy these mortgages. I know many investors who have established personal lines of credit with their bankers so that they can use the banker's money to pyramid and leverage their way to wealth. This is risky, but like real-estate investing, if it's done right, you can minimize the risk.

Suppose you don't have a line of credit with your banker but do have a house with sufficient equity to borrow $10,000 to $20,000 cash using the house as collateral. You locate a local financial institution that is willing to lend you $15,000 against your home equity. Then you locate a discounted mortgage for sale like the one mentioned in the previous example—a $20,000 note with monthly payments of $191 per month for the next twenty years, which can be bought for $15,000 cash. Using the borrowed $15,000 cash, you buy the discounted note. The income from the note makes the payments on your house loan. When the house loan is completely repaid, you receive the next several years' of payments absolutely free.

What did it cost you to get this? You borrowed against your equity in your own home. You don't have to worry about monthly payments, because payments on the loan are offset by the income from the note. If the purchased note is paid off early in full, the loan on the house can be paid off in cash, and you can pocket the profit.

Now let's get more sophisticated. As I have mentioned previously, one of the keys to success is to do the opposite of what others are doing. We used this principle in chapter 7 by placing a different kind of ad in the "Real Estate Wanted" section of the newspaper. Most ads read, "Have cash—would like to buy your house at a discount." Our ad read, "Full price—would like to buy your house on good terms with no discount in price." And we got results.

Let's try the same concept in buying mortgages. Instead of placing an ad in the "Mortgages Wanted" column, which will compete with other ads—"Have cash to buy your discounted mortgage"—let's try the opposite approach and make it, "Full price for your mortgage." I can guarantee that you will get calls, because this is the exact opposite of what your competition is doing.

But how can you profit from buying a mortgage at full price?

Let me give you an example.

Suppose you get a call from a mortgage holder. He sold his property recently and carried back paper. He is now the owner of a $10,000 second mortgage bearing a 12 percent interest rate with interest-only monthly payments of $100 and a balloon due in five years. He needs a few thousand dollars to solve a short-term cash problem. He realizes that if he sells this mortgage on the open market, it may bring him only $6,000 or $7,000. He is interested in what you have to offer.

You tell him that he can keep the five-year balloon of $10,000. You are interested only in the $100 per month for the next five years. You offer him $2,500 cash now for the right to receive his payments for the next five years. And he gets to keep the $10,000 cash at the end.

This seems to solve his need for short-term cash. But what does it do for you? Well, if you plug the figures into your calculator, you will find that an investment of $2,500 today for the right to receive an income stream of $100 per month for the next sixty months will give you a yield of 48 percent per year on your money. You could feasibly sell this income stream to another investor to yield a whopping 20 percent on his money and pocket $3,500 profit.

Believe me, we've just scratched the surface of the profit-making opportunities in discounted mortgages.

The Buy-High, Sell-Low Formula

To finish this chapter, let's discuss one of the most powerful money-making ideas that you will find in this book. I call it the buy high, sell low formula. It goes along nicely with the other money-making ideas (the "cookie cutters") mentioned in chapter 6.

In the next few paragraphs I'm going to show you how to buy a property for $180,000, sell it immediately for only $144,000, and make at least a $10,000 immediate cash profit. In the process, you will do nothing illegal. Everyone involved will feel he has won. And you will not do anything risky or dangerous. You're going to buy high and sell low without losing your shirt.

In this chapter I have taught you that it is customary in the discounted mortgage market for a mortgage seller to accept a significant discount in the face price of his mortgage for the privilege of receiving cash now. This is an important, money-making fact.

An even more important fact is that it is customary for real-estate sellers to accept mortgages at full face value in exchange for real-estate equity—dollar for dollar. In other words, in a large number of sales involving creative financing, sellers have accepted mortgages instead of cash for at least part of their equity.

Now, it is when you combine these two important facts about discounted mortgages and seller financing that the dollar signs really start to add up. Let me illustrate.

Suppose you are looking through the MLS book one day and notice a free-and-clear $180,000 house for sale. You notice in the remarks section below the picture of the property that the seller needs a 20 percent down payment but is willing to carry the balance of $144,000 in the form of a first mortgage at 7 percent for twenty years. Payments would be $1,116.43. You would like to buy the property because it is in your price range, but you don't have the $36,000 needed for the down payment. You write down the information and decide to mull it over to look for a solution.

About the same time, you get a call from a mortgage holder with a $148,000 first mortgage bearing an interest rate of 8 percent with monthly payments of $1,157.72. He needs some cash desperately and is willing to sell for about $100,000. The loan is secured by a $250,000 house, and the payments have been made for about two years with no problem. You take down the information and proceed to do your analysis.

The yield on this loan, according to my calculator, is 13.2 percent. Not bad. The physical inspection of the collateral property is very good. Good neighborhood. Great property. Good condition. Seems there is some wonderful potential here.

Then a brainstorm hits you. Wait a minute! What about that free-and-clear $180,000 house? The seller said he would carry a first mortgage of $144,000 for twenty years at 7 percent.

Would he accept a first mortgage for $148,000 with better terms secured by a larger and better property across town? Could these two circumstances be combined in an unusual way for profit? The wheels are churning. Let's see, the seller wants the terms shown for Property A (see the next page). And the mortgage holder wants to sell a mortgage for $100,000 under the terms shown for Property B.

If I could get the seller of property A to accept a mortgage secured by property B, then property A would still be free and clear. (Stick with me—this gets a bit complicated, but that is the stuff money is made of.)

If property A is still without a mortgage, perhaps I could refinance it with a new mortgage of, let's say, $150,000.

Where would the $150,000 loan proceeds go? Well, $100,000

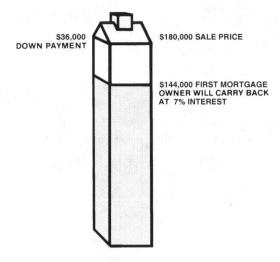

$36,000 DOWN PAYMENT

$180,000 SALE PRICE

$144,000 FIRST MORTGAGE OWNER WILL CARRY BACK AT 7% INTEREST

PROPERTY A FOR SALE

would go to buy the first mortgage at a discount on property B. That leaves $50,000. Then, $4,000 would go for closing costs on the new loan on property A. That leaves $46,000. The seller wants a down payment of $36,000 in cash. That leaves $10,000. Where does this go?

You guessed it: right into your pocket. Now, this doesn't sound quite right, does it? But everyone in this transaction won!

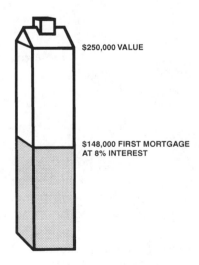

$250,000 VALUE

$148,000 FIRST MORTGAGE AT 8% INTEREST

PROPERTY B COLLATERAL FOR MORTGAGE

The seller of the discounted note got his $100,000 cash. He leaves happy.

The seller of the $180,000 house gets $36,000 down and a $148,000 mortgage ($4,000 more than he wanted) with monthly payments of $1,157.72 ($41.29 more per month than he wanted) bearing an interest rate of 8 percent (1 percent higher than he wanted) and secured by a better, more expensive house in a better location. And it has a track record showing that the payer on the mortgage is faithful in his payments! He is ecstatic.

The Realtor gets a full commission. That puts bread on his table.

The bank makes a new loan and earns fees. That's a bank's bread and butter.

And you end up with a $180,000 home mortgaged with a $150,000 loan—an equity of $30,000—plus $10,000 cash in your pocket. That's a profit of over $40,000 in one transaction where everyone got more than he wanted. Win-win-win-win.

But I can hear you saying, "OK, but you had to get a new mortgage on the property, which will mean high monthly payments and more than likely a very high negative cash flow. That's not so smart, is it?"

And my answer is simple. If you don't like to manage property with a high negative cash flow, just sell the property. The easiest way to sell would be to put an ad in the paper like this:

NOTHING DOWN AND $10,000 BELOW MARKET!

Take over payments on $150,000 mortgage. I will walk away from my $30,000 equity. You assume existing mortgage and get into property for *nothing down.* Hurry! Desperate.

Do you think you might get some response from an ad like this? I bet you would.

Therefore, your profit will be just the $10,000 cash. But do this once a month, and you've just created for yourself a handsome income stream that may beat your present job. If you make less than $120,000 per year, this money-making formula might interest you.

As I close this chapter, I don't want to leave you with the impression that all of this is easy. It isn't. It takes time and expertise to put together transactions like the one above. Timing is of the essence.

Each part has to fit together perfectly. That doesn't mean you should shy away from such transactions. It means that because they appear to be complicated, very few people do them.

It was not my intention to fill you in on every minor detail necessary to be totally successful in buying discounted mortgages. I wanted to alert you to the enormous profit potential. What you read in this chapter is really only enough information to get you in trouble. Dig deeper, please!

Thanks to Joe Land for generously providing the last example in this chapter.

As a final note, I do not suggest discounted mortgages as your starting place; they should not divert you from your primary goal of buying real estate. Discounted mortgages are an excellent tool for perpetuating wealth, with rates of return of 12 to 16 percent or more. Once you have your real-estate empire on automatic pilot, you can perpetuate it nicely with discounted mortgages.

CHAPTER 13

Numismatics: The Secret of the Midas Touch

King Midas was a fool. He didn't understand why things go up or down in value. And he paid the consequences.

If you remember the story, King Midas wished to become wealthy—to turn everything he touched into gold. One day, a stranger appeared and granted him his wish. The king was ecstatic. He touched a flower, and it turned to gold. He touched a vase, and it turned to gold. Everything he touched turned to gold. Everything.

Soon poor Midas began to realize that his gift was more a curse than a blessing. He couldn't even enjoy a simple breakfast. The food turned to inedible gold in his hands. Then, when even his own daughter, Marigold, was changed by his kiss into a lifeless gilded statue, the stranger felt that Midas had learned his lesson.

"Which of these two things," he asked, "do you think is really worth the most: the gift of the golden touch or one cup of clear, cold water?"

"O blessed water!" exclaimed Midas. "It will never moisten my parched throat again!"

"The golden touch," continued the stranger, "or a crust of bread?"

"A piece of bread," answered Midas, "is worth all the gold on earth!"

"The golden touch," asked the stranger, "or your own little Marigold; warm, soft, and loving as she was an hour ago?"

"Oh, my child, my dear child!" cried poor Midas, wringing his hands. "I would not have given that one small dimple in her chin for the power of changing this whole big earth into a solid lump of gold!"

The more gold he had, the less he wanted of it. And as even the most basic things of life were rendered scarce to him, the more precious they became in his eyes.

And so it will always be. Ask any economist.

Now, what does this have to do with investments? Every investor seeks to have in some small measure a golden touch. Whenever people talk about an extremely successful person, they often say that everything he or she touches turns to gold. The secret, of course, is to develop this Midas touch without losing perspective. I'll leave the perspective part up to you. As for the Midas touch, it seems to be fairly simple.

Concentrate on owning things that are in extremely short supply and for which there is an increasing demand. Housing is one such commodity. What are some others?

It seems to me there is at least one other commodity which fits this description exactly: rare coins.

The technical term for studying and collecting coins is *numismatics.* For centuries people have been collecting coins. As one commentator observed, "The Romans collected coins. The Medicis collected coins. The great master painter Peter Paul Rubens had a fabulous coin collection. The House of Rothschild started as a coin shop! There has been an active market for rare coins in this country since the Civil War."

It is one of the world's most established and profitable hobbies. For example, the Harold S. Bareford collection was sold some years ago at auction for $1.2 million. The entire collection was gathered and bought thirty years earlier for a total expenditure of $13,832. Not bad for a hobby!

And this hobby is ever expanding.

There are hundreds of thousands of collectors in the world, each competing for a fixed supply of rare coins. Added to this basic demand is an ever-increasing number of investors who recognize the marvelous growth potential of rare coins. We have here the makings of a Midas touch.

Before proceeding, let me caution you to consider your coin investments as a long-term venture. It's the long-term possibilities that should excite you, not the short-term fluctuations.

The first things you must understand about numismatics are what rare coins are and why they go up in value.

All U.S. coins minted from 1792 through 1964 are considered to be good investments. Why 1964? After that date the government significantly lowered the silver content in its minted coins. There are several reasons why these coins increase in value.

First, the silver and gold coins minted through 1964 have a value equal at least to their intrinsic bullion content. You could melt the coin and retrieve the precious metal, and sell it on the open market.

Second, coins have a rarity factor, in that only a fixed number of coins were minted each year, depending on the type and series of coins. This *mintage* factor is the starting point in determining rarity. But to understand the complete picture, you have to relate the concept of mintage to the availability of any given coin today. For instance, some coins had very large mintages but were not collected in their day, and thus are rare today because they are not available in large quantities.

For example, more than 5.2 million 1936-D Washington quarters were originally minted, but none was saved (it was during the depression, after all). Thus, this particular coin is very rare in uncirculated condition.

The 1884-S Morgan silver dollar is also very rare. There were 3.2 million originally minted, but apparently nobody cared about saving a new silver dollar.

The 1927-D $20 gold piece had an original mintage of 180,000, but only ten to fifteen specimens have survived.

Another determinant of value is condition. As I will explain later, there are several grades of coin condition, and just as with diamonds, these grades can significantly affect a coin's desirability and price. Two coins can have the same rare date and differ drastically in value depending upon the condition. One of the more dramatic examples of this is the 1892-S Morgan dollar, which had a recent value of $13 in "very good" condition, $190 in "extremely fine" condition, $26,500 in MS-60 condition (I'll explain the various gradings later in this chapter), and $150,000 in MS-65 condition.

This gives you a broad view of the "supply side" of rare-coin markets.

As for the "demand side," some coins enjoy enormous popularity with coin collectors even though the mintages were fairly large. This is true of almost all silver dollars minted between 1878 and 1935.

As for the price movements of the broad coin market, they have been affected greatly by the movements of the bullion markets—the prices of gold and silver.

The dramatic rise in rare-coin prices closely paralleled the dramatic rise in the prices of gold and silver bullion throughout the 1970s but did not fall as fast or as far when bullion prices collapsed in 1980 and 1981. This is a sign of the strength of the rare-coin markets. It is instructive nonetheless to understand the key factors that cause gold and silver prices to fluctuate.

Key Factors	Bullish for Metals	Bearish for Metals
Balance of payments	Large deficit	Deficit shrinks or in surplus
Dollar	Weak against foreign currency	Improving or strong
U.S. budget	Record deficits	Shrinking or balanced
Crops	Poor U.S. crops	World or Russian crop failure and U.S. abundance
Oil	Cartel raises prices	Large discoveries, weakness in cartel
Economy	Inflation/boom	Recession
Commodities	Prices up	Prices flat or down
Legislation	More controls, regulations, tax cut with no spending cut	Deregulation, lower taxes, positive legislation for free enterprise
Money supply	Expanding	Slow growth
Middle East/Africa/ SE Asia	War	Peace
Inflation	Overheated	Down or flat

Now let's consider the factors that would trigger a violent bullion price drop:

1. U.S. government gold stockpile sale (An extremely large sale of U.S. gold would drop prices.)
2. U.S. silver auction (The sale of the U.S. silver stockpile of 130 million ounces would depress silver prices.)
3. Prohibition of gold or silver ownership

4. Discovery of a silver substitute in photography
5. Rapid economic decline into recession or depression

Next, let's look at the factors that would trigger a sudden rise in bullion prices:

1. Single one-month high in the inflation index
2. Price controls implemented
3. Dramatic oil price hike
4. Banking-system problems
5. Severe crop failure
6. Heavy Mideastern buying
7. South African gold mines shut down

Once you understand the factors that influence the prices of gold and silver bullion, you will be better prepared to plan your rare-coin purchases.

In this context, realizing that numismatics has been somewhat affected by the rise of bullion prices, let's examine some of the fundamental benefits of owning rare coins. We can start by comparing numismatics with real estate.

In chapter 3, we determined that real estate is an excellent creator of beginning wealth because of two major attributes: power and stability. Through the use of leverage, real estate can produce high rates of return often in excess of 25 percent per year (power). And because of the enormous demand for and the limited supply of well-located property, a careful real-estate investor can sustain these high growth rates over long periods of time (stability). No other investment can even come close.

But real estate has its major drawbacks. It is very illiquid, and, compared to other traditional investments, it is enormously management intensive. Contrary to many investment advisers, I don't let these detriments divert my attention from real estate. Especially as a beginning wealth seeker, I would concentrate in real-estate investments and work to solve its problems.

However, there comes a time in the investment trajectory of every wealth seeker when it is wise to diversify into other investments. In the third stage of wealth, as discussed in chapter 4, I recommended putting up to 10 percent of your assets in gold and silver investments. Although gold and silver bullion are very popular investments, I think that owning gold and silver numismatic coins is an even better alternative. Why?

Like real estate, rare coins are a commodity in short supply with an ever-increasing demand. If you think about it, even the term *rare coins* connotes scarcity, which is an important attribute of all successful products, whether they be collectibles or everyday consumer items. Real estate increases in value in part because the demand far outstrips the supply, even though builders are constantly adding to the stock of housing.

With rare coins, however, the supply is fixed forever. They minted only a certain number of coins. This fixed supply is being distributed over an ever-increasing universe of collectors. Every day that goes by, an old coin gets older, thus increasing its desirability to collectors.

This fact is mirrored in the price history of rare coins. According to the 2000 coin index of prices for investment quality rare coins published by the Professional Coin Grading Service, $1,000 invested in rare coins in 1970 would now be worth $65,000. In fact, prices of high-quality rare U.S. coins have gone up consistently since 1950, with a few minor exceptions. It would be hard not to agree that rare coins have performed better than almost all other investments.

In recent years, rare coins have not enjoyed the spectacular gains of the last half of the 1970s. But it is easy to understand why. With rates of growth doubling and quadrupling in 1979 and 1980, it was time for a more stable, same atmosphere to develop. The sluggish real-estate market of the early 1980s was a result of the same phenomenon.

Residential real estate is a commodity that has three types of owners: users, investors, and speculators. Users live in the properties, investors buy and rent out properties for the long run, and speculators are the fast-buck artists who try to turn immediate profits.

The same holds true for rare coins. The users are the collectors who make up the stable base and source of constant demand for coins, the investors enter to make long-term profits, and the speculators drive prices upward in the hope of speculator short-term gains.

The real-estate market differs significantly from the coin market. Because of the basic illiquidity of real-estate investments, there are no broad fluctuations in the price of housing. It is a steady, relentless story of slow, consistent price advances marked by periods of price stagnation.

The coin market, by contrast, is the most liquid of all collectible markets. There is even a national electronic trading network, the Certified Coin Exchange, where dealers make daily bids and ask prices for the most frequently traded U.S. coins. There are several major auctions in the rare-coin market each month, with prices realized in the range of $5 million to $30 million per auction. It is a big, highly liquid marketplace.

As we learned also in chapter 4, any investment sacrifices something for the privilege of liquidity. What has the coin market sacrificed? It has sacrificed its stability, although only in small measure. The coin market moves in cycles: periods of broad price advances followed by sharp declines, and followed again by price advances.

You will notice that unlike the stock market, which fluctuates up and down wildly, the coin index sustained a long-term upward trend despite temporary dips or falters. Each market high was higher than the previous market high, and each market low was lower than the previous market low. This is the nature of a commodity that is in short supply but is subject to the speculative blowouts that can occur in a liquid market. Each time this market lets off steam, it is followed by continued upward price advances. Consequently, it provides the protection against inflation you get from real estate, while maintaining the liquidity you get from the stock market.

Although expertise is a must in both buying real estate and buying coins, the rare-coin investor is not burdened with the management problems of real-estate ownership. It doesn't take much savvy to place coins in a safety-deposit box. In addition, a large amount of wealth can be stored and transported in a very small amount of space. Since coin transactions are not subject to government regulation and paperwork, wealth can be stored in relative privacy and anonymity. The wealthier one becomes, the greater the need for such precautions.

Real estate is famous for three major benefits that few other investments possess: leverage, tax sheltering, and cash flow. The coin market is not recognized for any of these attributes, which is a drawback. But you have to admit that the long-range growth potential and liquidity of rare coins make them a marvelous companion investment to any real-estate portfolio.

There are four major points to a successful strategy of investing in rare coins:

Point 1: Concentrate in the Right Kind of Coins

Just as in real estate, we have our target properties. The coin market is vast and deep. You can collect anything from Transylvanian bus tokens to Lincoln pennies. The key to a successful strategy is to concentrate in certain areas and to make sure that these areas are characterized by broad interest and popularity. Stay away from the esoteric coins that only a handful of people in the world would want or could afford. You should also avoid foreign coins, coins minted after 1964, and private-mint or commemorative coins. Remember, you want broad U.S. coins with broad demand.

There are five broad "meat and potatoes" areas: rare gold, type coins, silver dollars, silver commemoratives, and modern twentieth-century singles. An investor should concentrate his buying activities in these five broad categories of rare coins for maximum upward price potential.

The rare gold coins are the most expensive coins that a collector can buy. All gold coins in rare condition (I'll explain *rare* in a moment) are hard to find. Thus they are very expensive. There are twelve major "brilliant uncirculated" gold-type coins. The cheapest gold coin will cost over $3,000 in top condition. Examples of the most common coins are the $1 gold piece, the $2.50 Liberty, the $2.50 Indian Head, and the $20 Saint-Gaudens. Your best bet is to stick with the more common dates, while not sacrificing on quality. The rare dates will be extremely expensive—some over $100,000. This would be analogous to buying a $5 million mansion in Beverly Hills. You can expect to find a definite price resistance to paying more than $20,000 for a single coin. Stick with the cheaper, more common gold coin—the three-bedroom house—that many more people can afford.

Type coins are coins in all denominations that were minted in the United States between 1793 and 1916. Roughly, type coins are nineteenth-century coins. Many collectors try to obtain an example of each type of coin minted during this period. There are twenty-three major brilliant uncirculated type coins and seventeen major proof issues. Some examples of these types of coins would be Barber dimes (1892 to 1916), Seated Liberty quarters (1838 to 1891), and Liberty Head nickels (1883 to 1913).

Silver dollars are the most commonly collected U.S. rare coin. The first silver dollar was minted in 1794, and mintage of these silver dollars continued through 1873. These coins are considered type coins. They are very rare and consequently very expensive. An investment-quality Seated Liberty 1873 silver dollar would cost more than $7,500.

In 1878 and continuing through 1935, the more common Morgan and Peace silver dollars were minted. There were 120 coins in the Morgan and Peace series. Because of larger mintages, one can obtain rare quality Morgan and Peace silver dollars starting from $100. Some of these series, however, are very expensive. Only a handful of the 1893 San Francisco silver dollars in rare condition exist. The last one on the market sold for over $500,000. Once again, it is not wise investment strategy to leave the broad mainstream of rare coins to purchase what only a few collectors can afford. The best strategy is to stay under the $20,000 price tag for a single silver coin.

Silver commemoratives are represented by the 144 different issues made between 1892 and 1954. Examples include the Texas Centennial half-dollar and the Daniel Boone half-dollar.

Twentieth century is the final area for consideration. These coins include:

> Lincoln cents (1909 to 1945)
> Buffalo nickels (1913 to 1938)
> Standing Liberty quarters (1916 to 1930)
> Mercury Head dimes (1916 to 1945)
> Earlier Washington quarters (1932 to 1945)
> Walking Liberty half-dollars (1916 to 1947)
> Franklin half-dollars (1948 to 1963)

These series of coins are seen to have the greatest numismatic value for investment.

Point 2: Concentrate in the Right Grade

All of the above coins exist in anywhere from poor quality to flawless or perfect quality. There are ten major categories of quality:

poor, fair, about good, good, very good, fine, very fine, extremely fine, almost uncirculated, and uncirculated. At one end of the spectrum, the poor-quality coin was once in circulation and has blemishes from the wear and tear. At the opposite end, the uncirculated coin was never in circulation and is in excellent condition. Coins are graded on a scale of 1 (the poorest quality) to 70 (perfect quality.) In the uncirculated mint-state (MS) category, there are eleven distinct conditions. These bear both a name and a number such as: average (60), choice (63), gem (65), superb (67), and flawless (70).

Coin experts disagree on which grade has the greatest potential for future appreciation. But the numbers do not lie. Numismatic expert David Hall undertook a massive study of each of these categories. His research showed conclusively that BU (brilliant uncirculated) gem-grade (65 or better) coins far outperformed any of the other grades. And he feels that the same reasons that caused this to happen over the past thirty years will hold true for the next thirty.

If you have only $1,000 to your name, your best bet is to start with real estate. But once you have an established portfolio of real estate, as in the third stage of wealth, it would be wise to diversify some of your assets into gem-quality rare coins.

A perfect portfolio distribution would be as follows:

> 20 percent gem-quality type coins
> 20 percent gem-quality rare gold
> 20 percent quality twentieth-century singles
> 20 percent quality silver dollars
> 20 percent gem-quality silver commemoratives

For your best strategy, stick with the right coin in the right gem grade.

Point 3: Concentrate Your Timing

Since the coin market moves in cycles, it would be wise to stick with the old stock-market adage, "Buy low, sell high." Buying coins at the top of a speculative blowoff (like April 18, 1980, the coin market's infamous Black Friday) would cause you to have to wait for the market to recover in order to start reaping profits. Fortunately, the rare coin market moves in fairly obvious cycles, and the outside influences on the rare-coin market such as the prices of gold and silver and the rate of inflation, also have somewhat obvious long-term trends. You want to buy when things look bullish for rare coins (and all tangible assets), and you want to stop buying or even sell when things start to look bearish. But it is better to buy a year too early than a day too late. It helps to have an expert on your side.

Point 4: Concentrate on the Right Experts

In order to capitalize on the right coin in the right type and at the right time, you have to deal with the right people. Unscrupulous dealers are not as rare as their coins. It helps to deal with dealers who possess great expertise, impeccable morals, and reasonable commissions. This is easier said than done. My favorite is David Hall, not merely because he is my personal dealer but because he understands a strategy for coin investment can fit comfortably within the principles of creating wealth. You can contact David Hall at: David Hall Rare Coins (DHRC), P.O. Box 6220, Newport Beach, CA 92658, 1-800-759-7575, www.davidhall.com.

There are many other reputable dealers. Look for a dealer who is both an authorized dealer and a member of the Professional Numismatists Guild (PNG.) A reputable dealer can help you to invest your dollars wisely and to resell your coins when the time is right. The cost will vary from 10 percent to 30 percent of the price of the coin. Other services that your dealer can provide are storage, appraisals, buybacks, and grading.

As a novice coin buyer, you should also be mindful of a few of the basic pitfalls of the numismatic field. All of these minefields can be avoided simply by dealing with the right people.

The most common problem in the rare-coin market is overgrading. This is the practice by some dealers of awarding coins higher grades than they actually deserve. Just as you wouldn't want to buy a house that had a termite problem, you wouldn't want to pay top dollar for an "uncirculated" coin only to find out later that it was "almost uncirculated." It means paying more for a coin than it is really worth.

How can you protect yourself?

There are rarely any bargains in the numismatic field. It is the last bastion of free enterprise, and the competition is fierce. If you come across a coin that seems significantly underpriced, you should be aware of overgrading, counterfeits, and treated coins. Once again, the experts can be of valuable service.

If you plan on exploring the field of rare coins, you would do well to visit any coin shows that pass through your area. Every year the American Numismatic Association sponsors a major coin show in a different major city. The multiday event buzzes with activity from start to finish and is always worth the trip. You can find out about this year's show by calling the ANA at 1-800-367-9723, or by visiting its Web site at www.money.org.

Obviously, this chapter cannot possibly explore the depths of the rare-coin market. I would highly recommend the following publications to those of you who want to explore this "gold" mine any further.

- *A Guide Book of United States Coins,* by R. S. Yeoman. The yearly "Red Book," now in its 59th edition, lists all U.S. coins along with very useful information on mintages and varieties. Though prices are listed, they aren't very accurate.
- *100 Greatest U.S. Coins,* by Jeff Garrett and Ron Guth. A large, richly photographed "coffee table" book that features details about the 100 most famous U.S. coin rarities. Fascinating reading.
- *Encyclopedia of United States and Colonial Proof Coins, 1722–1977* by Walter Breen. The Albert Einstein of coin research analyzes the "coiner's caviar." Out of print but available often via amazon.com or at local coin shops.

May you diversify into the right coins, in the right grade, at the right price, and with the right people.

CHAPTER 14

Liquid Money and Where to Pour It

This world is full of disappointed investors who couldn't hang on long enough. They didn't have staying power. They never *planned* to have staying power.

As an investor, you need staying power. You need to carry with you on your trek across the desert an ample supply of life-giving water to hedge against the times when the sun is too hot, the wind too dry, and when the oasis you had planned to reach is really another day or two away. Don't be like the unprepared prospector who ran out of money and abandoned the mine only to learn later that the pure vein of gold was just inches from the surface.

Cash is staying power. It is liquidity. And since you will be doing some major investing in illiquid assets like real estate, you will need to put some of this staying power away for the day that it fails to rain. Sometimes those droughts roll into months and even years. In the middle of major recessions, small businesses expire like so many flies in winter—because they don't have staying power.

I have recommended that during stage 2 of your investment trajectory you maintain a liquid staying-power fund equal to at least three surplus monthly payments for every property you own. In stages 3 and 4 you should try, if possible, to increase your cash holdings to as much as 10 percent of your net worth.

Where should you keep this staying-power fund? You need to place it where it can earn the highest rates of return with the greatest amount of liquidity and the least amount of risk. You don't want to play risky games with your staying-power fund.

Five types of institutions cater to these kinds of liquid investments:

1. Commercial banks
2. Money market funds
3. Treasury bills
4. Savings and loan associations
5. Thrift institutions

Commercial Banks

When I say commercial banks, I am referring to the institutions where you have your checking accounts. I think that it is always wise to have at least two or three different banks in your private banking system. I use two of them myself. At one bank, I do the bulk of my business activity with my business and corporate accounts. At another bank, we have our family and personal accounts as well as all of my rental-property accounts.

Why two banks? It's always wise to diversify your funds. And in addition, I have two sources for bank loans, if necessary. If I have trouble paying off a short-term loan at my main bank, I approach the other bank for a loan. Each of the banks should be willing to lend me money, because I am a valued customer: I have above-average checking-account balances, I pay my loans on time, and I am friends with the bank managers. It takes time to maintain relationships with several banks, but the fruits are worth it.

One of the prerequisites of a banking relationship is a win-win spirit between you and your banker. For instance, it does you little good to have a large checking-account balance if, when you are in need, your banker refuses to make you a loan. By the same token, a banker needs to feel that you are playing his or her ballgame also. The bank wins when it has customers who maintain healthy checking-account balances—for that is the bread and butter of the banking business. It should be reciprocal.

With this in mind, I often leave surplus funds sitting in my checking account earning only minimal interest when, if I were trying to squeeze out the last penny, I might shift these funds into accounts bearing higher interest. I am willing to sacrifice a few pennies in order to let my banker know that I will have his best interest at heart if he remembers me when I need him. And you can be sure that I remind him of this from time to time.

The most important time in a banking relationship is when you open your account. Sit your banker down for lunch, and let him or her know that you believe in the win-win philosophy. Because your banking relationship is so important, you should plan to leave a portion of your liquid staying-power fund in your checking account—perhaps as much as 10 percent of your liquid funds. Keep above-average checking-account balances. Another portion of your staying-power fund—maybe as much as 25 percent—can be distributed into one of the various high-yielding, low-risk investment alternatives available from any bank. I'll describe two of these: certificates of deposit and money market certificates.

Certificates of deposit are affectionately referred to as CDs. The funds are locked into maturities ranging anywhere from thirty days to five years. Although you can withdraw your money at any time, there are substantial interest penalties for early withdrawal. Check with your banker about current rates and maturity dates. But try not to lock in your money for longer than one year. CDs offer security commensurate with the bank's strength, so you should feel comfortable about the strength of the bank before you invest. Of course, your accounts are insured by the Federal Deposit Insurance Corporation (FDIC) up to $100,000.

Money market certificates (*not* the same thing as money market funds) generally earn one percentage point less than the previous week's six-month treasury bill rate and have maturities of three months, six months, one year, and three years. You should stick with short-term maturities for safety's sake, even though you may be sacrificing a little in yield. Minimum investment is $10,000, but a creative banker can sometimes lend you part of this. They are an excellent way of earning fairly high interest rates. Their disadvantage is, of course, their locked-in maturity dates.

With as much as 35 percent of your liquid funds in checking accounts and either CDs, money market certificates, or one of the many new money instruments being introduced regularly, your banker should be happy. Now you can go hunting for even higher yields and greater security and liquidity in other investments.

Money Market Funds

There has been a literal explosion in recent years in money market funds. And with good reason. The concept of a money market fund is to pool small amounts of money from hundreds of separate investors to enable them to buy jumbo CDs and government securities, which are available only in large denominations and earn significantly higher yields. In this way, a small investor can wield the same clout formerly available only to the very wealthy. And the concept has caught on in a big way. Tens of billions of dollars have poured into a plethora of various funds, each offering slightly different variations on the same concept.

With a money market fund, the small investor has the best of all worlds.

Liquidity: The funds can be withdrawn at any time without incurring a penalty. Many funds offer checking-account privileges with no charge for checks. Your money earns higher interest until your check clears.

Security: Money market funds invest in only short-maturity securities varying from a few weeks to no more than a few months. Even if there should be a "run" on the fund, the investors would only have to wait a few weeks for their money. Strict regulations protect from fraud and mismanagement, although it is impossible to remove all risk.

High yields: An investor can earn the highest available yield with the least amount of money. Many funds allow minimum investments as low as $1,000.

The safest funds and the ones with the highest ratings are those that invest in government-backed securities. The rationale is that a corporation can default on its debts and obligations, but the federal government can print its way out of any money crisis. The point is well taken. In 1970, Penn Central had the highest-rated commercial paper. When it went under, people began to realize the vulnerability of some of our largest corporations. Because of this fact, the money market funds that invest solely in government obligations have enjoyed growth rates near double those of funds invested in unsecured corporate notes. People are willing to give up the roughly one percentage point less in yield to pick up the extra security.

Rather than mention specific funds here, I recommend simply that you shift a heavy portion of your liquid assets into a high-interest-bearing liquid money market fund of your choice. Do some research on the Internet to track down the highest yielding, safest money market funds and CDs. And a casual glance at the advertisements in the *Wall Street Journal* and *Money Magazine* will tell you that the competition is fiercely fighting for your money.

Treasury Bills

Anyone with $10,000 to invest can go straight to the U.S. government and avoid money market funds entirely. Although there is an array of ways you can lend money to the government, the U.S. treasury bills (T-bills) are your best bet because of their short term—maturities varying anywhere from thirteen weeks to fifty-two weeks. It would not be wise to extend your staying-power liquid investments beyond one year, since the swings in interest could result in a capital loss if you needed quick access to your money.

Another advantage of buying T-bills is the exemption of any interest earned from state and local taxes. Obviously, the greatest advantage is their security.

But there are some disadvantages. Your money is locked in for the fixed period of time, and unless you have a creative banker, you will need a minimum of $10,000 to get into the game. The rates of return are a fraction higher than those of money market funds, but you pay for the privilege in added red tape. The money market funds are really the ultimate in convenience and availability.

How do you buy T-bills? You can buy them direct at the weekly auctions by submitting your own bid. A noncompetitive tender will allow you to buy your specified number of T-bills for the average of all of the bids tendered by the professional dealers, banks, and investors. You can obtain the necessary paperwork by writing the Bureau of the Public Debt, Securities Transactions Branch, Room 2134, Main Treasury, Washington, DC 20226, or by visiting its Web site at www.publicdebt.treas.gov.

If you don't like all of that work, you can go to your nearest Federal Reserve bank or branch and ask it to take care of it for you—for a fee, of course.

Savings and Loan Associations and Thrift Institutions

These are the two remaining major sources for liquid investments. My advice at this time is to refuse to be enticed by their slightly higher yields and tax-deferred instruments. However, the banking industry is in a constant state of flux. New savings instruments are constantly being introduced. Only recently, the banking industry, in an attempt to compete with the fast-growing money market funds, has been allowed by Congress to introduce money market checking accounts. These offer many of the same benefits of money market funds with the added benefit of federal deposit insurance. Just remember, your goal for your staying-power fund, after you have taken care of your banker, is to achieve maximum liquidity and safety.

To review, then, a sample distribution of your staying-power fund might be as follows:

> 10 percent checking-account balance
> 25 percent bank CDs or money market certificates
> 65 percent money market funds

When you fail to save for a dry spell, you jeopardize all that you have worked for. And that's no way to become wealthy.

CHAPTER 15

Limited Partnerships: Getting a Piece of the Action

What is a limited partnership?

Roughly, it is a group of investors who pool their resources for a specific purpose. For instance, ten investors may come up with $5,000 apiece and use the combined $50,000 as the down payment on a large apartment building or as exploration funds for an oil and gas drilling venture.

I have no doubt the idea to pool resources originated about 1,000,000 BC, when a group of cavemen accidentally joined forces to kill a mastodon and discovered that there was strength in numbers. None of them, individually, could have been successful. But together, it was a piece of cake. The mastodon didn't stand a chance.

Since that time, investment hunters everywhere have combined their limited talents and finances to make big things happen. This type of investment will become more and more popular in the years to come.

Sooner or later, someone is going to try to sell you a piece of a limited partnership, alias syndication. So you had better be aware of how such investments fit into the overall wealth trajectory. Otherwise, you may be tempted to jump into them too early.

In my opinion, limited partnerships are an ideal stage 4 investment. In other words, they are only for those who are trying to perpetuate lots of money, not for those who are trying to *create* wealth (stages 1, 2, 3). You'll understand better why I say this when you examine the benefits and detriments of limited partnerships.

There are six main benefits of limited partnership investments:

First of all, an investor can buy a small piece of a very large property, an investment in which the economies of scale are advantageous. Most investors could not afford to buy a large shopping center or a major apartment complex. But through the vehicle of a limited partnership, many smaller investors can pool their money to afford larger projects.

Second, as the name suggests, there is limited liability. A partner can lose only his investment and is not personally liable for the debts or obligations incurred by the partnership. This can be a very attractive feature if you have a lot of assets you are trying to protect.

The third benefit is each partner's limited involvement. Each partnership has one or more general partners and one or more limited partners. The general partner is usually responsible for gathering the funds, finding the property, putting together the deal, managing the property, and even disposing of the property. For this, the general partner receives fees and/or an ownership position. The limited partners, by law, have no voice in management. They just put up the cash. For them, it is a relatively passive investment.

The fourth benefit is expertise. It takes skill to capitalize on good opportunities. Many of the larger companies that specialize in syndication have large staffs of experts to handle each aspect of a successful purchase, including acquisition, tax planning, property management, and disposition. The average small investor does not have the same resources, and so many opportunities slip through his fingers.

Fifth, a good real-estate limited partnership can generally outperform almost any other traditional investment. Rates of return from 10 percent to over 25 percent are not uncommon. There is larger risk, but this is offset by a larger return on investment. Most real-estate partnerships also offer the added advantage of tax shelter. This fits nicely into the goals of a wealth perpetuator: namely, to beat inflation and taxes plus a little bit more.

Sixth, an investor with a large chunk of cash can achieve diversification by buying into several limited partnerships. Some limited partnerships also invest their funds into several different properties in different areas of the country to achieve an even further measure of diversification. There is an obvious advantage in spreading the risk.

Now what about the detriments?

First and most important, a limited partnership means limited control. Once you invest your money, you also lose the right to have a large say in what happens to it. You become one of many partners, each with an equal vote. Realistically, your positions are not always going to be shared by the majority. And what's one of the key wealth principles? To maintain control over your own destiny. In my opinion, if you are in the beginning stages of wealth, it would be wiser to own 100 percent of a $200,000 single-family house than to own 1 percent of a $20 million office complex. This would give you greater flexibility to move quickly to sell, trade, refinance, or take advantage of other opportunities. No need to ask permission of anyone. No strings attached. A limited partnership will not provide this flexibility.

However, in later wealth stages, when you are trying to find a less management-intensive investment alternative, you can afford to give up some control for a little automatic pilot pleasure.

The second major detriment to limited partnerships is lack of liquidity. There isn't much of a market for a limited partnership interest unless the general partner agrees to buy you out—and I can almost guarantee you that you won't get top dollar this way. The only way to get your money out is to wait until your property is sold, and the funds are redistributed to the partners. This may take years. So don't plan on seeing your money too soon. It is a long-haul investment that yields higher than average returns on your investments—provided that you have the patience and the staying power to hang around long enough.

Third, all of the expertise involved in setting up a limited partnership doesn't come cheap. The up-front fees to the general partner can get rather steep in some cases. That means that not all of your dollars are going to buy a great property. As much as 10 to 20 percent of your invested dollars can go directly to the general partner in fees. He deserves something, but you would do well to find out just how well he is doing at your expense. If the general partner gets a finder's fee for raising the money, plus a real-estate commission for both buying and selling the property (double dipping), *plus* a large percentage of the eventual profits, you may do better to put your money in a money market fund.

And fourth, although limited partnerships are very popular among investors, they are not very popular with the Internal Revenue Service. Recently, the IRS has singled out for audit any tax return boasting a limited partnership with a tax write-off in excess of $25,000. There will be more such scrutiny in the years to come. The odds that you will have a yearly visit from Uncle Sam are greatly increased if you invest in limited partnerships.

Notwithstanding these detriments, limited partnerships, if well selected, can provide secure and steady rates of growth for a person's portfolio in the later stages of wealth. You should plan on investing at least a portion of your funds there.

Now, how do you go about finding a good limited partnership?

You should first know that there are two kinds of partnerships, each with its unique method of distribution.

First, there is the private-placement limited partnership. With a private placement, the general partner can involve no more than thirty-five partners in the offering. He cannot advertise publicly. By limiting the partnership to only thirty-five individuals, the general partner can avoid the enormous red tape involved with getting an offering registered with the Securities and Exchange Commission.

The best way to find a good private-placement limited partnership is to visit the best accountants and attorneys in your area and ask them what they are recommending to their best clients. People who market limited partnerships contact these professionals regularly to tell them of the latest opportunities. I would ask around to determine which individual or company in your area has had a good track record of making consistent money. What you are thus buying is not the particular property but the know-how and expertise of a reputable syndicator. The word spreads rapidly. Unfortunately, the more successful this type of syndicator becomes, the more fees and ownership he can extract from his partners. Generally, these limited-partnership interests require an investment of at least $5,000 and normally higher.

The other type of syndication is a public offering. These are much larger affairs involving a full registration with the SEC, requiring a significant amount of time and money—which you eventually pay for. You will find public-offering limited-partnership interests being sold through all the brokerage houses. A Merrill Lynch stockbroker, for example, is licensed to sell limited partnerships, which can be sold in denominations as small as $500.

One advantage of a public offering is the lower amount of risk involved. As a rule, the large brokerage houses spend considerable amounts of money searching out the best opportunities for their clients (for a fee, of course), and the bad apples usually don't get past the eagle eyes of both the SEC and the due-diligence departments of most stock brokerage firms. This lower risk also means more conservative rates of return and higher fees, but you may settle for a lower return for the security of a safer bet.

What if you want to do more than just take the word of some accountant or stockbroker about the future of a limited-partnership investment? What should you do?

First of all, read the prospectus. All of it. Word for word. Don't be alarmed by all of the bad news. A prospectus is designed specifically to be long, boring, and full of boilerplate language, in the hope that most people won't read it. So you want to read the fine print.

Realize that the prospectus has only one purpose, and that is to protect the general partner. He wants to be completely covered should anything go wrong down the road. You should notice if the general partner has the right to approach the limited partners for additional funds to meet a balloon payment, an unanticipated capital improvement, or an unbudgeted negative cash flow. Will you be forced to sell your partnership interest at an inopportune time because you're unable to raise your share of an additional assessment? It is wise to plan for these things. The prospectus will outline various alternatives.

I also recommend that whenever possible, you analyze every real-estate limited partnership you are considering by running it through the analysis grid I taught you in chapter 7. Most private placements will describe the property to be purchased in the prospectus. You may not have total access to all information, but surely you can pass limited judgment on location, financing terms, price, and property condition. Make your investment decisions as if you were the sole owner—the time you invest here will pay handsome dividends.

On the other hand, many public-offering limited partnerships are blind pools. In other words, the money is raised without knowing what property will be purchased. You are, in effect, blindly giving your money to a syndicator with the hope that he will know how to invest your money wisely. In these instances, you should concentrate your analysis on the track record of the syndicator. Has this company been in existence long? What other successful projects has it completed? How strong is this company financially?

Now that you have some basic guidelines, let's run through a quick example. Suppose that you are in stage 4 of your wealth-building program, and you call your accountant to tell him that you have $25,000 you want to invest. You ask him to recommend a good limited partnership. He tells you of a young, aggressive syndicator who has just dropped off a prospectus of his latest offering. He has a good track record. You are interested and ask to read the prospectus in depth. Here is a summary of the pertinent details from a prospectus I received several years ago:

Subject property: 100-unit apartment complex in Orlando, Florida
Purchase price: $2 million
Mortgages:

First mortgage of $923,510 at 5.5 percent interest
Second mortgage of $136,397 at 7 percent interest
Third mortgage of $212,368 at 8.75 percent interest
Fourth mortgage of $227,725 at 12 percent interest

Total debt $1 million
(All mortgages are fully assumable.)

Down payment: $500,000
Total of capital contributions: $750,000 to be disbursed as follows:

$500,000 down payment
$250,000 closing costs, reserve accounts, and fees
$750,000 total cash from limited partners

The figure of $250,000 in closing costs, reserve accounts, and fees breaks down as follows:

$33,000	to reimburse general partner for interest cost of tying up property
$17,000	closing costs
$40,000	reserve account for unanticipated cash flows and repairs
$80,000	syndication fee
$80,000	capital-improvement account to upgrade each unit after acquisition, increase the rents and therefore the value

Now consider the following:

Tax information: land valued at $400,000, building at $1 million

Management fee: 5 percent of gross rents

Future costs and fees to general partner: General partner to receive 20 percent of all profits from appreciation and equity buildup at the time of sale but only 1 percent of the tax shelter and cash flow. This 20 percent equity interest is subordinated to the limited partners' profit. The limited partners must receive their money back first before the general partner can profit, assuming no sales commission at sale.

The five-year projections (minus the general partner's 20 percent interest) are as follows:

Total five-year positive cash flow	$151,305
Total five-year equity buildup	$164,454
Total five-year tax savings (50 percent bracket)	$175,372
Total five-year appreciation (7 percent annual growth)	$805,103
Totals in all areas for five-year projection	$1,296,234

Yearly average growth is projected at $259,247.

On an investment of $750,000, this equals a yearly average return on investment of 34.56 percent.

You are impressed by the numbers and decide to dig deeper.

First you call up a friend in Orlando and have him run over and inspect both the property and the neighborhood. The location is excellent, close to town and on a lake. The tenants show their appreciation by high occupancy rates. The structure is thirty-five to forty years old but was built to last. Red tile roofs, hardwood floors. Only minor cosmetic work needed. The rents are a bit low for the area, and an indication of the low rents is the fact that the building is 98 percent occupied.

Other units in the area have recently sold for $25,000 per unit. These units are being acquired for $22,500 per unit ($2 million acquisition price plus $250,000 in fees, renovation, and closing costs divided by 100 units). It is obviously an excellent price.

What was the seller's motivation to sell? The seller was actually another limited partnership that had bought these units several years previously for about $15,000 per unit. It was time to sell and take some profits. Because of the low price and excellent assumable mortgages, the property was on the market for only five days before being snapped up by the present general partner, who realized what a bargain it was. Without hesitation, he had gone to his bank and borrowed the necessary $500,000 to buy the property. He then formed the limited partnership to repay his bank.

With the excellent financing terms, the property shows a healthy positive cash flow and tax benefits as well as equity buildup.

The only question mark is the appreciation. Will this property appreciate significantly in value over the next five years? That is anyone's guess. But by buying the property right, the general partner almost assured his partners of a profit, regardless of appreciation. With only minimal appreciation, the partnership should do well.

On the strength of your positive analysis of each of the five areas of analysis, you decide that your $25,000 will be safe here. More than likely, this will prove to be a wise decision.

This is an actual example of an excellent syndication. Thirty partners came up with $25,000 apiece to form the $750,000 initial capital. In this example, you can notice many of the things you should be looking for in a limited-partnership investment: ungreedy general partners, good low-interest assumable financing, an excellent price, and a solid property in a good location.

You can see from this example how a passive investor could achieve a realistic 20 to 30 percent annual return on invested dollars in a well-secured investment. It may take some looking to put all of the right pieces in the puzzle, but once the pieces are in place, your passive dollars can grow on automatic pilot with a minimum of worry. This type of limited partnership deserves a portion of your investment dollars.

One last caution: don't be swayed into buying a limited partnership interest for the tax shelter alone. If it's not an economically viable investment, it won't be a good tax shelter.

Now let's proceed to the subject of taxes. We'll be leaving the area of how to make and perpetuate money and be entering the area of how to keep your wealth once you have acquired it. Although this is one of my least favorite subjects, second only to property management, it is crucial to the accumulation and preservation of wealth.

CHAPTER 16

How the Rich Pay Lower Taxes

The rich aren't like us. They pay less taxes.
　　　—Peter DeVries, *I Hear America Swinging*

Whether you like it or not, the IRS is your lifetime partner, following you wherever you go, demanding a patriotic share of whatever profit or salary you earn. No amount of moaning, groaning, beefing, or wailing will remove the tax shackles from your ankles. You had better get used to your yearly pilgrimage to the post office at precisely one minute to midnight every April 15 in order to send off a timely tax return (along with a handsome check). You are stuck in debtor's prison, serving a life sentence with no hope of parole.

No hope, that is, unless you are smart. Because if you are smart, you will realize that the taxpayer's prison in which you find yourself is locked from the inside—and you have been given the key. And it's not illegal to use it. Nor is it unpatriotic to think that by using this key you might drastically reduce the amount of taxes you are now paying, even perhaps to zero. In fact, you are encouraged to do so by some of the nicest people, including all of those nice lawmakers in Washington, DC. The rich have been using this key for decades with marvelous results. That is why they are rich.

Now, I don't intend to bore you with the minute details of form ABC and code XYZ, and so on. With the money you save in taxes, you will be able to hire the best accountant in town to do this for you. Instead, I want to have you step back with me and look at the broad picture.

If you are planning on becoming wealthy, you should have an inherent dislike for all destroyers of wealth. Paying taxes is one of the greatest wealth destroyers of all. Just as you work hard investing your dollars in wealth-producing assets, you also need to work hard to see that the fruits of your labor are protected from unnecessary and stifling "taxfixiation."

Don't get me wrong. I'm not a tax evader. I'm not a crusader walking the picket line or manning the barricades. I don't have any constitutional hang-ups against paying taxes. I file an honest return every year. But from a practical viewpoint, I don't like to pay money to the government in taxes if I can arrange my affairs, with a certain amount of time and effort, to pay a little less or much less in taxes.

As in my investing, I use a system to make sure that the amount I pay in taxes is kept to a minimum. I call it the "trickle-down theory of tax planning." Let me share it with you:

Let's suppose that you make, with your spouse (if you have one), a combined salary of $100,000. And, just for example, say you have two children. You allow your employer to withhold taxes from your regular paychecks, you file a joint return, you don't itemize deductions, you send in your tax returns early, and you look forward to receiving a small tax refund each year. Roughly, your picture looks something like this:

Total Income		**$100,000**
Less:		
Personal Exemptions:		
Husband	$3,000	
Wife	$3,000	
Dependents (2)	$6,000	
Standard Deduction	$10,000	
Total Deductions		**$22,000**
Taxable Income		**$78,000**
Taxes:		
Federal Income Tax	$13,000	
FICA (Social Security payroll taxes)	$7,000	
State Taxes	$2,000	
Less Child Tax Credit	$2,000	
Total Taxes		**$20,000**
Net Spendable after Taxes		**$80,000**
Effective Tax Rate: 20 percent		

*all figures rounded for simplification

Personal-Exemptions and Itemized-Deductions Faucet

This entire process is similar to a series of faucets or filters. As in the illustration below, the income is poured in the barrel or tank top. Various faucets along the way funnel off deductible expenses, thereby reducing the net taxable income. The taxable income is the figure that your accountant will use in determining your federal income tax, although the FICA (Federal Insurance Contributions Act) amount is determined from your gross income. In our example, you only have one faucet on your barrel: a deduction of approximately $3,000 for each dependent, which we call personal exemptions. In reality, many Americans also elect to deduct interest on home mortgages, charitable donations, and medical bills. These are called itemized deductions. To keep this chapter simpler, I have avoided a detailed analysis of these deductions. Your accountant will be able to fill you in on this at tax time.

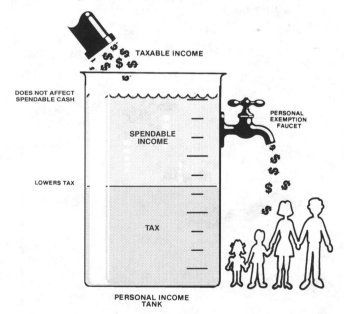

The aggressive tax planner is in constant search of new and legitimate filters to strain off taxable income and thereby reduce taxable income at the bottom of the tank. There are four main additional faucets or filters available to the individual, and some others that can be useful when income is high.

Business-Expense Faucet

As an investor, you accumulate expenses such as the cost of books (like this one), seminars, business travel, telephone charges, and so on—any expenditure for trade or business, including investment. These are dollar-for-dollar deductions. In other words, you spend a dollar of cash and reduce your taxable income by a dollar.

But you also reduce your spendable cash by a dollar. In other words, rather than paying taxes to the government, you end up with some books, office supplies, or memberships to professional organizations. Although this is preferable to flushing tax dollars down the drain, it still doesn't put any more spendable cash in your pocket. For every deductible dollar you spend, you are saving only a percentage of a dollar in taxes. Now, in our example, we put you in the 25 percent tax bracket. The next dollar you earn above $100,000 is taxed at 38 percent. If you should happen to spend your next available dollar for a business lunch, you can deduct the expense and thus save yourself 38¢ in taxes.

There must be a better way.

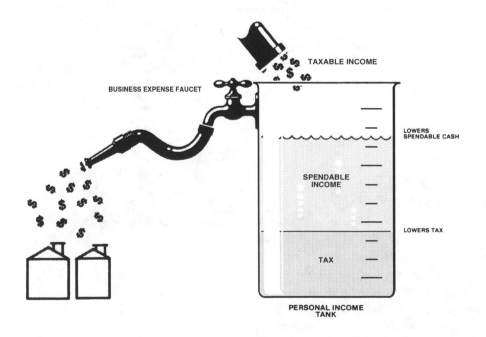

Business-Depreciation Filter

Things wear out. The IRS realizes this, and allows the businessman and investor to deduct an amount equal to the annual "wearing out" of any business equipment. A $15,000 van needed to help you manage your small real-estate holdings can be depreciated over five years. Your accountant may show you other ways of depreciating your assets, depending on your circumstances and the ever-changing nature of the tax code. Business depreciation is a filter that reduces taxable income.

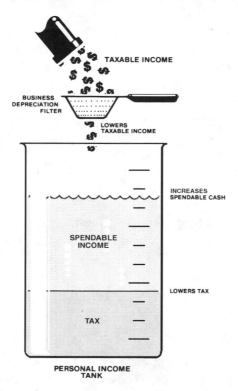

The key here was to buy something that depreciated, and this inserted filter siphoned off some of the taxable income and thereby reduced your taxes.

Let's delve deeper into this technique. What about real estate? It also qualifies for depreciation. But unlike cars and most equipment, it rarely declines in value. It usually appreciates instead of depreciating from a fair market-value perspective. But the government still pretends that a building wears out over time—and in reality it does. Also, it can be rented out to cover, or partly cover, the payments on the loans incurred to buy it.

For example, let's suppose that you buy a $200,000 single-family house. The land it sits upon is appraised at about $50,000. The sticks and stones are worth about $150,000. The government allows you to depreciate the sticks and stones part over eighteen years. Or, to say it another way, you can elect to depreciate 3.5 percent of your building each year for the next twenty-seven and a half years on a straight-line basis. That amounts to a tax deduction of approximately $5,000 per year.

Let's assume that you buy two excellent rental homes on January 1 with $10,000 you have been able to save—$5,000 down on each. You negotiate a reasonable interest rate so that your mortgage payments aren't too high, and you immediately rent out each with a break-even cash flow. That is, after paying all mortgages and expenses and collecting all rents, you pull no money out of your pocket. (Only the interest-payment portion of your regular mortgage payment is tax deductible. The principal portion is not. Since this principal portion is negligible in the first years of a mortgage, I have ignored it for our purposes.)

Owning this real estate made it possible for you to lower your federal income tax. You became the owner of two rental properties with future appreciation potential. In essence, the IRS is subsidizing your real-estate investing program.

Let's add a few more valves to our taxable-income tank, to see what this will do to the tax picture.

IRA-Account Siphon

Congress wants all Americans to provide for their own future security and therefore allows all taxpayers to deduct up to $4,000 from their income to be siphoned off and placed in an individual retirement account or IRA. (If you are over fifty, you can deduct an extra $1,000). You can create your own retirement fund. The money you put in this account and the income accumulating in it are tax deferred until you retire and begin to draw on the account. This is another device for reducing taxable income, although it also reduces available cash. Let's see how this has affected the overall tax picture:

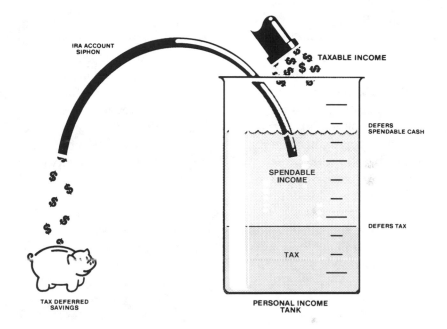

IRA ACCOUNT
SIPHON

TAXABLE INCOME

DEFERS
SPENDABLE CASH

SPENDABLE
INCOME

DEFERS TAX

TAX

TAX DEFERRED
SAVINGS

PERSONAL INCOME
TANK

As far as the IRS is concerned, as a married person you have to earn at least $40,000 to be subject to state and federal taxes. However, once your income goes over $40,000 per year, it becomes more and more difficult to shelter your money with only the few filters I have mentioned so far. For more wealthy investors, there are two other tax shelters that bear mentioning: partnerships with children, and corporations.

Partnerships-with-Children Siphon

This subject might be more meaningful if we relate it to a subject that strikes fear into every parent: the cost of a college education. Recent reports have indicated that the cost of raising a child through college age in the next few decades will exceed $100,000. A parent usually pays for these expenses in after-tax dollars. But there is a way to do it a lot more cheaply by using pretax dollars.

You could transfer some assets into your children's trust and lease these assets back from the children. For instance, as an author, I couldn't exist without my high-tech computer system. It cost me about $6,000. Once I had fully depreciated the machine myself, I could give this machine to my daughter, Aimee (I can give her up to $11,000 per year as an individual without gift tax, or $22,000 with my spouse). Aimee now becomes the owner of my computer. I make an agreement to lease the machine from her for $200 per month, or $2,400 per year. The lease payments are tax deductible to me as a business expense. My daughter's trust receives $2,400 in annual income, which is subject to little if any tax because it is not a significant amount. The $2,400 remains in the trust, gathering interest. If I start this process now, by the time she reaches college age in fifteen years, there will be more than enough in the trust to provide a respectable education.

Another method is to form a family limited partnership, with the parents as general partners and the children as limited partners. The parents put some of their real-estate holdings into the limited partnership—two free-and-clear mostly depreciated houses. (It may take several years of making gifts at $11,000 per year per child for the children to receive their full ownership of the partnership.) The $1,000 per month net income from each house goes into the limited partnership, which is owned 50 percent by the children and 25 percent by each spouse. That would mean the children would receive $12,000 cash distribution each year from the partnership (50 per-

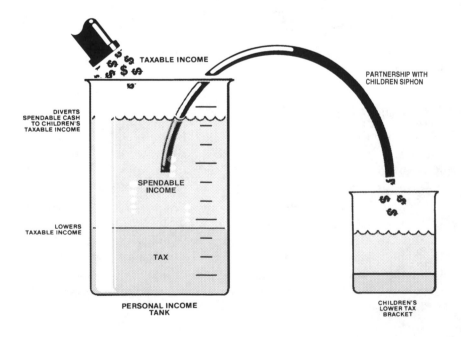

TAXABLE INCOME

DIVERTS SPENDABLE CASH TO CHILDREN'S TAXABLE INCOME

PARTNERSHIP WITH CHILDREN SIPHON

SPENDABLE INCOME

LOWERS TAXABLE INCOME

TAX

PERSONAL INCOME TANK

CHILDREN'S LOWER TAX BRACKET

cent ownership of $24,000 yearly cash flow from two houses rented out for $1,000 apiece). After deducting a mandatory salary to the parents for administering the partnership, this $12,000 cash flow—which used to go directly to the parents and was taxed at high rates—now goes to the children, who have much lower tax rates. The income could then be routed to a children's trust, which could accumulate the money to be used for their future needs. And the parents, who are the general partners of the family limited partnership, have total control of how the assets are managed. Remember, this is only an illustration. Your tax and legal advisers will point out the fine details.

But these are small-peanuts techniques compared with the most powerful and best-kept tax-shelter secret in America: a privately held corporation.

Incorporation Filter

If you aren't already familiar with the benefits of corporate life, you might be a little intimidated by the sound of the word *corporation.* After all, it conjures up visions of big boardrooms, fancy executive suites, high-powered lawyers, stockholders' meetings—and you wonder how you could afford all these trappings.

Well, you don't have to afford any of them. But you can't afford not to take advantage of all the other benefits of using a corporation. Even though you may be a little guy in the scheme of American business, you still inherit all the blessings that all of our country's multibillion-dollar corporations have negotiated from Congress over the years through multimillion-dollar lobbying efforts.

For a few hundred dollars, a small businessperson can be president of his or her own corporation and can enjoy all of the blessings of the rich without having to pay for them! Once the proper papers are filed, he or she can start to pay less in taxes. Of course, this should always be done after having examined your particular circumstances with proper counsel.

Let's imagine that your income is $100,000 per year. With such high earnings, you would want to implement your own private corporation. By the way, if your income isn't nearly that high, don't tune out. If you plan on being wealthy within the next ten years or less, you need to seriously consider forming your own corporation sooner or later.

The first step is to talk to your attorney about the benefits of forming your own corporation. Usually for less than $1,000, he can draw up the necessary papers and file them with the appropriate state offices. Or you can form your own corporation by mail for less than $300.

You will continue to operate as before. You receive income from your business and deposit it in your corporate bank account. From this bank account you will write yourself a salary check each month—enough to fit into your budget.

Of course, all business expenses are tax-deductible, as with a private individual. All such expenses reduce taxable income and lower the ultimate tax bill. But a corporation has two main tax advantages that are not available to the private citizen.

First of all, as a corporate officer, you are entitled to some special privileges. Your corporation is entitled to buy you a life insurance policy and to deduct the premiums as a tax-deductible expense—something a private citizen could not do. Other perks are medical reimbursement plans, child care plans, and health insurance, and so forth.

The second and most important benefit available in a corporation is a defined benefit pension plan. You are allowed, through various plans (see your attorney), to deduct a contribution to an employee pension plan—up to 25 percent of salary. This amount is a deductible expense and is totally tax deferred, in much the same way as an IRA account. The benefits of corporate pension plans have been substantially increased by Congress in recent years. Since the advantages of having a defined benefit pension plan are so great, you cannot have a pension plan *and* an IRA. One or the other, but not both. If 25 percent is contributed to the pension plan, then the IRA limit is zero.

Another reason to have a corporate entity is the lower corporate tax brackets on income below $50,000. Suppose your corporate income is $50,000. You have $5,000 in deductible expenses and plan on paying yourself the rest in personal salary. You can siphon off up to 25 percent or $11,250 and place it in your own personal pension plan. The remaining $33,750 would come directly to you as an individual salary. The money in your pension plan can be placed under your direction to invest as you see fit, with certain government-imposed limitations. You can't invest in wildly speculative ventures or risk it all on untenable business propositions. But you can invest in the stock market, or bond market, or money market certificates, or a host of other conventional vehicles. And all of the profit or interest earned in this pension plan is tax deferred until you draw out the money and go to Hawaii. (You must begin drawing out this money after age seventy and a half.) That means that you can deduct money from your taxable income, put it into a sheltered plan, and not even have to pay taxes on the money you earn from your tax deferred dollars for many years to come, when you can arrange your affairs so that you're in a low income tax bracket.

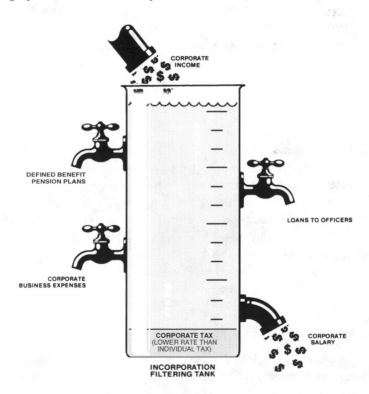

The most advantageous tax strategy using the corporate pension plan, in my opinion, goes as follows:

1. Deduct the maximum amount from your corporate salary and place it in your pension plan.
2. Make a loan from your corporate pension plan to yourself, as an individual, at a market interest rate—say, the prime rate. You will be required to repay the loan within five

years and can lend yourself no more than 50 percent at one time, with adequate collateral.

3. As an individual, take the borrowed dollars and buy real estate with it, using the property as collateral for the loan.

4. The interest payments on the loan you have taken out of your pension plan are deductible to you as an individual but are not immediately taxed to the corporate pension plan. In essence, what you are doing is lending yourself money, deducting the interest you pay from your personal income taxes, and not having to pay taxes on the interest you—or your pension funds—earn until age seventy and a half. As soon as you pay off the loan, borrow this same money plus the interest you have paid yourself and start the process all over again. In essence, you become your own bank!

Of course, setting up a corporation has its costs. There will be incorporation fees and maintenance costs. You can analyze these costs together with your accountant or attorney to see whether the benefits outweigh the detriments. With the passage of each new tax bill, some benefits of each strategy may be reduced or enhanced. Your advisers may recommend specific strategies to consider for your situation to keep you ahead of the tax man. Although the remaining benefits are still great, your attorney may recommend that instead of a corporation, you consider a simplified employee pension plan, or SEP IRA for short.

Putting the Filters to Work for You

What I have tried to illustrate here is the filtering process through which all tax dollars have to go. You have two choices. You can say that you don't like to complicate your life with such a complex system—and pay your taxes. Or you can begin to live a tax avoider's life, planning to use the government's tax laws to reduce or eliminate your tax liability. Once you learn to use this system and become proficient at it, keeping every dollar you earn instead of giving much of it away, you will see how easy it is to keep up. Your accountants and other expert advisers dot your *i*'s and cross your *t*'s. That's what they get paid to do.

Everyone has a tax threshold that he or she will not cross. Some people will pay $5,000 a year in taxes without squawking. Some more, some less. But sooner or later, no matter where your threshold is, you will cross it. You will begin to wonder why you should share so much of your wealth with the tax man. When you come to that point in your life, you will realize that however complicated my system may seem to you now, it will be worth the effort down the road.

I look upon this system as an extremely inexpensive way of earning money. If you owned a business that cost you less than $1,000 per year to operate, took up less than a hundred hours of your time, and earned you $5,000 to $10,000 per year or more, wouldn't you look into it? That's 500% to 1,000% profit; or to look at it differently, you would earn $50 to $100 per hour or more. The wealthy have long since learned that by buying real estate and funnelling their income through corporations and other elaborate vehicles set up by their accountants and attorneys, a hemorrhaging tax bill can be reduced to a mere trickle.

Let's go a step further to see what might happen to a man who earns $100,000 per year (the lucky devil). If this man isn't smart, his tax bill could be in excess of $25,000 and could go as high as $35,000. That's a lot of bread that won't be going on his table. Now, he can either get used to this fact and live on the remaining $75,000 or $65,000, which still isn't all that bad. Or he can start planning a filter system that will allow him to keep an extra $25,000 or more and invest it in things that will produce wealth for him and his family, and stimulate the economy as well.

The first filter is the corporate umbrella. Let's set up a corporation for him that receives all of his $100,000 income. We'll take off $5,000 in deductible business expenses and pay him a $70,000 salary. Of this salary amount, we will deduct 25 percent, or $17,500, and put it into a pension and profit-sharing plan. That will leave $52,500 to be paid out to this individual to plan for on his individual tax return. We also will have $25,000 of income left in the corporation to reckon with.

Since the first $25,000 of corporate income is taxed at only 15 percent, the man's total corporate tax bill will only be $3,750 plus state tax, if any. That leaves him $21,250 left over in the corporation after taxes—which he can lend to himself at low interest rate loans (with certain limits.)

Of course, we now have to worry about the $52,500 personal

income. Let's see how this flows through the system. (With this much income, the taxpayer will probably itemize deductions.) There are personal exemptions. Then come the two houses with depreciation. That leaves a much higher taxable income. The tax bill on this will be about $5,000.

The combined corporate and personal tax bills total about $10,000 as compared to as much as $35,000 without planning. This tax bill could be reduced even further by simply buying more real estate. If the taxpayer is worried about management, he only has to look at his tax bill to see that he could afford to pay a manager up to $25,000 per year to manage only four houses and still be ahead.

Obviously, the higher your income, the more importance you

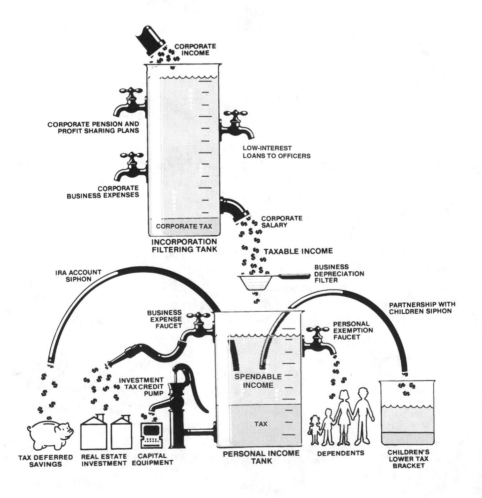

should place on your tax planning. Let's look at those filters again. As you read through this list, think about the money you have paid to the IRS in your lifetime. Could you now be using any of these to immediately reduce your tax bill?

1. Itemized deductions (beyond the scope of this chapter)
2. Personal exemptions (such as dependent deductions)
3. Business depreciation (such as real-estate depreciation)
4. Loss from business operations (such as negative cash flows)
5. IRA or defined-benefit pension plan
6. Family partnerships
7. Investment tax credit
8. Incorporation
9. Corporate business expenses
10. Low-interest loans to officers

These are just some of the possibilities worth exploring. You should explore all the possibilities you can, because the doors to tax savings won't open for you until you turn the knob.

CHAPTER 17

Insulating Your Assets from Lust, Liability, and Lawyers

A football player wouldn't think of going out on the field without shoulder pads and a helmet. Nor would a race-car driver race without a seat belt. Neither should you plan to make a lot of money without planning how to keep it once you make it. You'd be surprised how many people plan for one and forget the other. Once you've acquired wealth you need to think about protecting yourself. It's an unpleasant thought, but we live in a "sue-crazy" society.

The story is told of a farmer who had gone through a succession of incompetent farmhands. One day a new laborer arrived and was hired. All was fine for a few days until a terrible windstorm broke out in the middle of the night. The farmer, awoken by the thunder and wind, ran frantically out to the bunkhouse to tell the new farmhand to prepare for the storm. He found him sleeping peacefully. Nothing he could do would rouse him. Finally the slumbering man opened his sleepy eyes and said, "I can sleep when the wind blows." Then he rolled over and went back to sleep. The farmer, muttering under his breath about the lazy workers he had to put up with, ran out into the barnyard to do the job himself. But everywhere he looked, the job had already been done. The animals were all safely in the barn, and the barn doors and shutters were secured tightly. The hay was tied down. All the farm vehicles' windows were rolled up. There was nothing to do. Then he realized what the man had meant when he said, "I can sleep when the wind blows."

This chapter is designed to help you take three specific precautions that will enable you to sleep easier when the wind blows. In order to illustrate how to insulate yourself from lust, liability, and lawyers, let me make some assumptions.

Suppose that you have followed the basic investment guide-lines of this book. In ten years of careful investing, your net worth has increased from $0 to well over $1 million. You now own ten free-and-clear single-family houses, each producing $1,000 per month net cash flow. In addition, your portfolio includes $50,000 in rare coins, $100,000 cash in a money market fund, and $50,000 in discounted mortgages. Your cars, jewelry, furniture, and other miscellaneous assets are valued at $50,000. In essence, you are on automatic pilot—living off the income from your properties and dabbling comfortably in discounted mortgages and real estate.

Precaution 1: Maintain Adequate Insurance

Your first step in protecting yourself is to review your insurance needs. Have your insurance agent give you a complete insurance checkup. Common sense dictates that you should have more than adequate fire and liability insurance on each of your properties. This is no place to scrimp. Your cars should also have hefty liability insurance coverage. Better be prepared. For example, you can get a $1 million umbrella liability policy covering your personal home, cars, boat, and so on for just a few hundred dollars a year. In today's litigation-prone society, the typical coverage included in home-owner's insurance may not be adequate.

As for life insurance, you be the judge. With most of your assets free and clear of mortgages and with minimal debt, you may not need a lot of life insurance. Later in this chapter I'll show you ways to avoid probate and estate taxes, which are the main reasons why people buy extra life insurance. A $1 million term life insur-ance policy should be adequate.

Precaution 2: Avoid Signing Personally on Mortgages

This is easier said than done. But there are things you can do to limit your personal liability in signing your name to mortgages. This is a precautionary step. An ounce of prevention is worth a pound of cure.

You should have your attorney review all mortgages and/or trust deeds that you have signed on. (Let's use the word *mortgage* for this discussion.) In some states, like California, a property is the sole collateral for a mortgage. In other words, a creditor can look only to the property for repayment of the debt. The borrower is not personally liable to repay any deficiency if the mortgage debt is not fully paid off through a foreclosure proceeding.

Other states, like Utah, allow deficiency judgments. The borrower is personally liable to pay off the debt regardless of the collateral. Your goal in reviewing your documentation is to determine the extent of your liability.

Why should this bother you?

You never know when circumstances beyond your control will force you to lose one of your properties to foreclosure. For instance, let's suppose that a beginning investor buys a property and obtains a new mortgage. A few years later, for some unknown reason, the tenant goes off his rocker, destroys the property, and walks away, never to be heard from again. If the beginning investor wasn't adequately insured, this property damage could be devastating. The bank forecloses on the loan. The property is sold at a loss, and since the investor is still personally liable, the bank comes after him. Depending on which state he lives in, the bank may have the legal right to look to him for any losses it may incur. You wouldn't want an unfortunate situation like this to expose your other assets to risk.

How do you avoid this? If you live in California or any other nondeficiency-judgment state, you can breathe a little easier. If not, you may need to take some precautions.

The first and best precaution is to always include an exculpatory clause in any mortgage you sign. An exculpatory clause is a simple sentence stating that the property will be the sole collateral for the debt. This should limit your personal liability significantly. Have your attorney help you set this up.

If the seller refuses to allow an exculpatory clause, then you should try to buy the property in your name only, leaving your spouse's name off the mortgage. If worst comes to worst, and a foreclosure on this mortgage threatens all of your other assets, you can deed all of your property to your spouse. Then, if you are sued for the deficiency, there will not be any assets to seize. You will own nothing; your spouse will control it all.

Some couples deliberately split their assets so that all of the highly leveraged properties and high-risk assets (like boats, motorcycles, and cars) are placed solely in the husband's name and all of the low-risk assets (such as savings accounts and properties with large equities) are placed in the wife's name. Of course, limiting one's liability in this way should be done only with the advice of a competent attorney.

Precaution 3: Proceed as Soon as Possible to Transfer Most, if Not All, of Your Assets into One of the Legal Entities That Wealthy People Use*

There are just a handful of legitimate ways, time tested and court upheld, to protect your assets from frivolous lawsuits and unfair creditors. The entities and techniques that people of wealth use are: corporations, limited-liability companies (LLC), limited partnership (LC), and ERISA-qualified pension plans like the profit-sharing plan (which includes the 401 (k)) and defined benefit plan (*ERISA* stands for Employee Retirement Income Security Act). And to a much lesser extent, some complex and irrevocable trusts that are created by others for your benefit.

Aren't these things just for Rockefellers and Kennedys? Well, if such legal entities are good enough for the superrich, that should be evidence enough for you. As I once heard George Gilder observe, "The rich didn't get that way by being stupid."

Corporations are what asset-protection gurus call one-way or unidirectional protection devices. You see, lawsuits can come from many directions for a plethora of reasons. For example, you can be sued personally for something that you did to another (breach of contract, negligence, libel, slander, and so on). On the other hand, when a corporation does something wrong, the corporation gets sued, not the shareholders. Only the value of the assets in the corporation are at risk, not the personal assets of the shareholders, like their homes, IRAs, or cars.

Now, let's talk about the lawsuit from the other direction—that is, at you personally. The corporation at that point just becomes another asset for the creditor to take from you. The shares of common stock are just like the shares of stock you may own in your personal brokerage account at a broker-dealer. To the extent that the corporation has value in and of itself, it will be forced to be sold or taken over by the creditor through a postjudgment court procedure called the writ of execution. When a creditor wants to force you to pay his judgment, he goes back to the judge and asks for a writ of execution to sell or turn over your assets; namely, the common stock of your corporation.

---

* Thanks to my attorney, Anton Ewing, for providing this information.

The limited liability company (LLC) and the limited partnership (LP) are blessed with the charging-order rule. A judge is limited in the remedies against the ownership shares, called units, of these two entities. No writ of execution is allowed. In other words, the creditor cannot sell your LLC or LP, and he cannot become the actual owner. That is a pretty impressive rule. What that means for us is that if we have one of those entities, and it owns valuable investments, the personal creditor can not become the owner even if he has a judgment.

About one thousand years ago, judges decided that it was better if society encouraged people to come together and form partnerships to run businesses. In order to encourage individuals to come together, society wanted to ensure that partners would never become partners with their partner's creditors. Therefore the charging-order rule was created. This is what is known as the common law, or judge-made law. Since then most states have enacted statutes to codify the common-law rule regarding the charging order and LLCs or LPs.

These legal entities are essential to building and protecting your growing wealth. An advanced asset-protection strategy is called equity stripping. This is a technique where we use two LLCs. One LLC holds legal title to the asset or assets such as rental property that you have. The first LLC is important to protect the asset from attachment by personal creditors and to prevent creditors from getting at you personally. The second LLC is important to use as an entity that will file liens against the assets owned by the first LLC. In this manner, you can see that any creditor suing the first LLC will get nothing, because all of the equity, or value, of the first LLC has been stripped out. It is important to maintain the second LLC in good order. You want to treat the second LLC very carefully, in that you do not want it to be much more than a mere owner or a bank account and other intangible-type rights. To this day, I have yet to see a bank account get sued.

The last asset-protection device is the pension plan. There just happens to be a 1974 law, called the Employee Retirement Income Security Act, which stipulates that pension plans are off-limits to most creditors. The pension plan is a very powerful tool. Ask O.J. Simpson how he is able to live a very comfortable lifestyle even though he lost a massive civil judgment. It is because his retirement assets are protected by a pension plan. There is also a very good Supreme Court case upholding what is known as, in legal parlance, the antialienation rule of ERISA. In plain English, this means that the Supreme Court says that the ERISA law says that no general creditor can touch your pension money. ERISA is a very complex body of law, and a good tax lawyer is needed to make sure that your plan qualifies for these protections. Not all plans are drafted with expertise so as to take full advantage of the law's asset-protection features.

Note that an IRA is not part of the federal definition of a pension plan. Some commentators are stating that the new bankruptcy law exempts IRAs from attachment by creditors. This is true and false. It is true that an IRA can achieve some level of exemption from creditors; however, you would have to file bankruptcy to get the protection. While this works, I do not believe that your protection plan should ever rest on your being required to file for bankruptcy. I prefer to use devices that get us protection without having to file for bankruptcy.

Finally, I would like to dispel some asset-protection myths and rumors. First of all, self-created, revocable trusts do not afford you any protection from creditors at all. There are only a few states that have statutes that purportedly allow you to create a trust for asset protection. While this may be true academically, these laws are so new and untested in the courts that I would not bet my entire net worth on whether or not the mechanism in fact works. I certainly wouldn't want to be the test case.

Another asset-protection blunder would be to use a general partnership or joint tenancy type of situation. These are the worst ways to run a business or hold title. They beg and scream for lawsuits to come after you; then, the problem is that you lose everything, because you end up liable for your partner's actions or get sucked into a joint tenancy lawsuit.

In summary, follow these three steps in reducing the liability you have:

- Get proper insurance.
- Put exculpatory clauses in all your mortgages or use similar precautions.
- Use one of the many legal entities to protect your assets.

If you do so, you will not only be richer than most folks, you'll be infinitely safer too. And you'll be able to sleep when the wind blows.

CHAPTER 18

Do-It-Yourself Financial Counseling

Every day, dozens of graduates from my nationwide seminar call our toll-free number to ask our opinions concerning their problems and their opportunities. Their ultimate question is:

"Given my circumstances, what can I do to increase my wealth?"

As a roundabout way of answering, I would like to take you through a personal counseling session, much like the one you would receive if you were a graduate of my "Creating Wealth with Real Estate" seminar. I'll try to teach you the principles of personal financial counseling, at least as I understand them. Once you learn the principles, you won't have to rely so heavily on the experts—myself included. And when you do go to the experts, you will be better prepared.

There are four distinct steps to each counseling session:

Step 1: Determine What You Are Trying to Accomplish

On the continuum of wealth, you may be one of the many who have no assets to speak of (except a nice smile) or one of the few who can draw upon bulging bank accounts and plentiful equities. As we learned about leverage, it doesn't matter; if you don't have it, someone does.

There is nothing wrong with starting from scratch. Creating wealth may take a bit longer and require a bit of fancy footwork, but you can still get there from where you are.

The first principle to follow is: *Knowing where you're going is more important than how much you have at the start.*

What do I mean by "knowing where you're going"? Let me illustrate. While speaking at a convention recently, a woman approached me and asked for some advice.

"Mr. Allen, after a costly divorce, I have about a $300,000 net worth, a good job, good credit, a nice home. How can I use what I have to create real wealth?"

"Why do you want to become wealthy?"

"Because I want my children to be secure financially. I'd like to be able to leave them something."

"All the reports I have read indicate that leaving your children a lot of unearned wealth is about the worst thing you could do if your objective is to leave them financially secure. That is your objective, isn't it?"

"Yes, but how can I leave them financially secure?"

"Why don't we teach you and your children at the same time? If they're going to be the eventual stewards of all of your money, we might as well bring them into the picture right now. Then they'll know what to do with it when they get it. By the way, the first thing we'll be teaching you is that there is no such thing as financial security! As soon as we can deprogram you of that myth, the better off we all will be."

People want wealth for a host of different reasons. You'll notice in the above dialogue that I didn't care what assets this woman had until I had a better grasp of what she was trying to accomplish and why. This woman felt that her problem was that she needed to leave her children financially secure. She felt that the solution to her problem was to become a millionaire. She should have learned a lesson or two from our federal government: throwing money at a problem usually creates more problems than it solves. By involving her children in the wealth-building process at the outset, she will be more apt to reach her original goal.

That brings us to the next principle: *You can't solve a problem until you know what it is.*

The most neglected part of our decision-making process is spending time determining what the problem or objective is. Most of our time is usually spent coming up with obvious solutions to the wrong problems. According to my friend Lin Bothwell, a management consultant and author, the most important rule of problem solving is, "What is obviously the problem is obviously not the problem." The next most important rule of problem solving is:

"What is obviously the solution to the problem is obviously not the solution to the problem."

In other words, before you run off in all directions to make your fortune, it would be wise to make sure that you have chosen the correct solution to the correct problem. Or to say it a different way, make sure that you have chosen the correct program to reach the correct objective.

Let me give you another illustration:

A middle-aged couple approached me for some advice after hearing me speak on real-estate investment. They had a handsome net worth, enough to last a lifetime. The husband had built up a thriving business. They wanted to know what they should do with what they had. They felt that real estate was an excellent vehicle.

As always, my first question was, "What are you trying to accomplish?" After a few minutes of discussion, it became clear that they weren't trying to create wealth, they were trying to perpetuate or preserve the wealth they had been able to accumulate. They didn't need any more money. They just needed to hang on to what they had.

They were concerned about inflation and taxes. And while it is true that real estate is both an inflation hedge and a tax shelter, it is also a pain in the neck. Owning and managing your own real estate is hardly my idea of the carefree good life. This couple was in stage 4 of the wealth trajectory but were acting as if they were in stage 1. They were at a time in their lives when they needed to be winding down, carefully putting what they had on automatic pilot, and not starting all over again in a new field, learning new jargon, acquiring new headaches.

The solution to their problem was to slowly diversify their assets into safe, management-free investments that outpaced inflation and taxes. I gave them several alternatives to choose from, including carefully selected limited partnerships in real estate, money market funds, and, if they were a bit more venturesome, discounted second trust deeds.

Once I had gained a perspective on their problem, the solution was easy.

It has been said that the definition of a fanatic is "a person who once having lost sight of his goal redoubles his efforts." I sometimes feel as though we live in a country of fanatics living from day to day without the rudder of goals to guide them, chasing after solutions to problems they don't understand.

The first step in all counseling, financial or otherwise, is to understand the problem—the *real* problem. And then the solution is much easier to come by.

Step 2: Once You Know Where You Are Going, Focus All of Your Resources to Accomplish Your Objective

Your resources will be both financial and nonfinancial. List them all according to the guidelines below:

Financial Resources

1. Cash and "near cash." How much cash could you raise within thirty days without borrowing?
2. Credit. How much could you borrow on a short-term basis? How much could you borrow on a long-term basis?
3. Financial statement. What is your net worth? How many "borrowable" equities do you have?
4. Cash flow. How much cash could you divert from your monthly income to apply toward your financial goal?

Nonfinancial Resources

1. Time. How much time per week could you devote to accomplishing your financial goals?
2. Knowledge. Do you possess the specialized knowledge required for success in your chosen field of investment? Or do you know someone who possesses this knowledge and can share it with you?
3. People. Do you know the right people? Often, it's not what you know but who you know. If you are lacking in either financial or nonfinancial assets, do you know someone who will provide them for you at a reasonable cost?
4. Courage. Are you ready to swim upstream to get what you want? If not, quit daydreaming and find an easier hobby.

Step 3: List All Feasible Alternatives to Reaching
Your Goal Using Your Resources

I asked a group of seminar students what their goals were. One fellow raised his hand and said he wanted to be a billionaire. Everyone laughed. But I told them that this would be a very modest goal if the student had $500 million to start with.

Obviously, whether your goals are modest, ambitious, or superambitious depends on how you use your financial resources. For example, anyone with a net worth of less than $50,000 should be able to achieve a modest net worth of as much as $500,000 (a tenfold increase) in ten years just by following the programs outlined in chapter 5. On the other hand, the same person reaching for the magic $1 million mark (a twentyfold increase) has a much more ambitious goal requiring significantly more time and effort. And achieving a superambitious goal of $2 million (a fortyfold increase) in less than ten years would require maximum use of his resources.

Let's consider a modest goal and see how we could generate some alternative avenues to reaching it:

"Hello, Mr. Allen. I'm calling you to ask some advice about what I should do with an inheritance of $30,000 I just received."

"What would you like your windfall wealth to do for you and when?" (Step 1: Determine what your objective is.)

"I would like to be able to have enough income from my investments to supplement my retirement income when I take early retirement in ten years."

"How much supplemental income do you feel you need? Allow for inflation in your projections." (Get specific.)

"I think I will need about an extra $2,000 per month."

"So your goal is to take the $30,000 and invest it wisely enough to have it provide you a $2,000 monthly income in ten years?" (Clarify the goal, so there is no misunderstanding.)

"Yes."

"If conservative investments in ten years are yielding 10 percent, how much would you have to have in the bank to give you an interest income of $2,000 per month, or $24,000 per year?"

"Let's see: 10 percent of $240,000 would give me $24,000 per year."

"Then one solution to your goal would be to have your $30,000 grow to at least $240,000 in ten years, which you could then invest in something paying at least 10 percent return to give you $24,000 per year. Does that sound right?"

"Yes. How do I do that? That sounds like a lot of money!"

"Well, it may be a lot of money now, but in ten years . . ."

"I see what you mean."

"Now, let me put these figures into my calculator. If we want to take your $30,000 and have it compound into $240,000 in ten years, it looks like you'll have to have an after-tax rate of return of at least 23.11 percent per year." (Any calculator with financial functions can figure out the return on compounding dollars.)

"What can I invest $30,000 in that will yield me 23 percent per year after taxes?"

"You could probably get this rate of return by investing in carefully selected discounted mortgages [see chapter 12], well-selected rare coins [see chapter 13], or real estate [see chapter 6]. How much time do you have to devote to your investments?"

"My job is fairly light. I have a lot of free time."

"There could be a way for you to invest a lot of time in your investments without having to dip into your $30,000 nest egg. One alternative would be to invest in at least one single-family house each year for the next ten years. You would spend your extra time looking for motivated sellers who will sell with little or no money down, flexible terms, and a wholesale price. This wouldn't be easy, but your goal is modest—you only need to locate, buy, and rent out one new house each year. At the end of ten years, you would own at least ten properties with combined equities well in excess of your necessary $240,000 goal. If you were to sell these properties, your after-tax proceeds could be invested to give you the cash flow you require. If you bought all of your properties with nothing down, you would still have your original $30,000 cash, which would have grown to almost $78,000 if invested at only 10 percent rate of return after taxes."

"That sounds like a lot of work."

"Well, let's just say that you have several alternatives. You'll have to decide just how much of your money, time, and effort you want to invest to achieve your desired goal."

The above conversation is a fairly straightforward example of picking an objective, utilizing resources, and devising several alternative plans. It is rarely this simple.

It starts to get much more complicated when people ask questions like: "I have $30,000 equity in my home. Should I borrow it out to invest in real estate?"

Or: "I lost my credit rating a few years ago, but I would still like to start on the road to financial self-reliance. How should I begin?"

Or: "I don't have any money, but I am able to save a few hundred dollars a month. Where should I begin?"

Or: "I was just transferred from a city where prices are lower. I have an investment home there. Should I sell it and reinvest the proceeds in my new city, even though the prices here are higher?"

Without going into a complete discussion of what to do in each instance, let me give you some of the guidelines I use when people ask me what to do with their resources to maximize their goals.

One: *If you don't have it, you can get it.*

It doesn't hurt to repeat the motto of a leveraged investor that we learned in chapter 9. As soon as you realize that you are short on resources, your next step should be to go looking for someone who has what you need.

Two: *Try to use your own cash last.*

I jealously hoard my cash until it is absolutely necessary to use it. And I use it only for the best of deals. Why? To keep me in the bargain-hunting frame of mind. This way, I always wring out of myself the last bit of speculation. If I will risk my money only on the best buys, I am safer and more liquid.

Three: *When you resort to borrowing, always borrow the cheapest dollars first.*

Money has two basic costs: the financial costs such as interest rate and fees, and the time costs, including the time and trouble needed to arrange for the money.

What is the cheapest source of dollars? Buying real estate with the seller carrying back part of his equity in the form of a mortgage or trust deed. You can always negotiate a lower-than-market interest rate from a flexible seller, and you rarely have to go through the red tape required to get a loan through a lending institution.

The next cheapest source of funds is through a lending institution. You will have high interest rates, short-term paybacks, and plenty of red tape.

The most expensive source of funds is from equity partners. It takes time to find willing partners, and you generally have to give up a percentage of ownership. But that is how I got my start.

Four: *If you do borrow against your equity—in your home, for instance—only borrow an amount with monthly payments equal to the amount you can afford to repay out of your present monthly income.*

Suppose you have a home with a lot of equity in it, and you want to tap into this unused source of capital to fund an investment program. First determine how much you can afford to squeeze out of your monthly budget to go toward payments on your new loan. If you can afford only $150 per month, use this as a top limit for the monthly payments on your new loan. For example, if the money costs 20 percent interest with monthly payments over ten years, you shouldn't borrow more than $7,500.

In other words, don't rely on your investment program to make the payments on the money you borrow. If you follow this rule, you avoid the problem of getting overextended.

Five: *Start out slowly when using leverage.*

A novice investor asked me if he should borrow out the $50,000 surplus equity in his home to get started in his investment program. I told him he would do better to borrow only $5,000 get his feet wet, and return to borrow more later once he had learned what he was doing. This way he will avoid the temptation of dropping the entire $50,000 in an ill-advised investment.

In summary, then, the first three steps in financial counseling are (1) to determine what the problem or objective is, (2) to list the resources that can be used, and (3) to list the alternative solutions to the problem.

Step 4: Decide on an Alternative and Begin Using It

Deciding what to do is a snap if you have followed through on the first three steps. Putting your decision into practice is another story. In fact, it is the story of our lives—the doers versus the dreamers. Which are you?

PART FIVE

Real Wealth

CHAPTER 19

Education: The Shortest Distance Between Wealth and Poverty

Our educational system is a poorly adapted dinosaur in an age where knowledge is multiplying and changing at the speed of light. Most educational textbooks are obsolete before publication date—disseminating transistor knowledge for a silicon-chip society.

According to Marilyn Ferguson, author of *The Aquarian Conspiracy,* "Discoveries about the nature of the mind, unfortunately, have been like the slow-spreading news of armistice. Many die needlessly on the battlefield, long after the war is over. Young minds are dampened and diminished every day in numbers too great to bear thinking about, forced through a system that stunts the capacity for a lifetime of growth. In contrast to insects, as someone said, human beings start out as butterflies and end up as cocoons."

Why such waste?

Because our educational system is a lumbering bureaucracy stabilized with tenures and seniorities. The first rule of this hierarchy is to maintain the status quo, to offend no one, to not rock the boat. Being different is not professional or respectable. So educators continue to dish up doses of numb knowledge cafeteria style. Empty calories from a sterile kitchen.

And if you want to get specific, listen to what Neil Postman and Charles Weingartner wrote more than thirty-five years ago, about the way our young people are taught to learn. It is as true today as the day it was written. They call it the Vaccination Theory of Education: "English is not History and History is not Science and Science is not Art and Art is not Music, and Art and Music are minor subjects, and English, History and Science major subjects, and a subject is something you 'take' and when you have taken it, you have 'had' it, and if you have 'had' it, you are immune and need not take it again."

And what does a child learn during his whole educational experience about becoming wealthy? Does he learn how to become more creative? Does he learn how to devise solutions to changing problems, or just how to regurgitate fixed answers to problems that are irrelevant? Does he learn how to create long-term wealth, or just how to obtain the proper credentials to get a job for which a high-school education would have been sufficient?

Essential understanding of our economy and how it works is painfully absent. According to the National Center on Statistics, a few years ago only 16.6 percent of a large sample of high schools even offered a course that dealt specifically with economics, finance, or business management. And less than 1 percent of the students in these schools were enrolled in such courses.

Where will these students learn about the free-market system? About the right to fail, the need for sacrifice, and individual responsibility? Will they learn it when they go to college? More than likely, what they will get in college in the typical liberal-arts curriculum is a dismaying tendency to equate capitalism with greed, self-reliance with selfishness, and profit with cold-hearted plunder.

Is it any wonder, then, that so few Americans ever become self-sufficient? No one teaches them how—and if they ever learn how, they are embarrassed to act. Becoming wealthy carries a vague moral taint. Who wants to be considered greedy, selfish, or cold-hearted? In the rarefied air of aestheticism, we are led to believe it is purer and more respectable to be poor.

The purpose of this chapter is to introduce you to a new breed of educator that has no patience with this kind of flabby and self-indulgent thinking. What I am referring to is the wave of adult education that is sweeping the landscape. It is led by doers who are on the cutting edge of expanding knowledge, not the trailing edge. Rather than regurgitating nineteenth-century romanticism, they are sharing practical ideas for a changing world. They don't have to bow to bureaucracies. They are not bound with government red tape, because they beg for no government grants. For the most part, they are loners who love to preach what they practice. Their only tenure is excellence. Service is their seniority. And when they cease to provide that, they go quickly out of business. As they should.

The seminar format is the modern vehicle for adult learning. A few days, at the most, are all that is required. The working adult can arrange a short leave without disrupting his life much—surely not as much as taking night school over a long period of time or a whole semester of class work. The adult coming to a seminar is generally thirsty to learn, more concerned with obtaining specific answers to specific problems than with diplomas.

Adults who don't understand the value of education are skeptical about education sources that aren't "respectable" enough to have huge campuses and recognized diplomas. However, when it comes to gaining knowledge about wealth, the only diploma that counts is the one that increases your net worth.

You may have already attended one of the smorgasbord of money-making seminars offered weekly around the country; no doubt you have at least seen some of their advertising. My first contact with these maverick seminars happened in 1976. As a real-estate-investment counselor, I had studied everything I could about financing, taxes, and analysis. When an opportunity came up to go to a seminar in Los Angeles about creative real-estate financing—which was a relatively new field—I jumped at it. As I remember, with tuition and travel expenses, the cost came to about $1,000. It was money that I didn't have at the time. But I felt that I needed to obtain this knowledge. When I told my colleagues I was going to an expensive seminar, they looked at me as if my elevator didn't go to the top floor.

In retrospect, that seminar was the turning point for me. It was taught by a man named Bob Steele, one of the originators of creative financing in the United States. In all my college education, no one had dared say that a person could expect to become wealthy in ten years or less. Mr. Steele calmly told us how he had done it himself. And he showed us how we could do it. He shared techniques of creative financing that quite literally stunned me. This knowledge wasn't watered down but poured out fully concentrated, without apology or fear. Whereas I might have spent a year to harvest one money-making nugget from a university, this three-day seminar was a vein of pure gold.

I met other doers at this seminar and found out that there were other, equally good seminars being taught. In the next two years, I attended more than a dozen other such seminars, at great expense. But the knowledge that I gained gave me the confidence to strike out on my own. And I began to develop techniques of my own, which I organized into an expanded system of learning. As I compared the few weeks of time I had expended at these seminars with the six years expended gaining my college degrees, I was shocked at the differences. I have often said that the most important thing I learned in my MBA training was perseverance—enough to know that if I could make it through two boring years of Statistics, Policy, and Production Management, I could do anything.

I can't fault the general knowledge I gained at college. I realized that I must have matured and seasoned over those years, perhaps enough to make my later successes possible. But the motivation to action came by attending little-known, relatively "unrespectable" seminars taught without much fanfare in hotel conference rooms. It came by rubbing shoulders with the tough-minded pioneers of the twentieth century.

Let's explore three principles of education that will guide you in your search for knowledge and by which you will be able to judge what you learn.

Principle 1: If You Think Education Is Expensive, Try Ignorance

That statement is attributed to Derek Bok, former president of Harvard University but I am tempted to alter it slightly to make it more relevant to the goals of learning to create wealth: "If you think *the right kind of* education is expensive, try ignorance."

Some education *is* too expensive. In my opinion, much of what is taught at universities is enormously expensive, not only in money but in time. And the kind of education that takes a long time to make you ill prepared to deal with the harsh realities of life is almost worse than ignorance. Now, you may draw from this that I am opposed to formal education. Not so! But if you choose to be formally educated, please understand the strengths and weaknesses of the system.

In many ways, the seminar approach to adult education is much more efficient. Although seminars take much less time, they can be expensive. When you add up the tuition, travel, and hotel expenses, it is not difficult to drop much more than $1,000, as I did on my first seminar. But the best seminars teach more in two days about the real nitty-gritty of building wealth than most people learn in a decade of university training.

I am constantly surprised at how many people have a hard time paying even small amounts of money for knowledge—especially those who were "vaccinated" in college. So many will step over dollars to pick up pennies.

I was vividly reminded of this a few years ago at a seminar I was sponsoring in San Francisco. That evening over five hundred people had turned out to attend one of my free lectures on creative real-estate investing. Just before the lecture was to begin, I met a man in the elevator who was visibly upset. Not knowing who I was, he began complaining to me about the supposedly "free" lecture he had planned on attending. He had decided to leave before it started because he couldn't stand paying 85¢ per half hour for parking. As I watched him storm off the elevator toward his car, I just stood there and shook my head. This man, standing at the crossroads of wealth, had taken the wrong road. He had said no to wealth. He had the opportunity to pick the brains of an expert for free. And he was worried about an investment of less than $5.

I stood in a bookstore recently and watched a well-dressed man pick up an important financial book. He thumbed through the pages, saw the price, and set it back down. I asked him if he intended to buy the book. He said he was going to wait until it came out in paperback. In order to save a few dollars, this man also had said no to wealth. He stepped over thousands of dollars to pick up a few pennies. And thus, many a prudent, penny-watching business person will decide to remain ignorant, content to reinvent the wheel rather than going to the experts.

Going to the experts is expensive. Very expensive. But it is infinitely cheaper than experience.

My trip to the experts cost me perhaps $5,000 over a two-year period. I learned how to avoid the mistakes for which they had paid dearly. As a result, I have reaped a harvest of several million dollars. Even today, after having reached the top in my field, I still attend three to four seminars and conferences each year. Now the money is no object, it is the time that I have difficulty investing. But still I find that I cannot afford to stay away.

I have many people ask me why they should attend an expensive seminar when the words of most experts can be obtained from a $25 book. Books play an important part in the transfer of quick, inexpensive information, but one is never a total substitute for the other. What happens at a seminar is much more than the mere one-way transfer of book knowledge. The person who attends a seminar removes himself temporarily from the seduction of the world and allows himself to be totally immersed in a new philosophy. In such an environment, a person's mind-set can be unfrozen and allowed to refreeze with a new set of correct principles. If anything, a book and a seminar on the same subject enrich each other. Reading a book allows you to pause and reflect for as long as you like. But a book can sometimes raise more questions than it can answer. The seminar is the next logical step forward, for it allows for the give-and-take of questions and answers that allow you to apply the information to your own situation.

At a seminar, the student can engage in a two-way transfer of information not only with the instructor but also with fellow students. He can hear the testimonies of those who have used the new information. He can ask questions and defuse his insecurities. He can establish channels of friendships, people to call in case of emergency.

In short, what is taught at the seminar is the least important thing that happens. The networks that are set up, the questions that can be asked, the nurturing of confidence, and the display of courage necessary to invest time and money are the real bonuses.

How do you find the best seminars? The best way is through word of mouth. Talk to others who have attended various seminars. Ask them what each seminar did for them. If you ask several people and get the same negative response about a particular seminar, you know that there are others that offer a better way.

Don't forget, the right kind of education is expensive, but it is the shortest distance between poverty and wealth.

Principle 2: Learn from the Experts but Don't Pray to Them

Hero worship is one of the many signs of poverty mindedness. The best teacher is not a camp maker but a camp breaker. He doesn't want (or need) disciples to be huddled around the warm campfires of his specialized knowledge. He would rather motivate those he teaches to break camp and to move on up the mountains that we all have been put here to climb. If he has done his job well, he will soon be unemployed. Once you have drunk some humble water from his meager well of wisdom, you can be off on your journey.

You don't need him anymore. And that suits him just fine, since he is also just a student.

In fact, nothing would please him more than for you to become your own expert so that he can learn from *you.*

Principle 3: Become Your Own Expert

Ultimately, when it comes to creating wealth, you have to become your own expert. You can draw upon the collective wisdom of other experts, but you will still be responsible for incorporating the information into your own investment framework.

How do you become an expert? Well, I can only suggest what has worked best for me. Write a book about it.

I urge you to pick a subject that you feel will be vital to your ultimate financial success. Study everything that has been written on the subject, attend whatever seminars you need to attend, pick the brains of whatever experts you can find who will talk with you. Then sit down, organize your thoughts into twenty chapters, and start to write.

Why go to such effort? First of all, it will discipline your thinking. Trying to write it all down will help you to identify the weak spots in your knowledge. As you write, you will learn enormously. Your subconscious mind will help you notice, in even the most mundane details, lessons that will eventually pay off for you.

I heard a great religious leader talk about a book he had just written. He said, "I realize that the last thing this church needs is another book. But I needed to write it." He had learned a great secret: there is no better way to learn about a subject than to write a book about it.

If you are planning to attend a seminar, here are my five tips for getting the most out of each session.

1. While attending a seminar, don't plan anything else but education. Leave your business and daily concerns behind. Concentrate fully on what is being said. Leave your evenings free for extra study and fraternization with fellow attendees.
2. Make a list of the questions that pop into your mind during the seminar. They will be lost to you if you don't write them

down. Take time out to corner the instructor or others in the room until your questions are answered. If you don't act now, you may never have another chance.

3. Have a goal to find and get to know the five most experienced and successful fellow students at the seminar. Find out what makes them tick. Try to learn what their cookie cutter is—that is, the system they have developed to organize their efforts. Don't be shy. Nothing could be worse than to have been in the same room with several millionaires without asking them some questions. If possible, get their names and addresses. Start a correspondence with them once you return home. You may need a little moral support from time to time. It helps to know someone who speaks your language.

4. Ask at least ten people, including your instructor, to answer the following questions for you:

   What is the best investment book you have read?

   What is the best seminar you have ever taken?

   If you were me, what would you do right now to start on the road to financial independence?

   What investment idea has the greatest money-making potential in the next five years?

5. Once you return home, take half a day out to read through your notes and to write down the two or three solid money-making ideas that you will definitely implement. Set a goal to begin as soon as possible.

You can learn more about the seminars and trainings offered through my company, the Enlightened Millionaire Institute, by visiting www.robertallen.com or calling us at 1-801-852-8700.

Happy "seminaring!"

CHAPTER 20

Wealth Is Thoughts, Not Things

Human beings can alter their lives by altering their attitudes of mind.
—WILLIAM JAMES

You are what you think.

In order to help you become wealthy in every sense of the word, I have chosen fifty-two insightful thoughts on the subject, one for each week of the year. Read them regularly. May these thoughts help you, as they help me, to build a wealthy mind-set.

1. Our aspirations are our possibilities.—Robert Browning

2. The world turns aside to let any man pass who knows whither he is going.—David S. Jordan

3. The secret of success in life is for a man to be ready for his opportunity when it comes.—Benjamin Disraeli

4. All virtue lies in individual action, in inward energy, in self-determination. There is no moral worth in being swept away by a crowd even toward the best objective.—William Channing

5. Nothing in the world can take the place of persistence. Talent will not; nothing is more common than unsuccessful men with talent. Genius will not; the world is full of educated derelicts. Persistence and determination alone are omnipotent. The slogan "press on" has solved and always will solve the problems of the human race.—Calvin Coolidge

6. There's no such thing as a self-made man. I've had much help and have found that if you are willing to work, many people are willing to help you.—O. Wayne Rollins

7. There is a tide in the affairs of men,/Which, taken at the flood, leads on to fortune;/Omitted, all the voyage of their life/Is bound in shallows and in miseries.—William Shakespeare, *Julius Caesar*, IV, iii

8. Success seems to be largely a matter of hanging on after others have let go.—William Feather

9. Keep away from people who try to belittle your ambition. Small people always do that, but the really great make you feel that you, too, can become great.—Mark Twain

10. Do unto others as you would have them do unto you.—The Golden Rule

11. Let him who wants to move and convince others be first moved and convinced himself.—Thomas Carlyle

12. Every great man, every successful man, no matter what the field of endeavor, has known the magic that lies in these words: Every adversity has the seed of an equivalent or greater benefit.—W. Clement Stone

13. Inch by inch, anything's a cinch.—Dr. Robert Schuller

14. Don't let the opinions of the average man sway you. Dream, and he thinks you're crazy. Succeed, and he thinks you're lucky. Acquire wealth, and he thinks you're greedy. Pay no attention. He simply doesn't understand.—Robert G. Allen

15. Someday I hope to enjoy enough of what the world calls success so that someone will ask me, "What's the secret of it?" I shall say simply this: "I get up when I fall down."—Paul Harvey

16. One great, strong unselfish soul in every community could actually redeem the world.—Elbert Hubbard

17. It is not the critic who counts; not the man who points out how the strong man stumbles or where the doer of deeds could have done better. The credit belongs to the man who is actually in the arena, whose face is marred by dust and sweat and blood; who strives valiantly; who errs and comes up short again and again; who knows the great enthusiasms, the great devotions; who spends himself in a worthy cause; who, at the best, knows in the end the triumph of high achievement, and who, at the worst, if he fails, at least fails while daring greatly, so that his place shall never be with those timid souls who knew neither victory or defeat.—Theodore Roosevelt

18. History records the successes of men with objectives and a sense of direction. Oblivion is the position of small men overwhelmed by obstacles.—William H. Danforth

19. Industry, thrift, and self-control are not sought because they create wealth, but because they create character.—Calvin Coolidge

20. Give a man a fish, and you feed him for a day. Teach a man to fish, and you feed him for a lifetime.—Lao Tzu

21. Progress always involves risk. You can't steal second base and keep your foot on first.—Frederick B. Wilcox

22. Ultimately we know deeply that the other side of every fear is a freedom.—Marilyn Ferguson

23. Money is the seed of money and the first guinea is sometimes more difficult to acquire than the second million.—Jean-Jacques Rousseau

24. One man with courage makes a majority.—Andrew Jackson

25. The life which is unexamined is not worth living.—Plato

26. The more you do of what you've done, the more you'll have of what you've got.—Anonymous

27. The winners in life think constantly in terms of I can, I will, and I am. Losers, on the other hand, concentrate their waking thoughts

on what they should have or would have done, or what they can't do.—Dr. Dennis Waitley

28. To know and not to do is not yet to know.—Zen Saying

29. Wealth is when small efforts produce large results. Poverty is when large efforts produce small results.—George David, MD

30. Luck is a word used to describe the success of people you don't like.—Charles Jarvis

31. Success is not something that can be measured or worn on a watch or hung on the wall. It is not the esteem of colleagues, or the admiration of the community, or the appreciation of patients. Success is the certain knowledge that you have become yourself, the person you were meant to be from all time. That should be reward enough.—Dr. George Sheehan

32. The man who does not work for the love of work but only for money is not likely to make money nor to find much fun in life.—Charles M. Schwab

33. I would rather see a crooked furrow than a field unplowed!—Paul Jewkes

34. The road to hell is paved with good intentions.—Karl Marx

35. My life seems like one long obstacle course, with me as the chief obstacle.—Jack Paar

36. When the imagination and the will are in conflict, the imagination invariably gains the day.—Émile Coué

37. If money is your hope for independence, you will never have it. The only real security that a man can have in this world is a reserve of knowledge, experience, and ability.—Henry Ford

38. Don't compete. Create. Find out what everyone else is doing and then don't do it.—Joel Weldon

39. I shall be telling this with a sigh/Somewhere ages and ages hence:/Two roads diverged in a wood, and I—/I took the one less traveled by/And that has made all the difference.—Robert Frost

40. Goals are as essential to success as air is to life.—Dr. David Schwartz

41. There is no security on this earth; there is only opportunity.—Douglas MacArthur

42. Some men have thousands of reasons why they cannot do what they want to, when all they need is one reason why they can.—Dr. Willis R. Whitney

43. Men give me some credit for genius. All the genius I have lies in this: When I have a subject in hand, I study it profoundly. Day and night it is before me. I explore it in all its bearings. My mind becomes pervaded with it. Then the effort which I make the people are pleased to call the fruit of genius. It is the fruit of labor and thought.—Alexander Hamilton

44. No man is free who is not master of himself.—Epictetus

45. For what shall it profit a man, if he shall gain the whole world, and lose his own soul?—New Testament, Mark 8:36

46. We know too much and are convinced of too little.—T. S. Eliot

47. You can get everything in life that you want . . . if you'll just help enough other people get what they want.—Zig Ziglar

48. If I had eight hours to chop down a tree, I'd spend six sharpening my ax.—Abraham Lincoln

49. Successful people make decisions quickly (as soon as all the facts are available) and change them very slowly (if ever). Unsuccessful people make decisions very slowly and change them often and quickly.—Napoleon Hill

50. The way to develop decisiveness is to start right where you are, with the very next question you face.—Napoleon Hill

51. Unjust criticism is usually a disguised compliment. It often means that you have aroused jealousy and envy. Remember that no one ever kicks a dead dog.—Dale Carnegie

52. Come to the edge, He said.
    They said, We are afraid.
    Come to the edge, He said.
    They came.
    He pushed them . . . and they flew.
    　　　　—Guillaume Apollinaire

You *Can* Take It with You

Those who don't understand wealth are fond of saying, "You can't take it with you." But I disagree. Just the opposite is true. You *can* take it with you. In fact, that is the message of this entire book.

It is only the poverty minded who tend to think that wealth resides solely in material things. Those who look upon wealth as thoughts and attitudes will not be disappointed in death. For they will be able to carry their wealth with them.

My hope is that in creating the kind of wealth you can't take with you, you also create a generous portion of the kind of wealth you can take with you.

Good luck and Godspeed.

Index

About the Author

Robert G. Allen is an investor, author, and lecturer. His first book, *Nothing Down,* was a colossal number-one bestseller, remaining on the prestigious *New York Times* bestseller list for over one hundred weeks. His various seminars have been taught to over two million people, who buy billions of dollars' worth of real estate per year on their way to financial freedom. You can read their stories at www.millionairehalloffame.com.

Return to:
Enlightened Millionaire Institute
5072 North 300 West
Provo, Utah 84604
www.robertallen.com
1-801-852-8700
Robert Allen's **FREE** report:

For a free update of the latest creative investment techniques and strategies as my research uncovers them, simply mail this coupon to our address above.

Name ————————————————————

Address ————————————————————

City, State, Zip code ————————————————

Creating Wealth, Updated Edition